DIVIDED BY CHOICE

Divided by Choice

How Charter Schools Diminish Democracy

Ryane McAuliffe Straus

NEW YORK UNIVERSITY PRESS
New York

NEW YORK UNIVERSITY PRESS
New York
www.nyupress.org

© 2025 by New York University
All rights reserved

Please contact the Library of Congress for Cataloging-in-Publication data.
ISBN: 9781479835812 (hardback)
ISBN: 9781479835843 (paperback)
ISBN: 9781479835867 (library ebook)
ISBN: 9781479835850 (consumer ebook)

This book is printed on acid-free paper, and its binding materials are chosen for strength and durability. We strive to use environmentally responsible suppliers and materials to the greatest extent possible in publishing our books.

The manufacturer's authorized representative in the EU for product safety is
Mare Nostrum Group B.V., Mauritskade 21D, 1091 GC Amsterdam, The Netherlands.
Email: gpsr@mare-nostrum.co.uk.

Manufactured in the United States of America

10 9 8 7 6 5 4 3 2 1

Also available as an ebook

In memoriam

The College of Saint Rose, 1920–2024

Thank you, Sisters of Saint Joseph of Carondelet,
for establishing an institution to educate women,
for marching with Dr. King on the Edmund Pettus Bridge,
and for welcoming a nonbeliever like me into your community.

We were stronger together.

CONTENTS

A Note on Language   ix

Introduction   1

1. Reframing School Choice: The Double Helix of Race and Class   9
2. Not Quite Colorblind: How Racial Capitalism Shapes Education Politics   24
3. Segregation Lives On: The Supreme Court and Policy Failure   52
4. An Unequal City: Albany's Political Landscape   74
5. City Politics, Policy, and Power: How Charter Schools Develop   92
6. Why Parents Choose: The Limits of Public Education   118
7. Divided by Choice: Race, Class, and Inequality   156

Conclusion   195

Acknowledgments   203

Appendix A: Methods and the Case Study   207

Appendix B: Charter School Enrollment in Capital Cities   219

Notes   221

References   237

Index   251

About the Author   263

A NOTE ON LANGUAGE

Race (and, though to a lesser extent, class) is a social construct with shifting meaning. As "race" changes, so too does the language we use to refer to different categories of people. Throughout this text, I have tried to use the most current language possible. The language I use here will necessarily become dated as racial concepts continue to change.

Part of the current historic moment includes capitalizing words that refer to racial categories. Though this began as a way to provide the respect to Black groups that other groups (such as Latinx and Asian populations) already receive, shifting standards have led to frequent capitalization of "White," as well. This makes some people uncomfortable, largely because capitalizing "White" also has a significant history in White Power groups.

I recognize this difficulty, but I capitalize "White" throughout this text for two reasons. First, it provides some basic consistency to capitalize all racial and ethnic groups. A capital letter clearly indicates an identity, while a lower-case letter is more ambiguous. Second, while some people—especially Whites—might be uncomfortable with this, I think we need to sit with that discomfort. This discomfort stems from knowing that Whites have held power over other groups for centuries, and a desire among White individuals to separate ourselves from that history and claim colorblind innocence. But we can no more separate ourselves from history than we can ignore the political and social impact that race continues to have in the United States today.

I use these capitals in my own writing, and I use them when quoting respondents who use this language in interviews. I do not change quotations from written documents that use a lower-case letter.

Introduction

Separate educational facilities are inherently unequal.
—US Supreme Court, *Brown v. Board of Education*, 1954

People in my community don't have these things.
—Adeja, Albany teenager, quoted in Fessler 2019

In 2024, the United States celebrated the seventieth anniversary of the decision in *Brown v. Board of Education*. In that decision, common knowledge says, the Supreme Court outlawed segregated education because it violated the Equal Protection Clause of the Fourteenth Amendment. Less commonly acknowledged is how much the Supreme Court struggled to implement this decision over the next several decades, until it essentially gave up.[1] The retreat from requiring integration has led to a return to segregated schools,[2] especially for larger school districts,[3] and is framed by national income inequality.[4]

Americans today are split by many cleavages, but race and class remain among the strongest of our dividing issues. Both of these inequalities are found throughout our cities and in our schools. And, while they do not overlap perfectly, race and class remain strongly correlated. Census data show that, nationally, Asian and White households continue to earn higher incomes than Black and Latinx households.[5] In Albany, New York, the subject of this book, White household income is double Black household income.[6]

These divisions of race and class structure American society, including how and where children attend public school. This is the case across the country and in individual cities. In Albany, neighborhoods are so segregated by race and class that they provide very different opportunities for children living within the same city. According to a story aired by National Public Radio in 2019, students in the affluent, largely White neighborhood of Buckingham Pond have vastly better life chances than those who live in Arbor Hill, less than four miles away. One Albany teenager, interviewed for the story, found that "just a few blocks from her home, there was a whole other world."[7]

This is the context in which Albany parents and guardians strive to raise and educate their children. Middle-class White parents in Albany have many options, including traditional neighborhood public schools, magnet schools, and a variety of private institutions. They have always been able to choose how to educate their children, at least to some extent. Working-class parents of Color have very different options. Unhappy with their neighborhood schools and unable to afford private education, many have turned to enrolling their children in the city's large network of charter schools.

I found myself, and my family, faced with a school choice in 2015. Having outgrown our first Albany home, we looked for something larger. My oldest child, then in second grade, was enrolled in our neighborhood elementary school. He was very happy at the school, which was comparatively racially integrated and located about five blocks from our first home. When we moved, we deliberately looked for a home in the same area, so he and our younger child would be able to go to that school. The purchase of our second home was, fundamentally, a decision about school choice.

Not all families have the same options that my family, and others like us, had. While we were able to purchase a larger home in a neighborhood we desired, and while friends and neighbors tell multiple stories of other White families who left Albany when their children reached school age, not every family can change their residence in order to enroll their children in their preferred school. This, of course, is one of the primary motivators of the school-choice movement—those with means have been making choices about their children's schools for generations. Those without means are left with whatever is available.

This lack of choice led charter school advocates and proponents to develop a second school system in the city of Albany. Since 1999, the city has been home to a significant charter school movement. Charter schools are schools of choice that parents may apply for via lottery, and are authorized by one of two state agencies permitted to grant a "charter" to an individual or private organization. They are not subject to oversight by the district or school board. Charter schools offer a free alternative education for parents who are not happy with the city school district but cannot afford, or do not wish to pay, private school tuition.

There is another difference between traditional Albany schools and its charter system. Albany charter schools are overwhelmingly Black and Latinx. Most recent data show average Albany charter school enrollment at about 70 percent Black, 16 percent Latinx, and under 4 percent for both Asians and Whites.[8] This is quite different from Albany City School District enrollment, which most recent data show to be 45 percent Black, 20 percent Hispanic,[9] 9 percent Asian, and 19 percent White.[10]

Because Albany's elementary schools are primarily attended by those in the surrounding neighborhoods, the race and class composition of individual schools can vary widely. The city's most economically disadvantaged elementary school (with 93 percent of its students participating in one or more state or federal economic assistance programs) is 7 percent White at the time of this writing. The city's most economically advantaged elementary school, with only 36 percent of its students participating in economic assistance programs, is 43 percent White. These distinctions show significant segregation across elementary schools.

Schools in the Albany school district are predominantly attended by students of Color.[11] However, the racial balance at individual schools varies widely. Most middle-class parents who want their children to attend racially integrated schools have that option.[12] Those living in neighborhoods with higher poverty rates do not.

Although our decision to stay in Albany was frequently challenged, not one person used racial language when they asked why we were staying. Indeed, no one mentioned race at all. Those who wish to avoid Albany's schools, all of which are now primarily attended by students of Color, have multiple "nonracial" variables to point to. Instead of race or ethnicity, regional conversations about Albany schools generally focus on claims that they are simply not of good quality. Test scores are low. Until recently, the high school's graduation rate was well below the national average. Student fights are frequently featured in the local news. Like other urban school systems, many of Albany's schools are segregated.

The ways community members discuss Albany schools, and the ways many reacted to my family's relocation within Albany, are symbolic of how racial discussions occur in the contemporary United

States. The pervasive colorblind ideology that dominates our understanding of race makes it difficult, especially for White people, to talk about racial issues clearly and directly. There is a deep-seated fear among many that acknowledging race is tantamount to being racist. Anxious to avoid accusations of racism, many White people avoid discussing race at all. This colorblind approach makes it difficult—if not outright impossible—to challenge or change racial trajectories and hierarchies. We cannot dismantle racism if we cannot discuss it.

Although colorblind racism is the current national norm,[13] and although it shaped people's reactions to our move within Albany, there are also two distinct ideologies that are challenging colorblindness. The first is a Trumpish approach that reflects (and sometimes matches) previous overt racism. Although still far from the norm in most circles (and especially in Democratic Albany), this trend justifies references to "shithole countries" and assumptions that Mexican immigrants are "bringing drugs. They're bringing crime. They're rapists."[14] While rare among the individuals I interviewed for this project, such understandings of race were not absent. One woman, for example, explained that "everybody has their preconceived or their less favored group of people." Continuing, she explained that she did not like "White Asians," whom she defined as being from East Asia, as opposed to "Brown Asians" from Southern and Southeast Asia. "I don't think they're attractive," she said. "I don't necessarily like the smell of their food." She further explained that she avoided visiting a friend in her home because her roommate was Asian, and that she would never date an Asian man. Like racist language from America's Jim Crow past, this is a language of disparagement and disrespect.

Language like this, however, is not the norm, and it was rare in my interviews. While the vast majority of my discussions with Albany leaders and parents were solidly colorblind, there is also a clear group that is challenging colorblindness from a place of empowerment. This group, primarily composed of Blacks but also some Whites, took a decidedly race-conscious approach to understanding race relations and racial politics.[15] The race-conscious approach was celebrated by those who chose charter schools because they had a nearly all-Black student body, had more Black teachers, and used African words in their classrooms. This approach is exemplified by a Black mother who stated that she chose a charter school for her child because she was "impressed with the fact that they're very Afrocentric." Unlike Jim Crow language, this is a language of community and liberation.

Albany schools thus reflect the three basic frames that Americans have for discussing race. The most unusual in public (though likely not so rare in private conversations) is outwardly racist language. Although emboldened by the Trump administration, this approach remains rare in polite conversations. The most common frame for racial discussions is colorblindness, which allows people to maintain the racial hierarchy without having to acknowledge it.[16] Colorblind language frequently hides more traditional racism, as I show later in this book. Finally, a small group of people from different racial backgrounds are challenging colorblindness by recognizing race in a much more positive, community-building way.

I discuss this language, along with the broader American capitalist framework and public policies and institutions that are framed by racism and capitalism, by focusing on how community members in Albany, New York, understand educational offerings in a segregated setting. The Albany City School District provides multiple educational options at the elementary level; parents may enroll their children in a neighborhood elementary school, apply (via lottery) for one of the district's four elementary magnet schools with different themes, or, space permitting, request to enroll in a different school via open enrollment. Busing is offered to all children, beginning in kindergarten, if they live at least 1.5 miles from their school. There are fewer options beyond the elementary level, but the city offers three traditional middle schools and one large high school. There are also a handful of very specialized schools, including a school for recent refugees and a continuation middle/high school. In addition, there is a group of charter schools at the elementary, middle, and high school level. These schools are separate from the city school district. However, they are publicly funded and they remain, technically, public schools.

* * *

My questions about Albany charter schools originally developed because I live in the community and send my children to Albany public schools. My own experience was with a diverse elementary school with excellent teachers. Truthfully, I did not understand why so many parents would not only choose to leave Albany schools but also choose to enroll their children in segregated institutions. I soon learned that my experience, while common among other White professionals, was not repeated across the city.

My curiosity about charter schools gradually developed beyond that of a parent and community resident, and into a more traditional academic approach.[17] Why, I wondered, did Albany have so many charter schools? For several years, it ranked among the top ten cities in the United States for charter school attendance, per capita. At their peak, there were sixteen traditional schools in the city plus twelve additional charter schools. Why were there so many? Why did they focus on Albany? It is a relatively small city, and, other than being the seat of state government, it seems to have no inherent importance on its own. Why should the focus be on this city?

The second part of my question is the natural follow-up to the first. Once charter schools were built, they could not stay open without students. Why did so many parents choose them? Why were these parents predominantly Black, a significant group Latinx, and only a tiny smattering of them Asian or White? Given the importance of integrated public schools to the American civil rights movement, why would so many Black families today deliberately choose to put their children in highly segregated schools?

I discuss a lot of members of the Albany community in this book. To encourage my respondents to speak freely and openly, I guaranteed them anonymity and changed all of their names. Although I mention closed schools by name, I keep current schools anonymous because I do not want an Albany community member to see how disparagingly another individual discusses a school their children attend. I wanted to encourage free, unencumbered discussion of taboo topics such as race and class, and many people did take our meetings as an opportunity to make statements that I found surprising, even shocking. The conversations I discuss in this book contribute to maintaining an institutionalized hierarchy based on racial capitalism, even though I am confident that no individual with whom I spoke would call themselves either "racist" or "classist." I am grateful to the fifty-plus community members who took time to meet with me, especially those who will disagree vehemently with how I characterize their approach to school choice.

Most fundamentally, what I saw throughout Albany is a strong desire and motivation among all parents to do the absolute best they could for their children. For some people (including my own family), this meant a traditional neighborhood public school. For others, it meant a magnet school operated by the school district. And for still others, it meant rejecting the city's public schools entirely and enrolling their children in charter schools. I make no judgment about which school a family chooses; all of them are striving to do the best they can in the context they have.

1

Reframing School Choice

The Double Helix of Race and Class

Our nation is moving toward two societies, one black, one white—separate and unequal.
—Kerner Commission, 1968

This is like a tale of two cities. You get two different things going here.
—Billie, Albany, 2018

In 1968, after a series of racism-provoked rebellions erupted across American cities, the Kerner Commission warned that the United States was "moving toward two societies, one black, one white, separate and unequal."[1] Fifty years later, in 2018, an elderly Black activist in Albany, New York, made a similar claim, arguing that Albany was "a tale of two cities." To her, the city provided a microcosmic example of the effects of racial apartheid identified generations earlier. The fact that a national problem recognized in 1968 remained so strong in an individual city fifty years later shows how deeply engrained racial and economic divisions are in American society.

These divisions have hardly gone unnoticed. By the time Billie remarked on them in 2018, the United States had spent several decades implementing policies that are putatively designed to combat the racism and economic disempowerment indicated by both of these statements. And yet, racial and economic divisions continue to shape, frame, and motivate politics as they work together to maintain a society structured by racial and economic hierarchies. Further, these barriers occur and the hierarchies exist within a society framed as a capitalist democracy that purports to provide equal opportunity for all.

The complexity of modern society means that politics and economics are interwoven and mutually dependent. However, even with an interlocking structure, each realm symbolizes a different type of decision making. The goal of political decisions in a "democratic" nation is to follow the will of the people.[2] Democratic political decisions are supposed to be about promoting the common good and are, therefore, based on communities, both large and small. For example, political decisions include declarations of war and peace, large-scale decisions about where to concentrate the nation's financial and natural resources, and decisions about which industries to regulate or deregulate. These are decisions that affect the public, and are made and implemented through institutional practices.

Economic decisions have a different goal. If political decisions seek to benefit the common good, economic decisions in a capitalist nation seek to benefit the self. Rather than relying on the will of the people to guide decision making to promote the common good, as a democratic political decision would do, a capitalist economic decision relies on the individual to make market trades that are most beneficial to the self. These trades might be large- or small-scale, but they all have one thing in common: their goal is to benefit the individual actor (including corporations or small groups) that makes the decision. These are decisions that affect the self, and are made and implemented through individualized practices; any benefit to the public good comes from the amalgamation of individual goods. In simplistic terms, democratic politics is a transparent, public way to make decisions that affect the community; capitalist economics is a shrouded, private way to make decisions that affect the self.

Although the political and economic realms are separate, with different goals and processes, they are also very tightly intertwined. In the United States, they are so constitutive of each other that, together, they provide the genetic material of the entire American experiment. Like human genetic material, they are connected at multiple places and wrap around each other so that neither democracy nor capitalism can easily work without the support of the other. This mutually reliant "double helix" of political and economic realms is such an intrinsic part of American DNA that its hegemony prevents us from recognizing when it is in play.[3] So blind are we to these structures that we frequently blame individuals for actions (or inactions) of the polity. And so deep is the intrusion of each realm into the other that it is difficult to decipher when a decision is public or private, political or economic.

The Double Helix of Race and Class

The double helix of politics and economics shapes all American decisions, institutions, and relationships, public and private. It is strongest when we consider one specific aspect from each realm: race, for the politics side, and class, for the economic side. Race and class are intimately entwined in the United States. This relationship stems from centuries before the nation's official founding, when it began, in Nikole Hannah-Jones's language, as a "slavocracy."[4] Even as the twin concepts of race and class work together to shape national history and destiny, they work because American property rights, so central to our notion of economics, are "rooted in racial domination."[5]

There is no shortage of academic or popular discussion about race and class. Indeed, these concepts could easily replace the "chicken" and the "egg" as one asks which came first. Yet, as with that age-old riddle, distinguishing between "first" and "second" is not likely to lead to a satisfactory conclusion. Rather than attempting to determine which is "more important" or which "came first," approaches that rely on drawing clear lines *between* unclear concepts, it is incumbent upon scholars to "draw lines *connecting* race and class."[6] These are powerful concepts that work together to build and maintain hierarchy, power, and control. These systems of domination are integral to the concept of "intersectionality," which recognizes that oppression works on multiple levels.[7]

It is no secret that divisions based on wealth have dominated societies around the globe since ancient times. Class, based on wealth, has "objective dimensions"—an individual, a family, or a group either has riches or it does not. Race, a more ideological construct than class,[8] developed as a way to justify European conquest of the Western hemisphere.[9] If religion produced a "matrix conducive to the politics of race,"[10] the drive to seize the riches of the Americas led directly to the creation of a hierarchy of control built on visible differences among human bodies. This reliance on physicality was necessary because the violence inherent in the conquest required that European settlers be able to make quick distinctions between themselves and "others."[11]

This hierarchy developed and maintained relationships of power; those of European descent held clear and complete power over all those of non-European descent.[12] In this process, race began to take on properties of class. As the concept of "Whiteness" expanded to include more European groups, such as the Irish, Italians, and Jews,[13] previous differences based on class became less important to racial identity. Those with power, primarily the Anglo-Saxon Protestants, expanded their numbers in order to retain control. They did this by redefining who was "White."[14] This "amalgamation of various European strains into an American identity" was "central . . . to the republican project."[15] As this occurred, Whiteness continued to gain power and grew to become an element of property owned by those who could claim it.[16] This property was used by Whites as a "public and psychological wage."[17] Constructed Whiteness developed privileges, including higher wages, primarily because it was "other than" constructed Blackness.

Thus, in the United States, race took on elements of class. The two concepts were so fused together that to be a "worker" implied being "White."[18] The importance of race and the "psychological wage" it provided "stifle[d] class tensions among Whites."[19] This "stifling" was further aided by the division between work and community,[20] and the fact that American residential communities were deliberately segregated by public, putatively "democratic" decisions.[21] Because the United States has lacked a strong socialist movement, partly due to its lack of a feudal history,[22] the minimal class structure in the United States easily gave way to allow racial divisions to take precedence.

Race has therefore eclipsed class in the United States to become a "master category" that is so ingrained in human consciousness that it has become a notion of "common sense."[23] Race is "the front man" for the American caste system.[24] This "commonsense" idea that humans have different, and somehow meaningful, racial backgrounds and identities shapes the racial hegemony,[25] which makes it difficult to see when race and racism motivate public or private decisions.[26] Although a social construct without biological meaning, race remains a "social fact" with deep political importance.[27] This is not to say that other systems of oppression and domination, such as patriarchy, misogyny, antisemitism, heteronormativity, and others, have no role to play. Rather, the concept of race shapes how these other concepts work; race is a "*template* of both difference and inequality."[28]

The hegemonic common sense of race explains why race-based reforms follow a predictable pattern of expansion and containment. In the long trajectory of race as a political structure, groups gradually chip away at the expansive edifice of racial domination. Real gains are achieved. The successes of Reconstruction and of the civil rights movement are not to be discounted. However, we must also acknowledge that these events—the only really significant examples of challenging the racial hegemony in the United States—each resulted in a backlash that removed the power of their gains. Reconstruction was followed by northern withdrawal, and the South was permitted to end the racial gains that occurred after the Civil War. The civil rights movement, after the significant achievements of the Civil Rights Act (1964) and the Voting Rights Act (1965), instigated a reactionary movement of colorblindness and, eventually, the elections of Donald Trump in 2016 and 2024.

The predictable pattern of challenge on behalf of a group, acquiescence by the state, and incorporation of moderate group demands explains why the United States remains a racist society even generations after the successes of the civil rights movement. Fundamental racist structures are never fully challenged; they are only modified at the margins. The civil rights movement could not expunge the country's history and foundation as a slave-owning polity that generated immense capital for its enslavers. It did not attempt to redistribute capital. It could not challenge the construct of America as a White country or its workers as White men.[29] These concepts were already so deeply ingrained as "common sense" that the movement's demands were best understood as demands for a slice of the American pie, not challenges to that pie to insist on cake instead.

Therefore, focusing on race as a master category that is eminently political does not stop us from considering its development alongside economic dispossession. Racism and capitalism developed together in American history. They are inseparable. This inseparability means that the civil rights movement was set up to be limited from its beginning. The civil rights movement focused on using law and public opinion to broaden political, social, and economic access for non-White individuals. Its primary focus on law, including its successes with Supreme Court decisions, executive orders, and congressional legislation, kept it squarely within the political realm. But, because racism developed through politics *and* economics, maintaining a focus on political change kept the movement limited. To create full change, it would have had to work to fully redistribute capital as much as it worked to redistribute political access.

Public Policy in the Double Helix

Politics provides a process for making values-based decisions between competing views of broad, amorphous goals like justice and equality. These decisions are known as "public policy." Public policy is the mechanism through which we allocate values and resources and use government to indicate who is valued and who is not.[30] Those who are valued by the polity are provided with benefits, while un- or undervalued citizens and residents are targeted with burdens and stigma.[31] Moreover, public policy includes not only government action but also government *in*action.[32] In other words, a decision *not* to solve a given public problem, especially when there is significant evidence that it exists, is tantamount to a positive decision to let that problem stand.

Ultimately, the goal of politics is to have other people accept the meanings that help one's position because acceptance of meaning provides support for one's policy goals.[33] These goals usually involve decisions about how to distribute resources,[34] which are used to either support or diminish current hierarchies of power. Policy goals, problems, and solutions are defined through the use of symbols, stories, and narratives.[35] Leaders of the discourse-oriented approaches to the study of politics, policy, and race, among them Edelman (1985), Stone (2012), Yanow (1996), Schneider and Ingram (1997), Fischer (2003), and Omi and Winant (2015), argue that language not only reflects power structures but builds and reinforces these structures.

The political meanings that are the core of policy goals are represented by policy frames, which are "implicit organizing idea[s]" that provide a discursive shortcut for promoting power-laden political goals.[36] Frames do not simply reflect an empirical truth, but they are the very truth that political scientists seek to explain.[37] This construction of reality is at the heart of many policy, and political, controversies. In framing policy, both elected leaders and citizens promote their preferred political values over others. Their frequently sophisticated use of frames shows that citizens are not (or are not always) the political neophytes that many people presume.[38]

Divided Educational Opportunities

Defining public policy as including nondecisions means that a decision *not* to solve a given public problem is equivalent to a policy that supports exactly that issue. Although there are any number of political problems that are framed by the race and class double helix for which one could point to a lack of significant political action, I focus here on public education. Mounds of research have documented the policy problems that exist within public schools. For example, there is significant evidence that American public schools are segregated,[39] that they treat children differently on the basis of what teachers and administrators expect of them,[40] and that they vary drastically in terms of how much money is spent per student in spite of significant evidence that this investment matters.[41] This differential treatment and lack of equal opportunity are not oversights. When government does not act on the lack of equal opportunity present in American schools, the reason is that it is the policy of the United States to treat students differently.

It is no secret that American public schools were racially segregated before the 1954 Supreme Court decision *Brown v. Board of Education* declared these Jim Crow schools a violation of the Equal Protection Clause of the Fourteenth Amendment. Speaking for the Court, Chief Justice Earl Warren clearly stated that "separate educational facilities are inherently unequal." It is also well known that communities throughout the South fought this decision, which was not fully implemented until the 1964 Civil Rights Act threatened to remove federal funding from public schools that continued to maintain race-based segregation.

Similarly on the radar of many historically aware Americans is the northern response to later Supreme Court decisions that challenged not only southern-style legally segregated schools but the racial school segregation that occurred "naturally" due to residential segregation.

Boston's response to court-ordered racial integration of its public schools remains legendary. Los Angeles also underwent significant political turmoil when ordered to integrate public schools across residentially segregated boundaries.

And yet, there seems to be a collective sense of "giving up" among the American population and on the Supreme Court.[42] Jonathan Kozol's best-selling book *Savage Inequalities* (1991) documented stark differences in racially segregated schools across the country, with majority-White schools having pristine buildings and working equipment while majority-Black schools suffered from neglect and underfunding. But later Supreme Court decisions, such as *Parents Involved in Community Schools v. Seattle School District No. 1* (2007), make it virtually impossible to integrate public schools because, except for schools still under a court desegregation order, it forbids the use of race in making school assignments. Some districts have moved to relying on economic measurements instead of racial ones in order to accomplish the same goal.[43]

Charter Schools and Public Policy

The frustration felt by many parents, community leaders, and politicians over the multiple entrenched problems in public schools led directly to the charter school movement. Charter schools are a nationwide movement that impacts children, families, and communities throughout the United States. By definition, they are all part of a neoliberal, market-based movement that focuses priorities on individuals over communities. Nationally, they also share very high rates of segregation.[44] Charter schools thus personify the racial and class-based hierarchies that have long motivated American politics and society.

As with other complex public policies, there are mirroring ways to understand charter schools. In one version, charter schools provide an easy "exit" option for parents who are disappointed with their local public schools but cannot afford (or do not wish to take advantage of) private schools.[45] In this view, charter schools allow parents to avoid democratic education policies and focus instead on their own, individual needs. They are, in other words, a way to privilege economic decisions over political ones.

At the same time, however, the political context in which these parents make their decisions must be carefully considered. If a parent is unhappy enough with their public school that they move to a charter school instead, and if there are enough parents engaging in this action to support that charter school, we must also consider the lack of the public school's change as a public policy. Given that public policy includes nondecisions and that school districts are well aware of how many of their students leave them for a charter school, it is incumbent on those schools to make changes that satisfy parents' democratic demands. When they decline to do so, we can read that as a school district ignoring parental pleas, at best, or deliberately pushing them out, at worst.

Charter school policies also provide one example where both elites and ordinary citizens mobilize policy frames to serve their own political goals. Although the market and the community (or the "polis") are frequently discussed as separate entities,[46] public policy crosses these boundaries routinely. School-choice advocates deliberately blur the lines between the two spheres. In an attempt to promote their preferred, market-oriented policy, school-choice advocates use community-based language—especially that of civil rights and equal opportunity. As Scott argues, "Corporate and private sector supporters of market reforms have embraced the language and moral authority of civil rights to champion reforms," even when these reforms do not benefit—and frequently harm—traditionally underserved communities.[47] In other words, charter-school advocates frame their policies as progressive beacons of equality and opportunity. Detractors do the opposite; due to their reliance on market choice and minimal public oversight, they frame charter schools as yet one more capitalist intrusion on the community. Both of these frames reflect a different "truth" for different communities.

These disparate frames of the charter school movement, and the ease with which they move between the marketplace and the polis, explain the odd political place they hold today. Charter schools continue to usurp community-based language when they demand equal funding from the state as providers of an important social good. At the same time, they also use language from the market when they claim to be independent entities that should not be subject to state regulations.[48] These interlocking realms, the community and the market, provide a hook for multiple players. Claims of efficiency, quality, and access are used together to deliberately meld the community with the market. Without a clear distinction between these frames, both major American political parties support school choice broadly and charter schools specifically.

That racial and economic hierarchies are so central to education should concern anyone with a stake in American democracy. When applied to erstwhile public education, market opportunities encourage parents who are unhappy with their public school—no matter what motivates that lack of satisfaction—to leave the democratic structure altogether. When this population leaves the public institution, their voice is no longer available for discussion. And because American politics is so racialized, the vast majority of parents who leave their public school are people of Color, or have children of Color. This removes the voice of people who might otherwise provide alternative visions for democratic institutions, even while it maintains segregation and a racial hierarchy.

The Research

The social and political worlds are socially constructed and deeply entrenched with layers of meaning and power. Parents' decisions are structured by a broader context that includes constructed knowledge of academic options within a world that is limited by power, race, and class. In this study, I use documents and interviews to build knowledge about how people make decisions about an important policy in an urban setting. The individuals and the decisions I study are congregated around two questions: First, how and why did Albany become home to so many charter schools? Given that charter school policy is written at the state level, there is no reason to expect Albany (rather than New York City, Buffalo, Rochester, or any other urban area operating under New York State policy) to be at the forefront of this issue. Second, once charter schools were available, why did so many parents in Albany flock to them? Why was this decision so unbalanced across racial and class lines, occurring almost exclusively among families of Color?

These issues—who decides where charter schools should be built and how this occurs, and which parents select them—are limited by the context in which they occur. In the United States, policy contexts are always limited by the double helix of race and class. This is the context that shapes political and social decisions, and these decisions and actions are then fed back into the original context, strengthening it further. This constructed context, reified with every decision made by the polity and the individuals within it, shapes and reflects the human activity that is laden with intent. Because humans are different from chemicals, a science of human behavior—that is, a social science—must include consideration of this intent, the meaning it conveys, and the way others understand it. Following the interpretivists, then, I begin with the understanding and meaning that are crucial to a more complete explanation of a complex phenomenon.[49]

Most of the data I build on in this study come from personal interviews. Altogether, I interviewed fifty-five people in Albany, divided into two samples. The first sample, constructed of twenty-three people over twenty-two interviews, was a group of local leaders who were involved with or close watchers of the charter school development process. This group included elected officials at multiple levels, activists, journalists, and policy entrepreneurs. Averaging an hour each, these interviews occurred in respondents' homes, offices, or local coffee shops. The second sample, constructed of thirty-two people over thirty-one interviews,[50] was a group of parents who had children attending school in Albany. This group included parents who chose charter schools, magnet schools, or their assigned public school.[51] Also averaging an hour, most of these interviews occurred in private rooms available at neighborhood branches of the Albany public library.

*　*　*

While positivist-oriented scholars frequently argue that data should be analyzed without bias, those of a more interpretivist persuasion recognize that their material is embedded in socially constructed relationships. This requires "critical self-scrutiny on the part of researchers" rather than the researcher serving as a "neutral, detached observer."[52] Such reflexivity is particularly important when there might be an implied hierarchy (such as that imposed by race and class) between the interviewer and the respondent. Throughout the interviews, I remained reflective on the impact my own presence had on the individuals with whom I spoke.

I was not especially concerned about the role of my own identity with the first sample. With few exceptions, this was a group of middle-class professionals who are not likely to recognize a hierarchy when speaking with a college professor. However, I was somewhat concerned about establishing trust in my interviews with parents, especially those who chose charter schools. Charter schools in Albany are a political lightning rod, and parents who look like me (White and middle-class) are among the most vociferously opposed to them. Although we would have natural connections and similarities because we live in the same city and are raising children,[53] my identity, along with my role as a researcher, was a clear marker of difference in a very segregated community.

In deliberately reflecting upon my interview experiences, however, I have come to believe that my identity provided more benefits than costs. I did not sense a feeling of unease among charter school parents or respondents of Color. Many of them brought up race-related issues on their own, before I asked these questions. No one hesitated when I asked questions about race or racism. Therefore, while of course I cannot detail how interviews might have been different had I had a different skin color, I am confident that the arguments I build from respondents of Color are complete.

What I found to be even more interesting, however, was the assumed connections that my own race provided with my White respondents in the second sample. Just as White individuals are more comfortable telling racist jokes to other Whites than to people of Color, my White respondents did not hold back when discussing race. Many of their comments were racially coded, as is required by polite society. But some were much less coded than others. One White mother, for example, referred to "violent kids" at her children's elementary school, and blamed their presence on the fact that the school has a high level of open enrollment. "Everyone gets bused over," she said. "That's a problem." This is coded language that accuses students in the sending neighborhoods (which are downtown, high-poverty neighborhoods predominantly populated by people of Color) of being violent. Another White parent was more open, declaring that children of Color in a high-poverty school were not "peers" to her children, and their parents were not her peers. The same parent was concerned about gang violence in her child's future kindergarten class.

This language is barely coded, and is clearly an indication that this individual views populations of Color, especially if they are living in poverty, as beneath her.

I will come back to these conversations later, as I discuss the role of race, class, and the double helix in school-choice decisions. I bring them up now as a point of reflection. I was surprised to hear both of these statements, and considered a counterfactual. Had I been a person of Color, would these parents have felt comfortable enough to make these statements? My guess is that they would not. While I cannot say for certain how my interviews would have differed under different racial dynamics, my experiences with Black and Latina parents suggests that parents of Color were comfortable discussing race with me, *and* so were White parents. I believe my own race served as a benefit to this study, and allowed a much more open, honest discussion from White parents than I would have heard otherwise.[54]

Plan of the Book

This is a study of how various forms of race and class frame school choice in a small, segregated urban setting. In chapter 2, I explain what I mean by "race," "class," and their different iterations. Building on the work of Du Bois, Robinson, and other scholars, I establish that the United States is built on and founded by *racial capitalism*. I argue that racial capitalism has evolved into the newer concept of *colorblind individualism*, but that both are reliant on the United States' genetic material as a slavocracy. While major developments have occurred in both race and class relations and hierarchies, these changes have not been strong enough to abolish the original double helix.

Chapter 3 explains how racial capitalism and colorblind individualism impact public policy, especially policy purportedly designed to create strong, equalized public schools. I further argue in this chapter that the Supreme Court, the creator of significant federal school desegregation policy, is subject to the same policy theories as elected legislatures. Legal and other policy decisions are framed by the same concepts of race and class that formed the nation and continue to dominate its politics. Although the Court showed an early possibility of dismantling public education systems that separated children by race and class, this goal soon proved too politically difficult, and the Court remained fully entrenched in racial capitalism.

Chapter 4 develops the City of Albany, which serves as the book's case study, into a character of its own. I explain the city's demographic and political history, describe the city's current populations, and explain how these factors help us understand the classic relationship between politics and policy. This background is important for understanding the remainder of the book and provides context for the interviews I share.

Chapter 5 explains how and why charter schools, the current darling of the school-reform movement, gained traction in Albany. Albany is not a large city, and, other than being the capital of New York State, has no inherent importance of its own. After evaluating two competing theories, I explain in this chapter how the city's historical political machine, its traditional political treatment of public education, and its status as the state capital all combined to create a community ripe for charter school growth.

Once Albany is explained in detail, I use chapter 6 to explain why parents choose specific schools. I argue that all parents in Albany are looking for the best options for their children, though these options are constrained by the racial capitalism and colorblind individualism that continue to provide hegemonic structure of day-to-day life in the United States. In this chapter, I show that parents who select charter schools are not dramatically different from those who choose the city's magnet schools or those who remain in their neighborhood public schools. All parents want the schools to provide their children with a solid academic background in a safe environment with a strong sense of community. Those with fewer economic resources have the additional need of school days and academic years that best match their work schedules.

Chapter 7 continues the discussion begun in chapter 6, but with a clear focus on the roles of race and class in parents' school-choice decisions. This chapter argues that racial capitalism and its descendent, colorblind individualism, continue to shape how people view public education and their role within it. In this chapter, I provide evidence for the common academic claim that colorblindness is simply a modern form of racism, and that colorblind language hides racist intent. This chapter also provides evidence of a growing challenge to these trends by a small but growing population that recognizes race consciousness.

Finally, the conclusion returns to the book's central claims that race- and class-based hierarchies continue to shape political decisions. We can make small changes at the margins, but without full reformation of the American institutional structure, these hierarchies will not simply disappear. Racial capitalism, the nation's foundation, is here to stay.

2

Not Quite Colorblind

How Racial Capitalism Shapes Education Politics

Your debts are paid because you don't pay for labor.
—Lin-Manuel Miranda as Alexander Hamilton to
Thomas Jefferson in *Hamilton*

In the United States it is just not possible to fully understand the role, success, and proposed function of education without weaving a tale inclusive of how segregation, race, and economics have combined to become the story of public education in America.
—Noliwe Rooks, *Cutting School*

Though it was populated by millions of people in the pre-Columbian era,[1] common wisdom has long held that the United States, birthed from a revolution and the deliberate formation of a new nation, began to exist in 1776 with the Declaration of Independence or 1789 with the ratification of the Constitution. Recent conversations place this birthdate earlier, at 1619 or 1526,[2] with the introduction of enslaved African peoples in land that eventually became part of the United States. No matter which date we select, it is clear that the United States began not as a democracy that promoted equality and human dignity, but as a "slavocracy" that exists only because enslaved peoples built it.[3]

The establishment of this slavocracy relied on and promoted two fundamental concepts. The first, racism, permitted wealthy White settlers to justify their enslavement of darker-skinned peoples. The very concept of race developed only after Columbus interacted with Indigenous populations of the "New World,"[4] which was, of course, only "new" to European knowledge. Previous "othering" by European powers had been based on religion, not phenotypic "racial" attributes.[5] The people Columbus and others encountered "challenged their discoverers' preexisting conceptions of the origins and possibilities of the human species."[6] Racial "othering" thus permitted the cruelties of enslavement and extermination that organized New World societies for centuries.

To justify that enslavement in a land theoretically based on liberty (especially after 1776), Americans claimed that "the black men were not men in the sense that white men were."[7] The theory of *polygenesis* argued that there were multiple human origins; under this theory, Native Americans and Africans "descended from a different Adam."[8] Even those who challenged polygenesis by maintaining the biblical notion that all humans descended from Adam and Eve and were, therefore, one human family, had a way to promote ideas of Black inferiority; the story of the "curse of Ham" maintained that Ham was punished by God, who turned his descendants "blacke and loathsome."[9]

Multiple theories of racial inequality thus developed to justify enslavement and extermination of whole populations. Not only that, but the African continent was constructed to be so harsh that enslavement was viewed (by Whites) as a better option for Blacks: on plantations, the argument goes, enslaved peoples were "well-treated and cared for, [and] far happier and safer . . . than in their own land."[10] Such claims remain common today; witness Ron DeSantis, while running for the Republican presidential nomination in 2023, who claimed that "some Black people benefited from being enslaved" because the brutal system taught them "skills."[11] The state of Texas has been controversial for well over a decade, as it used a textbook that referred to enslaved people as "immigrant 'workers,'"[12] state educators proposed calling slavery "involuntary relocation,"[13] and the state bans the teaching of the *1619 Project*.[14]

In addition to racism, the developing US slavocracy relied on and supported capitalism. Capitalism provided the early possibility for slavery's development, because slavery required that some people have enough surplus capital to purchase other human beings. Once established, slavery also promoted capitalism because it permitted and encouraged the creation and hoarding of immense wealth.[15] Slavery permitted landowners to reap extraordinarily high profits. The inherent linkage of racism and capitalism in the United States means that we cannot divide race and class, or the impacts of racism from the impacts of capitalism. Race and class are "fundamentally . . . intertwined."[16] Indeed, our task "is not to draw precise lines separating race and class but to draw lines *connecting* race and class."[17]

Although some of the Framers and other colonial Americans were troubled by the juxtaposition of slavery with a document that extolled innate human equality, those who wrote the Constitution were not concerned enough to overthrow slavocracy when they developed the nation's founding documents. Slavocracy, an institutionalized form of racism that serves in the expansion of capital, *is* the American experiment. Racism and capitalism created the context that permitted the American Revolution and subsequent founding to occur. They are central to an understanding of American history, development, and contemporary political events.

Racism and capitalism rely on and reinforce one another. Each concept contributes to the other, and the twin constructs unite to form the double helix of American DNA. This means that the United States is not, and never has been, a democracy. Indeed, its very founding documents would make it difficult to reach that goal.[18] Instead, I argue in this chapter that the United States is beset with racial capitalism, even if racial capitalism has evolved over time.[19] As the nation went through significant policy change, including the end of legal slavery and the civil rights movement, overt racial capitalism became less socially acceptable. Along with policy developments, American DNA evolved from racial capitalism to a contemporary incarnation, which I label "colorblind individualism."[20] Colorblind individualism is enabled by neoliberalism, a form of capitalism that relies on and even idolizes individual choices in a marketplace that purports to ignore race even while it is built on racial hierarchy. Even some of neoliberalism's most significant academic critics focus on class and divide it from racism,[21] but doing so "artificially separates class from race."[22]

The United States is not a formerly democratic nation that lost its way, but a nation built on racial capitalism, which has morphed into colorblind individualism. Both racialism and its modern incarnation, colorblindness, violate the democratic thesis. "Racialism," the noun form of the adjective "racial" that comprises the first part of "racial capitalism," is the belief that "race" is a biological human trait with important, inherent meaning. It is different from, but necessary for, the related concept of *racism*, which organizes human "races" into a hierarchy of intelligence or other variables. Colorblindness, the contemporary antidote to racialism, rejects not only the concept of race as an inherent trait but also the very real social impacts that different human skin tones create and experience. Similarly, capitalism and its modern version, neoliberalism, violate the democratic thesis. At its core, capitalism is an economic structure based on private ownership and the pursuit of profit. In the contemporary neoliberal version of capitalism, individuals and their market choices are given paramount importance. The centrality of the individual, or *individualism*, motivates economic and political decisions.

When combined, race-related and capitalism-related concepts form either racial capitalism or colorblind individualism. Both violate democracy, because both of them lead to oppression—whether that oppression is of a racial group, a class, or both—which is frequent. In the United States, these concepts are inseparable. American capitalism developed because the racist system of slavery permitted the accumulation of inordinate amounts of profit. Colorblind individualism continues the same process, but without the transparent cruelty of slavery. Colorblind individualism is a more opaque version of racial capitalism, and its opaqueness makes it difficult to identify, challenge, and destroy.

Racial capitalism and colorblind individualism are the roots of American social and political life. This means that all American political decisions are framed by these powerful ideologies. They are self-limiting, in that they only permit discussions about policy options that fit within their frameworks. These discussions include policies related to public education, especially the contemporary focus on charter schools. Charter schools are part and parcel of colorblind individualism, and they serve to promote this ideology rather than challenge it.

Racial Capitalism

At its most fundamental level, the United States is built on two structures of power: racism and capitalism. "Racial capitalism" recognizes that neither racism nor capitalism can stand on its own. Each structure reinforces the other, and the state provides the resources, authority, and hegemonic normalization that keep racial capitalism in place.[23] Racial capitalism is woven within and negotiated by state institutions through public policy, which is a collection of both decisions and nondecisions by public officials.[24]

Cedric Robinson, whose seminal work *Black Marxism* is broadly acknowledged as providing the introduction of the term "racial capitalism,"[25] argued that "the development, organization, and expansion of capitalist society pursued essentially racial directions."[26] Racial capitalism is a "global phenomenon" that can be traced to "the beginning of European expansion."[27] In other words, Robinson fundamentally disagreed with Marx and Engels's view that "capitalism was a revolutionary negation of feudalism":[28]

> Instead, [capitalism] merged within the feudal order and flowered in the cultural soil of a Western civilization already thoroughly infused with racialism. Capitalism and racism, in other words, did not break from the old order but rather evolved from it to produce a modern world system of "racial capitalism" dependent on slavery, violence, imperialism, and genocide. Capitalism was "racial" not because of some conspiracy to divide workers or justify slavery and dispossession, but because racialism had already permeated Western feudal society.[29]

Marx and Engels missed the racial component of capitalism, Robinson argues, because they were so focused on male European laborers that they "consigned race, gender, culture, and history to the dustbin."[30] In Robinson's argument, Marx did not understand slavery to be a critical part of capitalism, but rather saw it as part of a "precapitalist" developmental process. In relegating slavery to a precapitalist phase, Marx was blinded to the fundamental role it played in global capitalist development.[31] While not all scholars agree with Robinson's scathing critique of Marx,[32] there is wide agreement among both his supporters and his critics that racism permits capitalism to function and that the resulting racial capitalism is a powerful force in global, national, and local politics. Most recently, Nancy Fraser made this claim clearly when she said that "capitalism harbors a structural basis for racial oppression."[33]

If capitalism is inherently racial, then slavery was not an aberration to an otherwise race-neutral system. Rather, chattel slavery permitted and even encouraged capitalism to flourish. The accumulation of capital, particularly though not only in the nascent United States, relied on the extremely profitable institution of slavery because the acquisition of capital requires "severe inequality among human groups."[34] Those who amassed great tracts of land and enslaved others to use it to produce cash crops like tobacco and cotton reaped great financial rewards. Indeed, "From the dawn of capitalism, white supremacy was mobilized for the accumulation of capital."[35]

With their accumulation of wealth, large land owners in the American South created a new capitalist class. In order to protect their investments in land and human flesh, they also created institutions to support and maintain their power. These institutions became the modern state; indeed, "'expanded bureaucratic state structures' became the major conduits of capitalist expansion."[36] Racial capitalism needed institutional support, and racial capitalists developed the modern American state to provide that support. The United States was founded on the basis of various forms of "despotism," including slavery.[37]

Racial capitalism provided the overarching structure to the developing United States, including its early school system. Colonial and early American schools were minimal, as most education occurred in the home,[38] but that began to change shortly before the Civil War. By the time the war broke out, the primary mode of production had moved out of the family home and into much more public spaces. As production moved out of the home, the newly developing labor force required more detailed training than could be provided in the home or in traditional apprenticeships.[39] Bowles and Gintis argue, quite persuasively, that the developing public schools were designed to provide capital with trained workers and to promote the political stability necessary for a developing economy.[40]

And yet, not all children were eligible for the training that public schools provided. Before the Civil War, enslaved children were not permitted to attend school in most parts of the South. Much of the public education provided to Indigenous children was designed to "civilize" them into the American structure, including its economy;[41] a small group of Indigenous children still attends boarding schools managed by the federal Bureau of Indian Education. Northern and western schools were also legally segregated. For example, the Massachusetts Supreme Judicial Court ruled in 1849 that Sarah Roberts, a five-year-old Black student, would be better served in a segregated school and denied her father's attempt to enroll her at the school closest to her home,[42] even though she had to pass five White schools to reach her Black school.[43] In the West, California's School Law of 1860 required that Black, Chinese, and Indigenous children attend schools separate from White students. The state legislature later amended this law to provide schools for Black and Indigenous children only, leaving Asian students without guaranteed education.[44]

Even the Civil War, a strong positive part of the great democratic leap forward in the traditional American narrative because it brought with it the end of legal slavery and the formal establishment of citizenship and voting rights for men of Color, was as much about promoting racial capitalism as it was about ending racial apartheid. This is the central argument in Du Bois's *Black Reconstruction*, originally published in 1935. In Du Bois's capable hands, the Civil War is a war over control of capital, not (or at least not fundamentally) over emancipating enslaved peoples. Southern planters, whose ability to increase capital was limited primarily by the amount of land they could exploit, wanted to expand slavery to new territories. Northern industrialists wanted to limit slavery to the South and forbid expansion, because free Black labor challenged even low-paid White labor. The Union had too much capital embedded in southern plantations and agricultural products to allow seceding states to leave.[45] The abolition movement was a fringe group in this war over control of capital, and was added to the narrative about the Civil War later.[46]

Even after the Civil War and the technical end of slavery, racial capitalism permeated American public policy and political institutions. This was especially true in public education, the structure of which changed very little in the next century.[47] By that point, "Public education was universal, tax-supported, free, compulsory, bureaucratically arranged, class-biased, and racist."[48] Although public education in the South increased dramatically after the Civil War, it was significantly influenced by northern philanthropists and teachers.[49] It was also fully segregated by race, and Black students frequently had shorter school years and inferior facilities.[50]

Post–Civil War educational reforms were designed to confront many different social ills. The Progressive movement, in particular, had a significant influence on public education, and led to greater high school attendance, testing, student activities within a school structure, and other changes.[51] These changes remained fully entrenched within the United States' racial capitalism. Capital supported these changes in order to discipline a potentially radical labor group, while labor supported the changes because they seemed to be "the only remaining path toward mobility, security, and social responsibility."[52] And yet, schools throughout the country remained segregated.

Students in public schools were divided by both class and race. White students were "tracked" into different types of coursework to permit future capitalists and future laborers to each attain an education relevant to their social roles.[53] Many Black students, particularly in the South, remained in segregated, underfunded, unequal Negro schools. Other groups experienced similar segregation and discrimination; California permitted students of Mexican descent to enroll in previously White schools only with the 1947 case *Mendez v. Westminster*.[54]

Racial capitalism provided the political context for pre–civil rights movement public policy decisions. Racial capitalism, and the policies it engenders, fundamentally challenges the liberal democratic thesis. Rather than the sovereignty and equality that form the foundation of democratic community, racial capitalism lays a foundation of division, discrimination, and antipathy. Under this narrative, "The state *is* inherently racial. Far from *intervening* in racial conflicts, the state is itself increasingly the preeminent site of racial conflict."[55] State actions, both official and unofficial, are the core of public policy. Thus, *the state uses public policy to maintain hierarchies built on racial capitalism*.

Developing the Narratives: Racial Capitalism to Colorblind Individualism

Racism and racial capitalism built the foundation of the United States, and they remain entrenched in its structures and institutions.[56] However, in the United States today, it is no longer socially acceptable in most circles to make outwardly racist remarks. While racist jokes and commentary certainly remain active in closed circles, public discussions of race have changed dramatically since the mid-twentieth-century civil rights movement. Outright public racism has declined, and claims of colorblindness have taken its place as the norm.[57] Most fundamentally, colorblind racism "explains contemporary racial inequality as the outcome of nonracial dynamics."[58] Rather than pointing to "Whites Only" signs or deeply segregated and underfunded schools as the cause of racial hierarchy, Americans today have few such clear causes to explain racial difference. As public policy has become fully colorblind,[59] reasons for racial differences have become more difficult to pinpoint. As a result, colorblindness maintains the racial hierarchy *without the need for racist actions*.

Colorblindness has overtaken traditional, Jim Crow–style racism. This has occurred in two distinct ways. First, for some people, the very concept of race has lost its power. And second, for those who remain strongly racist in their ideology, clearly racist language is forced underground and "colorblind" approaches take its place as a way to actively, deliberately maintain racialized discourse.[60] Both of these processes make it difficult to have conversations about race at all, as many people (especially Whites) shy away from having what they now think of as "difficult" discussions.[61]

This reticence to engage in clear discussions of race is a "defensive strategy" from people who are anxious to avoid being labeled "racist."[62] However, because open racism is much less socially acceptable today than it was decades ago, much of it has moved online. This is especially common in anonymous conversations, where the "the hood comes off" otherwise masked racist attitudes. While much more difficult to pinpoint than old-fashioned racism, colorblind racism is evidence that "manifestations of the racial hierarchy" continue to shape everyday American life.[63]

Stripping Race of Its Power

Although racism itself remains a powerful force in American politics and society, discussions of race and outwardly racist claims have declined since the legislative successes of the civil rights movement.[64] This may have occurred because criticisms of the very concept of race have worked *too* well. There is growing acknowledgment, not only among academics but also in broader society, that race is a social construct. For some, this leads very naturally to a denial of the power of race. Because it is a social construct, the logic goes, race itself is inherently nonexistent. As a nonexistent entity invented by humans, race must not have power. And if it has no power, there is no need to discuss race any further.

This reticence to talk about race is reinforced by social norms that imply that even talking about race is a racist act.[65] Because of this, many Whites avoid discussing race at all, at least in a clear and direct way.[66] This is sometimes the case because they honestly believe that their statements or belief systems are divorced from old-fashioned racism as they understand it. In other cases, colorblind discussions allow Whites to continue to discuss race without being explicit. Without explicitly racialized language, they have a ready excuse or justification if they are called out for their behavior. As Bonilla-Silva puts it, "Shielded by colorblindness, whites can express resentment toward minorities; criticize their morality, values, and work ethic; and even claim to be the victims of 'reverse racism.'"[67] Colorblind language permits these ideas to continue while also providing cover for those who spread them.

Colorblindness is not merely a social trend; public policy and court decisions have followed colorblind ideology since at least the mid-1970s. While the banner policies of the civil rights era, including the Civil Rights Act (1964), Voting Rights Act (1965), and Fair Housing Act (1968), "involved both race-neutral and race-conscious components,"[68] public policy soon began focusing on colorblindness. Whether this focus is due to Supreme Court decisions or the growing conservative movement,[69] it is clear that colorblindness became the norm—particularly in education policy and judicial decision making. Most famously, in *Parents Involved v. Seattle School District* (2007), the Supreme Court argued that race cannot be used even as a tie breaker in assigning students to schools. In the words of Chief Justice John Roberts, "The way to stop discrimination on the basis of race is to stop discriminating on the basis of race."[70] For the chief justice and a plurality of the Court, *any* recognition of race in educational policy was necessarily a violation of the Fourteenth Amendment. This forces public policy into colorblind language while removing the possibility of race-targeted improvements. This approach was strengthened and extended to higher education, including private universities, when the Supreme Court ended affirmative action programs in 2023.[71]

Colorblind language allows people to discuss race in carefully guarded ways, without risking being labeled racist and without acknowledging the power that race continues to hold. Although race is a social construct "that signifies and symbolizes social conflicts and interests by referring to different types of human bodies,"[72] it remains extremely powerful. As Omi and Winant put it, "Race is indeed real as a social category with definite social consequences."[73] Bonilla-Silva, similarly, argues that the social construct of race does have a "social reality."[74] Supreme Court justice Ketanji Brown Jackson made a similar claim with very clear language as the Court ended affirmative action programs in higher education. As she put it, "Deeming race irrelevant in law does not make it so in life."[75] Indeed, because race is such a powerful concept, we *must* continue to discuss it at length.

Those who have fallen for the hegemonic argument that the United States either is or should be a colorblind polity are unable to hold these important discussions.[76] When people, especially those at the higher end of the American (and global) racial hierarchy, cannot or will not use language to examine and discuss the racial differences that structure American society, they turn a blind eye to social forces that maintain these racial (and racist) hierarchies. When individuals refuse to acknowledge the power of race, they are forced to "[explain] contemporary racial inequality as the outcome of nonracial dynamics."[77]

This is where references to "culture" frequently come into the discussion. To understand "race" as "culture" is to reduce the power of race to a different concept. This reduction of the power of race makes it less crucial that we as a nation confront race and racism. As Omi and Winant explain, "culture" is less immutable than race. Unlike skin tone, facial features, or other phenotypical markers, "one can speak a different language, repudiate a previous religious adherence or convert to another, adopt a new 'lifestyle,' switch cuisines, [or] learn new dances."[78] In other words, culture is not necessarily fixed. Because culture is not always fixed, "ethnicity theories of race tend to regard racial status as more voluntary and consequently less imposed, less 'ascribed.'"[79] And if culture creates the racial differences in income, education, home ownership, and other variables that have remained so fixed in American society, then the problem becomes identified with those who own that culture rather than with society itself.

Even Barack Obama is guilty of blaming Blacks' lower socioeconomic status on Blacks themselves. While still on the campaign trail in 2008, then senator Obama spoke at the Apostolic Church of God in Chicago. In that speech, given on Father's Day, Obama reminded the large, predominantly Black congregation that "of all the rocks upon which we build our lives ... family is the most important." Obama continued:

> And we are called to recognize and honor how critical every father is to that foundation. They are teachers and coaches. They are mentors and role models. They are examples of success and the men who constantly push us toward it.
>
> But if we are honest with ourselves, we'll admit that what too many fathers also are is missing—missing from too many lives and too many homes. They have abandoned their responsibilities, acting like boys instead of men. And the foundations of our families are weaker because of it.
>
> You and I know how true this is in the African-American community. We know that more than half of all black children live in single-parent households, a number that has doubled—doubled—since we were children. We know the statistics—that children who grow up without a father are five times more likely to live in poverty and commit crime; nine times more likely to drop out of schools and 20 times more likely to end up in prison. They are more likely to have behavioral problems, or run away from home or become teenage parents themselves. And the foundations of our community are weaker because of it.[80]

In this speech, Obama blames problems in the Black community squarely on the Black community itself, particularly on absent fathers. There is no attempt here to understand *why* "more than half of all black children live in single-parent households." There is no criticism of unequal educational structures that provide different opportunities for Blacks and Whites, no critique of the system of mass incarceration that targets Black men.[81] In this speech, Obama reduces the power of race to culture and implores Black men, in particular, to change.

Contemporary discussions of race frequently follow one of these two paths: either race is reduced to culture, or race is ignored completely in colorblind justifications of racial hierarchy. For many Americans of all races, it is not difficult to discuss race without using clearly race-based language. One need not refer to skin tone (black, white), use racist epithets,[82] or refer to an individual's assumed racial or ethnic heritage (African American, Latinx, Asian) in order to carefully share with others which group one is discussing and how one views that group. This includes language that is facially neutral, characterized by words like "urban" or "underprivileged" and references to language fluency ("English as a Second Language/ESL" or the now more accepted "English Language Learner/ELL"). As an example from my Albany case study, one parent described a middle school principal in this way: "He does about as best of a job with an urban school that I've seen. I mean, he's tough love, but really empathetic dealing with the whole diverse crowd that goes to [the school]. I don't think he's perfect, but he certainly has an understanding of what he's dealing with." This comment came up in a conversation I had with two White parents, a married couple with two children in Albany public schools. This couple presented as progressive Whites; they had enrolled their two children in multiple Albany public schools, including the least economically advantaged magnet elementary school, by choice. While similar statements came from parents with less clearly progressive, antiracist leanings, this statement is an example of how even Whites who are otherwise comfortable with conversations about race use colorblind language like "urban" and "diverse." Parents of all racial backgrounds, as well as city officials and school leaders, used similar colorblind language to avoid discussing race. This language provides them a way of communicating their ideas and thoughts about race without taking the risk that is now thought to be attached to language that more clearly identifies race.

Colorblind language also includes geographic terms, such as the pervasive use of the word "ghetto." Not only people but also entire neighborhoods are subject to this type of language. Some neighborhoods are clean, tree-lined, and filled with middle-class, single-family homes. Others are strewn with litter and graffiti, crowded, and dominated by renters with high residential density. Indeed, in American and other cities, "the cycle of neglect, racial containment, and redevelopment of central cities is justified by the pathologizing racial discourse of the 'ghetto.'"[83] The idea of "blight" and related concepts is a social construct, and this construct manifests power in such a way that those who already have capital are able to benefit from urban renewal projects. With the proper framing, an area formerly considered "blighted" or "run-down" by some might become "hip" and "edgy" to others, thereby bringing in fresh resources.[84] All of these images are laden with racial symbolism and meaning.

As another Albany example, consider a statement from Gloria, a mother of a charter school student. Gloria identifies as White and Latina, and her child's father is Black. I asked Gloria why she thought so many White families in Albany did not choose charter schools, and she said, "I honestly think that a lot of White families don't consider charter, because that's the ghetto school. They're not going to send their kids." Gloria did not have to say what she really meant—that charter schools in Albany are overwhelmingly Black, and White families avoid them because of this racial dynamic. Colorblind language allowed her to make that argument without saying it explicitly. Through colorblindness, racial hierarchies are maintained *without* the need to use explicitly racial language.

Rejecting Colorblindness

While colorblindness has become the norm in most American social circles and is fully entrenched in American public policy, there are also groups of people who reject it and embrace race consciousness as an alternative. This movement has clear connections to Black Lives Matter, as well as the Black Power and Black Is Beautiful movements of previous generations, but it remains a relatively small objection to colorblindness. This view challenged colorblind ideology among charter school parents who selected a majority-Black school for their child or children. An example comes from Catie, a single Black mother with a child in a majority-Black charter school. When I asked Catie why she chose that school, she brought up race completely unprompted: "I was also impressed with the fact that they're very Afrocentric. And I find this extremely important for [my son] to be very close to his race. Not separating wise. I want him to be more aware than I was in elementary school." Similarly, Tabitha, a middle-class Black professional with two children, moved her children from an integrated, low-economic-need neighborhood school to a charter school partly due to its racial composition. The student body at her children's new school had a stronger impact on her children than she had expected:

> TABITHA: One of the reasons... for how I chose [their charter school] was that my kids also are a lot around a lot more African Americans in charter schools. And at first it didn't occur to me that that made a difference, but I think it does now.
> RYANE: In what way?
> TABITHA: Well, they really didn't get exposed too much to a lot of African Americans at [their neighborhood school]. And you know I think sometimes when we were around like our other family members and other friends they wouldn't really know how to, like, interact.

Although Tabitha begins to frame her discussion in a race-positive way, it is important to remember that racism is a structural problem that impacts all people. While she appreciated that the predominantly Black student body made her children more comfortable around their family members, she wanted to ensure that this did not go too far. She worked to ensure that her children, especially her older child, knew that they were not the stereotypical African American kids "growing up in the typical ghetto, you know, project type environment. And I want him to think that he's not the African American that's seen on TV, he's a young man that happens to be African American who lives in this part of town."

While Tabitha's language shows the beginning of a move toward race consciousness, Catie provides an example of the full rejection of colorblindness present among some Blacks and a handful of progressive Whites. As members of all groups challenge the danger of colorblindness, the concept is losing its power in some communities. Throughout this book, I provide examples of Black, White, and Latinx individuals using racist, colorblind, and race-conscious language.

Capitalism, Neoliberalism, and the Role of Individualism

Racialism, whether in its original or in its current colorblind form, does not act on its own. At the United States' founding, as well as in its colonial period, racism and racialism were deeply intertwined with capitalism.

If Jefferson completely missed that "all men are created equal,"[85] he and other founders also placed an inordinate amount of emphasis on the right to property, especially protecting their ownership of other humans. Indeed, some scholars see the Constitution as a "slaveholders' compact" that was designed to protect slavery.[86]

Like race, capitalism has seen its share of challenges and changes over the past centuries. All of these iterations, however, have a common foundation in classical liberal thought. Classical liberalism is fundamentally focused on the rights and importance of the individual, and the decisions that individual makes in the market economy.[87] This focus on individualism is a fundamental part of multiple versions of capitalist ideology. Marx noticed this as early as 1843, when he criticized capitalism's and democracy's tendency to divide individual from community demands: "By partitioning off where people see and act as collective (as abstract citizens of the state) from where they see and act as individuals (in their everyday participation in economic and civil life), capitalist political democracy divides people from their social forces and leads 'each man to see in other men not the realization but the limitation of his own freedom.'"[88]

Capitalism's focus on individualism, noted by Marx, has long been recognized as a crucial part of the American civic religion. Alexis de Tocqueville discussed his concerns about the tendency toward individualism in American democracy in his two-volume tome *Democracy in America*. Tocqueville's concerns were prescient of Marx, as he noted that American democracy encouraged a tendency toward isolation of individuals and led them to focus on themselves over society. The counterbalance to this, in Tocqueville's understanding, was the American propensity to form groups and to be closely involved with religion, both of which had the potential to lead an otherwise individualistic society to focus on community.

The centrality of individualism continued through different iterations of capitalism, including the nation's experiment with Keynesian economics. Although the United States began experimenting with the government-supported broad economic investments promoted by Keynesian theory during the Great Depression,[89] the postwar period saw the United States and other wealthy nations much more fully committed to adopting its tenets.[90] While the goal of capitalism is always to maximize profits, different forms of capitalism approach this maximization in different ways. Under Keynesian capitalism, "production, sales and growth are central to profits."[91] In this approach, stability is key and strikes are costly, so there is an attempt to placate workers by including them (at least to some extent) in growing profits.[92] And yet, not everyone benefited from this attempt to placate workers in the same way. The stability that Keynesianism provided focused on benefiting unionized, White, male workers.[93] This unbalanced support relied on patriarchy and racism.[94] The Keynesian approach began to lose ground in the United States in the late 1960s and 1970s as profits fell and as the "poverty, racism, oppression of women, imperialism and social alienation seething beneath the surface of economic growth and political stability erupted in the social movements of the 1960s and 1970s."[95] Newer economic theories to replace Keynesian policies fundamentally challenged the government spending that was not just authorized but fully encouraged under Keynesian economics. If Keynesian economics encourages government investment in infrastructure and other large projects to stimulate the economy,[96] neoliberalism, capitalism's next iteration, "is an ideological rejection of egalitarian liberalism in general and the Keynesian welfare state in particular."[97] Neoliberalism, which is "at its core a racial project,"[98] narrows traditional capitalism to a clear focus on the power of free markets to distribute all sorts of goods, while removing government from that role. David Harvey, one of neoliberalism's strongest academic critics, defines it as a theory of political economic practices that proposes that human well-being can best be advanced by liberating individual entrepreneurial freedoms and skills within an institutional framework characterized by strong private property rights, free markets, and free trade. The role of the state is to create and preserve an institutional framework appropriate to such practices.[99]

Neoliberalism, then, is "a reorganisation of capitalism" that shaped global and national politics and economics,[100] and was solidified by around 1980 (Harvey puts the date at 1978–1980; Omi and Winant place it at 1981; Hackworth claims neoliberalism was "naturalized" in the United States by the 1990s).[101] By the point it became fully solidified, the "neoliberal project . . . had destroyed aspects . . . of a host of . . . American cities."[102] The criticism of government inherent in neoliberalism led to a decline in government programs, especially those that had motivated the American economy,[103] and showcased the end of the "American century."[104]

Neoliberal theorists such as Hayek and Friedman returned to classical liberal thought in their arguments that government power should be limited to its ability to protect the market.[105] Ultimately, neoliberalism holds that "government spending should only be on those things markets cannot do."[106] And on the rare occasion when a market does not exist, government should use its power to create one.[107]

Neoliberalism is ultimately racial. If Keynesian economics recognized and encouraged an active government to promote at least a semblance of equality, neoliberalism rejects this capacity and relies on the market to distribute all goods and services. Its reliance on and trust in the market make it difficult for neoliberal ideology to recognize market failure. Instead, neoliberalism is much more inclined to blame these failures on government,[108] even as it has stripped government of much of its power. This hegemonic assumption that the market is "good" and government is "bad" is enshrined through the neoliberal thought process. This idea was most famously promoted by President Ronald Reagan. His first inaugural address, in 1981, squarely blamed American economic problems on government action. In this speech, Reagan argued, in part,

> These United States are confronted with an economic affliction of great proportions. We suffer from the longest and one of the worst sustained inflations in our national history. It distorts our economic decisions, penalizes thrift, and crushes the struggling young and the fixed-income elderly alike. It threatens to shatter the lives of millions of our people.
>
> Idle industries have cast workers into unemployment, causing human misery and personal indignity. Those who do work are denied a fair return for their labor by a tax system which penalizes successful achievement and keeps us from maintaining full productivity.
>
> But great as our tax burden is, it has not kept pace with public spending. For decades we have piled deficit upon deficit, mortgaging our future and our children's future for the temporary convenience of the present. To continue this long trend is to guarantee tremendous social, cultural, political, and economic upheavals.
>
> You and I, as individuals, can, by borrowing, live beyond our means, but for only a limited period of time. Why, then, should we think that

collectively, as a nation, we're not bound by that same limitation? We must act today in order to preserve tomorrow. And let there be no misunderstanding: We are going to begin to act, beginning today.

The economic ills we suffer have come upon us over several decades. They will not go away in days, weeks, or months, but they will go away. They will go away because we as Americans have the capacity now, as we've had in the past, to do whatever needs to be done to preserve this last and greatest bastion of freedom.

In this present crisis, government is not the solution to our problem; government is the problem.[109]

In this historic speech, President Reagan blames economic ills not on capitalism, individualism, or corporate greed but squarely on government spending and regulation. In Reagan's argument, the United States had borrowed so much money (the idolatry of work included here implies that the borrowing was for social programs) that it ruined the economy. The solution, in his mind, was to *reduce government power*. Indeed, the Reagan administration deregulated business and cut corporate taxes in an attempt to stabilize the economy. Capitalists won with these neoliberal developments; citizens did not.[110]

The neoliberal focus on markets and disparagement of government mean that markets are inescapable, and they are assumed to operate in an apolitical space. Market ideology ignores the historical and political context in which markets exist; it promotes "amnesia" about how the strength of government helped the United States prosper.[111] Under neoliberal theory, government is the problem, and the key to American success is reducing government power. This reduction of government power and control extends to all factions of American public policy, including education. Neoliberalism took the form of deregulation in the already-private corporate world, but for education and other public institutions, the change was much more dramatic. Neoliberal theory insists not only on deregulation of private entities but also on the privatization of public entities.[112] Privatization of public entities fits with neoliberalism's focus on private property rights and distrust of government.

Neoliberalism was critically applied to public education policy. The neoliberal turn occurred around the same time as the publication of *A Nation at Risk* (1983), a government-sponsored report that argued that

American schools were falling behind those of other nations, risking the strength of the future American economy. In response, "Parents, students, teachers, principals, superintendents, schools, and school districts are expected to adhere to the values of the market, changing the purpose of education itself."[113] Under neoliberal capitalism, education is not about preparing future citizens. It is a competition that creates and rewards schools that succeed according to standardized measures, and punishes those that do not. The difference between Keynesianism and neoliberalism is that, under Keynesian economics, schools that do not succeed would be provided with additional resources. Under neoliberalism, they are failures that are—and that should be—completely shut down.

This turn toward neoliberalism led directly to the creation and growth of charter schools.[114] The development of market-based school-choice options, particularly charter schools, reinforced the role of public education in the larger political struggles. This is not new, of course; education has long been part of the civil rights struggle, and some place the beginning of the midcentury civil rights movement at the 1954 *Brown v. Board of Education* decision. Yet this movement is different. Charter schools are not fundamentally about equality or justice, the symbols that framed school desegregation discussions during the civil rights movement. Rather, charter schools "are part of a larger deregulation reform agenda in public policy that has seen broad political support—not just in education and not just in the United States, but also in many other sectors around the globe."[115] They are about deregulation and the reduction of government power, not the use of government power to promote equity. In other words, charter schools reflect the capitalist turn to neoliberalism, not its earlier Keynesian form.

For some parents, the idea that charter schools must compete for students shows that they must prove their worth. This is the core of the neoliberal focus on the market; consumers choose their preferred goods, and corporations compete in the market to supply and sell those goods. The drive for success assumed to be built into the market model is seen as a positive side of the market economy. For some Albany parents, a school's potential to be closed provides evidence that charter schools are successful; if they were not, they would not be available. Tracy, a White mother of two children whom she identified as half-Black, chose a charter school after trying a neighborhood elementary school and a magnet elementary school. Unhappy with both, she explained why she thinks charter schools are inherently better:

> TRACY: I don't feel like the public school system holds up to charter, or even private school, or anything like that because I feel like the standards are different.
> RYANE: What kind of standards?
> TRACY: I know that they all have to teach the core, common core and all that, but I feel like because the charter schools get federally funded, they have to get higher, they have to reach a certain score, or they can get shut down. Where I feel like the public schools, they're not going to get shut down. It's always going to be there. I feel like kids can get lost in the mix of that without getting the proper education. I just feel like charter schools, and private schools, they work for their money, kind of thing. I'm not saying . . . because I know a lot of teachers. But I feel like, I don't know. I just feel like once they get tenured, or whenever, they just kind of get to a point in their career, where they're just doing it just to do it. I don't think they're doing it for the kids, or knowing that they'll make a difference in their lives. I haven't experienced it, but I just feel like, that's what it is.

In this discussion, Tracy is uncomfortable and a bit unsure about how truthful she can be. It takes her a few attempts to make her case; she thinks charter schools are better because, if they do not succeed in educating their students, they will be shut down. In the next breath, she also indicates a concern with the public-school tenure system, a frequent target of school reformers. Although Tracy is not correct in all of her assumptions (charter schools do not receive significantly more federal funding than other public schools in the same area), her focus matches that of neoliberal charter school reformers.

Idolization of the market is shown directly in some Albany charter schools, not only in their organization. Some charter schools reward children for good behavior with a "paycheck." Students use their paychecks to purchase access to pizza parties, college trips, and other rewards. Generally, parents with children in schools that provided student paychecks were happy with that system and thought it served as a positive incentive. Tabitha, for instance, with two children in charter schools, noted that one child could not go on a college trip because his paycheck was short due to a behavioral issue. Tabitha did not criticize the school for this; rather, she accepted it as a simple institutional structure when she stated that "according to their policies, according to the paycheck system that they have, he had to go home." The market is so internalized that many Americans have difficulty challenging it, even when it does not have a natural place.

Ofelia began to criticize a similar program, but quickly walked that back. She purchased two extra uniform shirts for her son from the school, but was frustrated that he would not wear them. Her son enjoyed walking to school in nice weather, and, as she put it, "because of his stage of development . . . sometimes he would be sweaty when he arrived, and he stunk." Ofelia notes that spending thirty dollars on two polo shirts was a financial sacrifice, but she did not want her son to be in dirty clothing. She asked him why he refused to wear the shirts, and he said he could not wear the purchased shirts because he had to earn them. "He needs to earn that polo through homework, exams, they give you points." Even though she paid for them, Ofelia's son would not wear shirts she purchased because of the school's norm that they had to be "purchased" with a "paycheck" that he could earn.

Tracy, Tabitha, and Ofelia all provide examples of parents who support a neoliberal, marketized system. While Ofelia found it a bit frustrating, she did not challenge the system itself; for all three, the market is simply a normal institutional structure. For them, the market belongs in the schools just as much as it belongs in consumer products.

Colorblind Individualism: This Is Not What a Democracy Looks Like

On January 21, 2017, the United States erupted in protests over the election and inauguration of Donald Trump, an avowed harasser who bragged about assaulting women. Joined by protestors around the globe, these women's marches were dominated by demonstrators in homemade "pussy hats," waving signs and chanting. One of the most common chants at these and follow-up protests was, "This is what a democracy looks like." Democracy looks like a community coming together to fight for equality, justice, and representation.

Democracy is not a group of colorblind, individual exchanges in an unregulated market. Particularly (though not only) in the United States, "neoliberals redefined democracy as choice in the marketplace and freedom as personal freedom to consume."[116] The idea of "democracy" has become an idolatry of the individual negotiating an unregulated market, a focus on allowing each person to achieve whatever they want to the best of their own abilities. It has become fundamentally about individual choices and actions, not community. The focus on "freedom" is routinely understood to mean "individual freedom" and liberty to choose, not the freedom or liberty that might encourage a community to flourish. With an unregulated market, there is no way to guarantee equal access by racial identity or other important factors. In Deborah Stone's language,[117] our concept of "democracy" is firmly entrenched in the marketplace, not the polis. The "marketplace" is a sterile, cold location where buyers and sellers trade products and services. It is divorced from the "polis," where human relationships and emotions matter greatly.

Outside of neoliberal challenges, democracy is a political concept, not an economic one. It belongs in the polis. But democracy has been redefined, in the marketplace, as colorblind individualism. This redefinition of democracy is exactly what occurred with the privatization, marketization, and charterization of American public schools. As hegemonic neoliberalism embraced education policy, its goal was "to bring education, along with other public sectors, in line with the goals of capital accumulation and managerial governance and administration."[118] A polity, especially a democratic one, enables unhappy citizens to voice their concerns in order to push for and create change. A market is different in that an unhappy consumer can simply leave a company and take their purchasing dollars elsewhere, but they remain within the market, making only market-defined choices. These are the two fundamental approaches to creating change; in a political community, unhappy citizens can use their voice. In an economic market, unhappy customers can exit.[119] For neoliberal theorists, the idea of exit is more efficient than voice, and it avoids the "cumbrous" nature of politics.[120]

Even as neoliberal policies, like school choice, allow citizens to exit the polity, they also point to a decline of democracy. Neoliberalism supports plutocracy, or a government "of, by, and for the rich."[121] While some scholars point to the Republican Party specifically for its role in promoting plutocracy by motivating racism,[122] it is important to remember that both American political parties have a racist past.[123] And, while race is hardly the only divisive issue in American politics today, it is part of what polarizes us.[124]

Extreme polarization permitted the unusual 2016 Republican primary win for Donald Trump.[125] Once elected through constitutional means, Trump joined other world leaders in having the opportunity to replace democracy (or what existed of it) with authoritarianism.[126] Because race and class remain so intertwined in the United States, Trump's "plutocratic populism" permitted his party to use economic means to motivate racial animus.[127] Democracy was pushed aside by multiple Trump policies, perhaps most clearly with the weakening of the right to vote.[128]

This weakening of democracy, exemplified by the Trump elections but with much deeper roots, is the context in which American children attend school. It is also the context in which their parents and guardians make decisions about those schools. Although markets are theorized to exist in an apolitical space, the ability of unhappy parents to leave the public school system for a charter school is layered with political meaning. After all, charter schools exist only because of the political structures that authorize them.[129] The simplest way to understand this process is to view these parents as choosing exit, as giving up their voice as citizens and embracing their power as market consumers instead. This is not incorrect, but it is also not complete.

When neoliberal policies create the option of exiting public goods, as charter schools do for public education, this is a policy decision by government *not* to respond to the voices raised by those who are unhappy with their public goods. Rather than responding to voices demanding change, the polity offers them a different option: an exit. If you're not happy, the polity says, you may leave. This is not a democratic response to a public need but an evasion of difficult politics. It cannot be overstated that this evasion of difficult politics—of democracy—is exactly what neoliberal theorists and elected officials propose and support. The result is antidemocratic policies that "take root in a culture of possessive individualism and White supremacy that makes them seem natural and inevitable, and contesting them involves actively challenging this culture."[130]

Friedman and other neoliberal thinkers praise not only the efficiency of the market but also its supposed racial neutrality. In the logic of the market, racial animus hurts not only those upon whom the hatred is placed but also those engaging in negative actions toward others. Racism interferes with the market's stability, predictability, and efficiency. Because of this, Friedman predicted, market-driven education would be racially integrated and equitable.[131] While he did not yet use this language, a market is one of the earliest examples of a colorblind approach to policy. Race can and should be ignored, because there is no way to quantify what to add to or subtract from a good's value.

Friedman's prediction that a colorblind market would lead naturally to integrated schools did not come true. Rather than natural integration, privatization through charter schools "reveals how destructive the culture of the market is to children of Color and the neighborhood public schools they traditionally have attended."[132] Further, this privatization, which leads nearly always to racial segregation, frequently provides a way for the upper class to reap a profit from the education of students of Color. This process of *segrenomics* is an apartheid structure that privileges—and financially compensates—one group over another.[133] This is how "accumulation by dispossession" works in public education policy.[134] In the process of "accumulation by dispossession," "assets previously belonging to one group are put in circulation as capital for another group."[135] Charter schools remove public institutions from the democratic landscape and move them, instead, to investors with enough capital to build, organize, and operate a school that, while publicly funded, has much less public oversight than traditional schools.

Charter schools typically develop in communities that have "failing" public schools. They use language of the civil rights movement to promote school choice.[136] This is deliberate, but it also has roots in reality. Charter schools are not *only* neoliberal attempts to reduce government power. In many cities, including Albany, they are strongly supported by communities of Color. The irony, and the political difficulty, of charter schools is that they are conservative, even far-right, attempts to end public education *with the support of parents of Color seeking the best options for their children.* Democratic, civil-rights language works to draw students and their families to charter schools when public schools have failed them miserably. When parents are desperate to do anything for their children, when they want them in safe environments with attentive teachers, when they need to know that their children are safe in a building and not on the streets while the parents are at work, charter schools and their promises of a college-preparatory education in a racially sensitive community are simply a better option for many families. It is the failure of the state and its branches, including urban school districts, that have pushed urban families of Color out of the democratic process of public institutions. And the state is doing very little to bring them back in.

In fact, quite the opposite is the case. Rather than trying to bring families back *in* to the public-school fold, legislation was specifically designed to push them *out*. One of the primary policy entrepreneurs, who worked with Governor Pataki on drafting the original New York State charter school authorization law, deliberately placed "reverse creaming" in the legislation. As he put it in my interview with him, "You couldn't run a gifted or talented charter school, but if you wanted to take harder-to-serve kids, you could create a lottery within a lottery to favor the harder-to-serve kids." The same entrepreneur later opened one of the early charter schools in Albany, and he proudly stated that "we were one of the first schools that had school lunch eligibility as a screen to get into the school." This structure, to provide first priority to children with high economic need, coupled with the locations of the schools, led to a segregated system. Acknowledging that location, coupled with income preference, led to segregated schools, he continued:

> That's the result of economics and housing that I have no control over. . . . In this city, race and economics are almost totally synonymous. Our whole theory of education is we were trying to break the link between those two factors. If we can serve primarily the people who are being misserved, and they were highly educated, as highly educated as everybody else, but not more highly educated, then the next generation there'd be no segregation.

> They would be able to get any job they wanted, live wherever they wanted, have whatever resources they wanted to take care of their own kids. You first had to get them a good education. There's nothing I could do about the racial segregation in their neighborhoods, unless I bought them all houses.
>
> We joked, we didn't buy anybody a house, we didn't change anybody's income, we didn't marry anybody off, and the kids were outperforming everybody in the district. To us that confirmed that a well-run school can overcome a lot of the disadvantages of poverty.
>
> If I was trying to make it diverse, I would have no income threshold whatsoever. The price of that is, for the sake of diversity, I would have sacrificed a whole bunch of low-income minority kids, who would have been shut out of the school.

This policy entrepreneur, along with Governor Pataki (who signed the law) and the majority of the New York State legislature, is White. The passage quoted here suggests a strong tendency toward White saviorism, a racist trope that assumes people of Color need Whites to help them escape poverty and other ills. Even while acknowledging the segregation that this policy caused, the entrepreneur refuses responsibility ("that's the result of economics and housing I have no control over") and clearly states that he and others "joked" about the work they were doing. Charter schools in Albany, as in almost every other city where they exist, are a way of taking politically active families out of the public system so the polity does not have to address their needs.

Policy entrepreneurs acknowledged that they were engaging in White saviorism discourse and policies. Another entrepreneur, discussing the fact that none of the charter school policy architects lived in the city of Albany, made his approach clear. This entrepreneur, discussing the primary architect of charter school legislation who is quoted above, stated that he once said, "I don't understand the concept where a person from one geography couldn't possibly care about the welfare of somebody in another." The second entrepreneur continued, "So does this mean that no one from North America should ever step foot on the continent of Africa to help out?" Policy entrepreneurs applied their paternalistic view to the education of children of Color.

Conclusion

Structured by racial capitalism, the American polity has limited options to combat these founding forces. While the state has evolved from a clear slavocracy to a nation limited by colorblind individualism, the country's DNA, built of racism and capitalism, remains firmly in place. These structures determine not only broad policies and social relations but the very nature of the state itself.

In the following chapter, I challenge the notion that the state serves as a neutral arbiter among competing interests. Instead, the state has its own interests and goals. These goals, coupled with the state's genetic code, have made fundamental change impossible. Racial capitalism lives on, and it structures not only the American polity but the choices we make within it.

3

Segregation Lives On

The Supreme Court and Policy Failure

We conclude that, in the field of public education, the doctrine of "separate but equal" has no place. Separate educational facilities are inherently unequal.
—US Supreme Court, *Brown v. Board of Education*, 1954

I was . . . impressed with the fact that they're very Afrocentric. And I find this extremely important for [my son] to be very close to his race.
—Catie, Albany Parent, 2018

In 1954, the Supreme Court declared that "separate but equal" facilities had no place in public education. In 2018, an Albany mother indicated that she chose a publicly funded charter school for her child partly because it was overwhelmingly Black. How did the United States move from being a country that demanded desegregation to being one where some Black parents deliberately choose Black schools?[1] To understand this, it is critical to trace the development of desegregation policies after *Brown v. Board of Education*. *Brown* was never the panacea that many Americans assume it was, because the Supreme Court is a political institution that writes policy, and is subject to the same policy theories we use to understand congressional and other legislative policies.

Public decisions, and their implications, are rarely clear and straightforward. This is the case regardless of which institution makes the decision. Although we are used to thinking of legislative bodies as being the primary policy makers, other institutions also write policy. These institutions include courts and executive agencies at the national level, and their counterparts in the states. This multiplicity of institutions, a result of American federalism and separation of powers, permits people to "venue shop" for the institution they think will best accommodate their demands.[2] This is why the NAACP pursued litigation rather than other political methods such as legislation in their quest to desegregate schools; the courts were more likely to end segregation than the legislators that relied on reelection.[3]

The sheer multiplicity of policy-writing institutions, along with the very nature of politics, makes it difficult to define public decisions and to identify the goals that motivate them. Political goals are paradoxical—they often strive to meet two conflicting concepts at the same time. This paradox comes from the fact that policies and goals are inherently political.[4] Sometimes defined as the "allocation of values" (or sometimes the "*authoritative* allocation of values"),[5] politics is bigger than government decisions or party affiliations. As the feminist movement reminds us, *the personal is political*. Politics infuses public and private decisions at all levels of institutional and daily life, and it affects the average person as well as those who work within government. Public policy, the formal result of government decisions and nondecisions made by people whose own lives are as shaped by politics as anyone else's, is frequently the result of political wrangling. This is especially true for controversial legislation passed by a body of elected representatives. However, even when policy comes from a court or government agency, it is based on politically constructed notions of power, deservingness, and deviancy.[6]

Public policy has failed to solve public problems because policy is part of a degenerative political process. The contents of any given policy, or its "policy design,"[7] are, by definition, written by people who are part of the political system. They are subject to the same assumptions about values, and part of the very power relationships that their policy attempts to change. Not only does this make it difficult for policy to solve deeply entrenched problems—and problems related to race and economics are among our deepest—but it prevents policy from fundamentally challenging dominant social constructs and the power relationships upon which they are built. This explains why *Brown v. Board of Education*, although symbolically important, did not end segregation in American schools. It also explains the paradox that evolved from *Brown*—that schools of choice can now provide Black families with a desired Afrocentric education.

54 | THE SUPREME COURT AND POLICY FAILURE

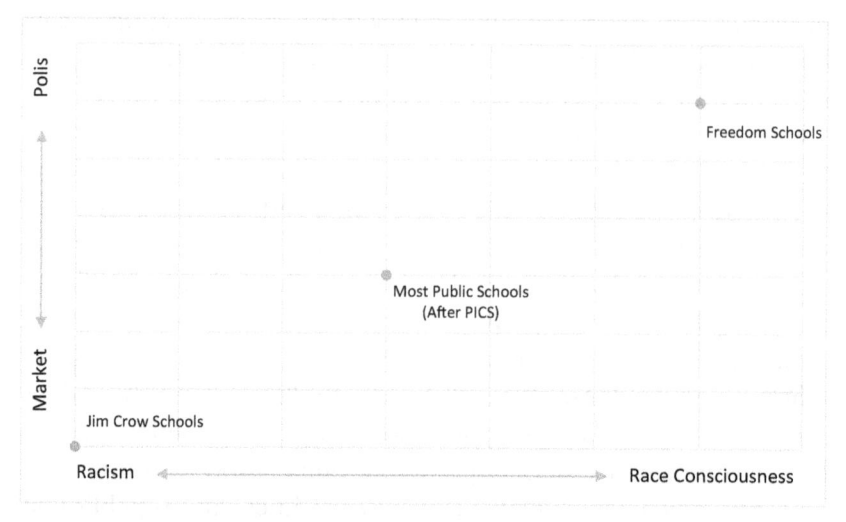

[Figure: A two-dimensional plot with vertical axis labeled "Polis" (top) to "Market" (bottom), and horizontal axis labeled "Racism" (left) to "Race Consciousness" (right). Three points are plotted: "Freedom Schools" in the upper right, "Most Public Schools (After PICS)" in the middle, and "Jim Crow Schools" in the lower left.]

Figure 3.1. Illustration of Policy "Change." Policy remains within a set frame, and change is limited by the context in which it occurs. In the United States, this context is framed by race and capitalism.

Public policy in the United States, like other political and nonpolitical decisions and actions, is framed by race and capitalism. Race and capitalism provide the boundaries within which policy may change. If we consider the interaction of race and capitalism to create a field for policy activity, we can see that these hegemonic forces place limits on how far policy change can reach.

Although it was largely developed by courts, school desegregation policy follows the example shown in figure 3.1. The scales of race and capitalism provide the framework within which policy changes. On the race scale, policy has two possibilities. First, it can focus on racial identification. This identification might be positive or negative; a positive racial identification, frequently referred to as "race consciousness,"[8] is exemplified by racial pride and tends to be justice oriented. Examples of this type of identification include the Black Is Beautiful movement and the more contemporary Black Lives Matter movement. A negative racial identity was showcased by Jim Crow and pre-*Brown* school segregation policies; they deliberately separated groups on the basis of a notion of racial hierarchy. At the other end of the race scale stands colorblindness. This, too, can be positive (such as MLK Jr.'s famous statement that we must focus on the content of character rather than the color of skin) or negative (including claims that affirmative action policies lead to "reverse discrimination").

Similarly, the capitalism scale can focus on one of two sides. At one end is community, or what Deborah Stone refers to as the "polis." At the other end is individualism, which is characterized by common American goals of individual wealth and power. The capitalism scale interacts with the race scale as it determines how race is applied. Racial identification can be used and applied in positive or negative ways. Note that positive racial identification (such as the Black Is Beautiful movement, or the freedom schools noted in figure 3.1) is associated with less capitalist, more community-focused orientation. As capitalism increases and becomes more individualistic, racial identification becomes more negative. The freedom schools used racial identification in a much more positive way than did the Jim Crow schools, for which race was a marker of powerful Whites and exploited Blacks.

Different types of schools fall in different places within the race/capitalism framework. For example, the Jim Crow schools of the pre-*Brown* South are framed by individualism and a negative racial identification. These schools promoted individual (White) rights over the (Black) community. They used racial identification in a negative way, assuming that Whites were better and deserved their own schools apart from the Black children, who were lower on the racial hierarchy.

Most contemporary public schools are open to students without regard to racial identification. After 2007, it became difficult to use race to promote an integrated school, so most of these schools now operate in a colorblind fashion. This is not the colorblindness promoted by Dr. King but a colorblindness that ignores race and the importance it continues to hold in US society. Schools in this category are expressly about the individual; there are standardized tests, a move toward a standardized curriculum, and a focus on individual achievement. The needs of the community are rarely considered.

The "freedom schools" of the 1960s were not traditional year-round schools but summer programs designed to combat the poor education provided in Black public schools. They were about community, as they taught children empowerment and ways to fight injustices. Race was important in freedom schools because it defined and promoted community in a positive way. In that way, racial identification could be promoted in order to build people up, not to tear them down (as was common in the Jim Crow schools).

It was within this framework of race and capitalism that, by 2007, the Supreme Court had all but given up on desegregation policy. Of course, the format today is different. State laws no longer authorize, or demand, separate schools for Black and White children. Individualistic, Jim Crow schools are long gone. But, even without those laws, racial capitalism has produced populations that live separate lives. Racial groups frequently live apart from each other, and experience different levels of political power, wealth, and other markers of American understandings of "success."

The extremes shown in figure 3.1 have been voiced by the Supreme Court. Chief Justice Earl Warren, in ending Jim Crow schools, said that "separate educational facilities are inherently unequal." Chief Justice John Roberts, in blocking a Seattle policy that permitted voluntary desegregation, showcased colorblind individualism when he said that "the way to stop discrimination on the basis of race is to stop discriminating on the basis of race." This decision (*Parents Involved in Community Schools v. Seattle School District No. 1*, 2007) made it difficult for school districts to create racially integrated student bodies. Instead, many districts placed their focus on economic integration as a proxy for racial integration.[9]

Separate educational facilities are now not just permitted but the norm. And while there is no specific policy demanding them, as was common before *Brown*, policies that try to fight these separate facilities rarely pass constitutional muster. Far from demanding integration, or even an end to segregation, the Supreme Court now condones choices that can be constructed as "individual." America's colorblind individualism, built on centuries of racial capitalism, continues to lead to segregated schools. This is the context in which some Black families now choose Black schools in a positive, race-conscious decision. The desire for an Afrocentric education held by some Black families developed in the same context that condoned segregated education, the same context that allowed schools and states to ignore *Brown*'s desegregation requirement for a solid decade, and the same context in which the Supreme Court gave up on pursuing integration as a national policy. This context is framed by the same two factors that frame all American decisions: the race and capitalism that formed the nation itself.

Brown's Failures: Power, Policy, and the State

There is no need to repeat the many accolades that scholars, journalists, activists, and others have given *Brown*. The decision itself symbolizes an important break with the past, as the state indicated an end to its willingness to not just overlook but support apartheid racial segregation. Chief Justice Earl Warren's language leaves little room for misunderstanding. Segregated educational facilities are inherently unequal, they are morally wrong, they violate the US Constitution, and they will no longer be tolerated. This is the common understanding of *Brown*, and it is not wrong.

However, it is also not complete. Seventy years after the Supreme Court ruled segregation unconstitutional, scholars and journalists continue to note how segregated American schools are. Prolific work by Gary Orfield and his colleagues at the UCLA Civil Rights Project/Proyecto Derechos Civiles finds continued segregation by race and ethnicity in all types of schools and in all regions of the country.[10] Nikole Hannah-Jones, the journalist who would later lead the 1619 Project at the *New York Times*,[11] wrote of her difficulty finding an integrated school for her daughter in New York City.[12] National Public Radio released a podcast in 2020 about how "nice White parents" in Brooklyn continue to hoard resources in public schools, and their fear that integration would lead to a decline in academic quality.[13]

All of this evidence points to one conclusion: while an important symbolic break, *Brown* did not end segregation. The meaning of *Brown* has shifted over time, even on the Supreme Court itself.[14] While *Brown* might have supported the Court's tenuous thoughts of demanding real integration (as it suggested in the later cases *Green* and *Swann*), it much more fully embraced the idea of symbolic desegregation (as the Court did in *Milliken*, just a few years after its forceful argument in *Swann*). The Court's decision to condone more symbolic desegregation, fully in place as early as 1974, allows school districts to ignore the context that made the *Green* plan unconstitutional. I argue that this is due to the Supreme Court's status as a political institution and its design of *Brown* and later policies. Like all American institutions, the Supreme Court remains stuck in the context provided by America's DNA, especially the double helix of racism and capitalism.

Centering the State

The story of the United States' failed nonattempt to create quality, integrated schools for all students does not begin or end with the decision in *Brown v. Board of Education*. The context in which *Brown* was decided is crucial and must also be considered. As discussed in the previous chapter, the American state developed to protect property rights ... including ownership of other people. Protection of property occurs through public policy. Public policy is a series of decisions and nondecisions that affect everybody in a geographic region (whether the nation, state, or local jurisdiction), made by elected and appointed officials who are ostensibly responsible to the public (especially for elected officials, but also for appointed and career government employees who carry out elected officials' decisions) or to the country's founding documents (especially for judges appointed to federal courts).

There are multiple ways to understand how the state creates public policies. Usually, these policies are thought to develop through state interactions with voters, interests (whether organized or not), capital, and other constructs such as race and class. In some of these theories, the state is a mere referee, mitigating competing demands and serving the loudest, best-organized interests. In these approaches, characterized by classic American pluralist doctrine such as Dahl's *Who Governs?* (1961), the understanding of the state as a mediator between competing interests is fundamentally democratic. The state, in these constructs, is a mere neutral arbiter between competing interests. It has no particular views or goals of its own. Its previous decisions are irrelevant, because each new political challenge is (and should be) decided on its own merits. Since elections do not allow Americans a voice on policy, those interested in a particular area organize to promote their preferred policy choices. In this understanding, policy is the goal. The analysis ends when policy is decided and implemented.[15]

Others, however, are critical of the assumption that all organized interests come from a space of equal power. Schattschneider's classic claim that "the flaw in the pluralist heaven is that it sings with a strong upper-class accent" reminds us that some groups are more organized than others.[16] This is due not to a stronger claim or a more sincere interest but to availability of time and resources. This is why organized interests have a strong tendency to overrepresent those who already have power. In this understanding, the state's previous decisions are not irrelevant, and later decisions do not occur in a vacuum. Instead, previous decisions are crucial because they have led to the different levels of power held by different groups. Once power is gained, it is used to continue to organize for more decisions and more power. (Clearly, those struggling to feed their families and pay the rent have less time and fewer resources for organization than those who do not worry about the size of their grocery bill.)

In this understanding, the state is not a neutral arbiter between equally neutral organized interests. Instead, the state is deeply influenced and impacted by the organized interests that are competing to win its favors. The state, as a collection of both formal and informal institutions, also seeks to maintain its own power. This makes it not a neutral arbiter between other nonstate groups but a competing player with interests of its own. The state, in this understanding, is crucial to the development and maintenance of power and the political positions held by groups and individuals. In this approach, state decisions are inherently conflicts of interest. Each decision the state makes impacts its own future power. The state, therefore, has an interest in maintaining (and even expanding) its own power, and will make decisions that facilitate that power.

Thus, organized interests have different levels of power. They compete on an unequal playing field in their quest to convince the state—itself a product of power and constructed knowledge and interests—that their own views should influence policy. The decisions they impact remain important and structure the polity for the foreseeable future. The pluralist approach, with its focus on organization and negotiation among groups and the referee state, misses the forest for the trees. More critical approaches consider what happens to the polity when the policy in question is adopted and implemented. Analysis does not end when one group wins the policy prize, but continues to see how policies impact future politics.[17]

The state and its policies provided the context in which *Brown* was decided. While desegregation studies frequently start with *Brown v.*

Board of Education (1954), this approach ignores the political and policy contexts that had been developing in the United States since at least 1619.[18] Studies such as these treat the state as the neutral arbiter, not as a set of institutions with their own history and interests. *Brown* was not decided in a vacuum, and no policy—including Supreme Court decisions—is strong enough to change centuries of history, political institutions, and social norms embedded in the nation's genetic code. Indeed, as I argued in the previous chapter, race and capitalism are so ingrained in the United States that they form the double helix of the nation's very DNA. The structure of race and capitalism, enshrined in the United States since the first Indigenous people were dispossessed and exponentially expanded when the first Africans were sold at Jamestown, provided the context in which *Brown* was decided. The same structure of race and capitalism also determined the context in which *Brown* was implemented and eventually eclipsed.

The Supreme Court as a Political Institution

Far from an insulated body of legal scholars, the Supreme Court is a political institution.[19] While cloaked in a much thicker veil of secrecy than public congressional fighting, and even name calling, the Court is made up of nine people who view US politics through a legal lens. While they are affiliated with different political parties, the Court's institutional structure (members are nominated by the president and confirmed by the Senate) ensures that they respect basic American values. As a political institution that holds one third of the federal government's divided power, the Court's political nature demands political analysis.

Because public policy is inherently political,[20] a policy-centered analysis of *Brown* and later desegregation cases places politics at the forefront.[21] This explains several parts of the decision that have motivated countless discussions among scholars, journalists, and activists. For example, the decision in *Brown* was delayed and the case reheard before the Court issued its first opinion. In the second opinion, known colloquially as *Brown II* (1955), the Court ordered that desegregation occur with the infamous "all deliberate speed." Later decisions toyed with a potential demand for full integration—regardless of whether a state had ever required segregated schools or not—before giving up entirely.

The Supreme Court could give up on desegregation—politically pleasing those who came to power with the Nixon administration and, later, the Reagan Revolution—without overturning *Brown* because none of their policies ever strayed beyond the landscape defined by race and capitalism as shown in figure 3.1. From 1954 to 1971, Court decisions could be reasonably placed in the upper-right portion of figure 3.1. Race was important to student-placement policies, and the Court-supported policies considered schools' impact on the entire community. By 1973, however, Court decisions were firmly placed in the lower left area of the same figure. It became difficult to acknowledge race, and policies focused on how they impacted individuals rather than communities.

Applying Policy Theories to the Judicial Branch

Theories of policy design remind us to focus on the content of public policy. Public policies are complex bodies of works, including "texts, practices, symbols, and discourses."[22] Policy designs are contextual; they are based on a constructed body of knowledge within a given geographic region at a specific point in time. (As one example, a policy designed to increase the number of teachers of Color in modern-day California would make little sense in ancient China.) Classic political science argues that policies allocate values,[23] and they do this by encouraging or discouraging specific behaviors by particular groups.[24] Within a given context, policy designs are composed of five specific items: the policy's "target population" is the group whose behavior it attempts to change or maintain; its "goals" are the "problems to be solved"; its "rules" explain who is to do what; its "rationales" explain why the policy is required; and its "assumptions" pull everything together and connect the policy directly to its context.[25]

Although this list makes it seem that policy is clear and straightforward, composed of identifiable components, Deborah Stone reminds us that each element of public policy is contested, constructed, and political.[26] Further, of course, language itself is a social construct that does not always achieve full clarity and directness. When each element of a complex policy is (or can be) contested, and when each of its various elements have multiple possible meanings, policy becomes an extremely complex way of building, maintaining, and distributing power. This complexity means that language can have multiple interpretations, even when an author strives for clarity. Providing this clarity was the Supreme Court's job in its school desegregation decisions. Of these decisions, *Brown* is the most symbolic; it is the policy that most clearly offered a break from past constructs and power relationships. It is the policy that most clearly offered a different interpretation of morality than the context in which it was decided.

Chief Justice Earl Warren, who authored *Brown*, clarified the importance of context when he said that the Supreme Court could not make its decision on the basis of 1868, when the Fourteenth Amendment was adopted, or 1896, when *Plessy v. Ferguson*, justifying "separate but equal" public facilities, was decided. Instead, he insisted, the Court "must consider public education in the light of its full development and its present place in American life throughout the Nation."[27] He continued by expounding the importance of education and its contributions to democratic citizenship and stating clearly that separation of children was inherently unequal.

However, other parts of the policy are less clear, and these parts permitted the drastic shift that would occur in 1973. For example, Warren begins the opinion with a reference to the plaintiffs of the consolidated cases, indicating that all of them "had been denied admission to schools attended by white children under laws requiring or permitting segregation according to race."[28] This statement implies that the intended beneficiary of desegregation was Black children who attended de jure segregated schools, or schools that were segregated due to state or local laws requiring separate schools.

Later statements in the decision, however, imply that de facto segregation, which affects children attending schools in states without explicit laws requiring racial segregation, might also be included. In explaining that some of the consolidated cases included schools that were (or had been) equalized, Warren indicates that "we must look . . . to the effect of segregation itself on public education."[29] This focus on effects leaves open the possibility that not only de jure but also de facto segregation might be included within the Court's decision. Warren's language throughout most of the decision remains broad enough to include both types of segregation, even if it also indicates that "the impact [of segregation] is greater when it has the sanction of the law."[30]

Reading *Brown* through a policy design lens, with a focus on target groups, goals, problems, rules, and rationales, highlights the difficulty Warren and other Court members had in creating clear, strong policy. There are at least two different target groups; the most obvious is the Black children who wished to attend a nonsegregated school. However, it is not the children's behavior that the Court attempted to change but the behavior of state and local lawmakers who built and maintained segregated schools. The Court suggests that the goal of the policy is to end segregated schools, and that the problem is that these schools have a strong negative impact on Black children.

However, the Court struggled with its definition of "rules." Is the new rule, after *Brown*, to stop segregating children by race? Is the new rule simply that districts remove "Black" and "White" schools from their communities, and instead build "just schools"? Or is the new rule that districts and states actively encourage integration, and not just legal desegregation? An active encouragement of integration, in order to respond to the Court's concerns about the "effect of segregation itself," requires much more from districts and states than simply opening up schools to children of any race. This lack of clarity provided the Court with ample room to greatly expand its desegregation requirements, which it did for a brief time.

Beyond *Brown*: Integration in *Green* and *Swann*

The next major school desegregation decision, *Green v. New Kent County* (1968), took on the question of what to do when a district reacted to *Brown*'s mandate not by desegregating its schools but by putting the burden on families to decide which school their children should attend. New Kent County, in eastern Virginia, had one school for Blacks and one school for Whites. With no residential segregation, children were bused to their school according to their racial identification. This structure, authorized under Virginia state law, was ruled unconstitutional in 1954 as one of the cases consolidated with *Brown*.

Like many other districts, New Kent County maintained its segregated system in the face of *Brown*. In 1964, fed up with the lack of enforcement of *Brown*, Congress included in the Civil Rights Act a provision to withdraw federal funds from schools that continued to maintain segregation.[31] In 1965, the New Kent County school board reacted by instituting a "freedom of choice" plan in order to maintain eligibility for federal funding.[32]

Policy design reminds us to consider context and power. Without context, a law permitting students to choose which school to attend might make logical sense. However, New Kent County had a history of segregated education, and it maintained this segregation for a solid decade after it was ruled unconstitutional in *Brown*. It is no surprise, then, that zero White children moved to the Black school, and 85 percent of Black children remained in the Black school, by the time the Court issued its opinion in *Green*.[33] Although the Civil Rights Act had mentioned "freedom of choice" plans as an option to meet the obligations of *Brown*, the Court indicated in *Green* that this will not work in every context. Race-neutral colorblind policy, in this case, did not lead to a race-neutral outcome.[34]

The *Green* case provides early evidence that colorblind individualism, the current incarnation of racial capitalism (see chapter 2), does not lead to racial equity. In a context like that of *Green*, colorblindness (the simple removal of racial enrollment requirements) maintained a segregated school system that differed very little from what had been present when the district had official "Black" and "White" schools.

Fundamentally, the Court used the *Green* decision to push *Brown* further than it had in 1954. Perhaps buoyed by the Civil Rights Act and Voting Rights Act, or perhaps chastened by the assassinations of the 1960s, *Green* and *Swann*, which came soon after, issued a demand not just to *desegregate* but to more fully *integrate* American schools. Wolters argues that *Green v. New Kent County* changed the Court's understanding of "desegregation" from "assignment without regard to race," or a colorblind policy, to "assignment according to race to produce greater racial mixing."[35] This is a much stronger standard, and a different policy than that offered in *Brown*. In *Green*, the Court acknowledged that *Brown* and *Brown II* were really about permitting Black children to attend White schools.[36] However, they claim, that "was only the first step."[37] Beyond removing restrictions, the Court says in *Green* that the original goal of *Brown* was a "transition to a unitary, nonracial system of public education."[38] The Court could make this claim in *Green* because its policy design for *Brown* was vague enough to include de facto segregation.

Three years later, in *Swann v. Charlotte-Mecklenburg Board of Education* (1971), the Court continued its demand that school districts take affirmative action to fully end school segregation. While reminding readers that cases like *Swann* "arose in States having a long history of maintaining two sets of schools in a single school system deliberately operated to carry out a government policy to separate pupils in schools solely on the basis of race," the Court also recognized that lower courts and school districts had struggled to implement its demands that these policies be put aside. Part of the goal of *Swann*, therefore, was to provide better guidelines "for the assistance of school authorities and courts." At the same time, the primary "objective . . . [is] to eliminate from the public schools all vestiges of state-imposed segregation."[39]

The Court also used *Swann* to explain that a colorblind solution to student assignment is not always a valid way to avoid segregation. Although this would change in 2007 with the *Parents Involved in Community Schools* case, the Court said in *Swann* that "the objective is to dismantle the dual school system." Because this system had been "deliberately constructed and maintained to enforce racial segregation,"[40] colorblind policies might not allow a district to reach the Court's goal. "'Racially neutral' assignment plans proposed by school authorities to a district court may be inadequate; such plans may fail to counteract the continuing effects of past school segregation resulting from discriminatory location of school sites or distortion of school size in order to achieve or maintain an artificial racial separation."[41] This is a clear acknowledgment from the Court that race-neutral policy does not always lead to a race-neutral outcome.

Finally, in 1973 the Court extended desegregation requirements to areas without clearly racially motivated laws. In *Keyes* (1973), the Court ruled that, even without clear laws mandating separate schools, the district in Denver, Colorado, had maintained segregation through decisions related to student placement and school locations. Even without starkly labeled Black and White schools, other decisions might effectively create de jure segregation.

From 1954 to 1973, the Court established a clear trajectory toward demanding significant integration. This was not a colorblind policy but a firm commitment to placing students of different racial identifications in the same schools. However, this began to shift in 1973. In

TABLE 3.1. Supreme Court School Desegregation Cases

Case	Year	Central Finding	Racial View
Brown v. Board	1954	Segregation is inherently unequal.	Race-positive
Brown v. Board II	1955	All deliberate speed	Race-positive
Green v. New Kent County	1968	"Freedom of choice" is not enough. Eliminate segregation "root and branch."	Race-positive
Swann v. Charlotte-Mecklenburg	1971	OK to require busing for integration. Colorblind policies are not sufficient.	Race-positive
Keyes v. School Dist. No. 1	1973	De jure segregation includes school placement, attendance, and other policies.	Race-positive
San Antonio v. Rodriguez	1973	Unequal funding is OK.	Colorblind
Milliken v. Bradley	1974	Suburbs can't be forced to integrate.	Colorblind
Parents Involved in Community Schools v. Seattle	2007	Cannot use racial identification to voluntarily desegregate. Ends districts' ability to desegregate without a court order to do so.	Colorblind

the same term that the Court extended its interpretation of de jure segregation with *Keyes*, it also began its slow retrenchment from its race-positive decisions.

Race, Class, Segregation, and the State

The 1973 case *San Antonio v. Rodriguez* may seem, at first, to be rather distinct from the line of school desegregation cases that started with *Brown*. In *San Antonio*, the Supreme Court was tasked not with a traditional implementation question but with a funding question. Texas, like many states, funded its public schools partly through a local property tax. Those with more capital have larger, more expensive homes and, therefore, can contribute higher dollar amounts of taxes even while keeping their tax rates fairly low. Those with less (or zero) capital have small homes or, more likely, rent their residences from landlords. Their tax rates may be as high as, or even higher than, those of communities with greater wealth, but the lower property valuation makes it difficult to raise as much money. This problem leads directly to less money for schools.

There are two distinct problems with funding schools on the basis of property taxes. First, those with more money contribute more in taxes, and therefore their schools have greater resources. This is why areas in wealthy communities often have schools with better facilities. Second, however, property taxes are inherently regressive. Although those with greater wealth pay a greater amount and, therefore, raise more money for their schools, they typically do this by paying a *lower* percentage of their overall income. Those in impoverished communities pay a higher rate to raise less money and, therefore, fund inferior schools.

The state remains at the core of this dichotomy. Residential segregation did not result from people simply choosing to be with others who look like them. Residential segregation, now the greatest cause of school segregation even when some policies might counteract it,[42] developed because state and federal laws encouraged it.[43] Residential segregation, coupled with racism, led to the creation of "inner-city" neighborhoods with high poverty rates and high populations of people of Color. As discussed in the previous chapter, race and class are not separable concepts. They are intertwined and supportive of each other.

Therefore, the 1973 Supreme Court decision that the Texas statute permitting local school districts to fund their schools partly with property taxes did not violate the Constitution should be seen as a clear break with the trend the same Court began in 1954. Rather than treating education as a right, as it had since *Brown*, the Court now backpedaled and clearly stated in *San Antonio* that education "is not within the limited category of rights recognized by this Court as guaranteed by the Constitution."[44] The Court could have used this as an opportunity to further the approach it solidified in *Green* and *Swann*, but here we see it beginning to walk back from these decisions.

Like other decisions, *San Antonio* provides evidence that the Supreme Court is an inherently political institution. Around this time, the desegregation "controversy" had moved out of the South and into the North and West. In September 1974, violence erupted in Boston as students were bused to integrate the city's schools.[45] School desegregation rocked Los Angeles and motivated antibusing social movements throughout the 1970s.[46] Federal leaders on both sides of the aisle began questioning the utility of desegregation once it affected areas of the country outside the South.[47] The same year that the Supreme Court permitted unequal funding to remain in Texas, it also held that a nonsouthern school district (Denver, Colorado) had engaged in segregation that violated the Constitution. Within three months, the Court issued these two contradictory decisions. This suggests a Court that is beginning to question its previous decisions, and beginning to wonder how far it could push the concepts in *Brown*.

The Court finalized its trend away from *Brown* in 1974, when it ruled in *Milliken* that Detroit suburbs could not be held liable for segregated schools within the city limits. Because these suburbs had not actively created the segregated schools in Detroit, the Court reasoned, they could not be forced to integrate across municipal boundaries. Ignoring the impacts of redlining and White flight, the Court in this case made it very difficult to integrate most urban areas. The Court, here, continues the blindness it showed in *San Antonio*, by ignoring the role the state played in creating segregated cities and neighborhoods.

The first several desegregation cases, including *Brown*, *Green*, and *Swann*, placed Black students as the primary beneficiaries. If public policy is the allocation of values, Black students received the valued good in question—an equal, integrated education. By 1973, the Court began to position middle-class White students and residents as its primary beneficiaries instead. We can see this in *San Antonio*, when the Court ruled that the state was under no obligation to ensure equal funding for schools and that White residents could keep the tax revenues they raised for their own schools. We see this move more fully established in *Milliken*. Here, the lower courts continued to position Black children as the primary beneficiary, arguing that "desegregation" squarely within the city of Detroit was impossible. Residential segregation had ensured that Detroit had a strong majority-Black population, and therefore racial integration without the surrounding suburbs was impossible.

The Supreme Court, however, overturned these lower decisions. White families and communities, the Court argued, had not caused the segregation in Detroit by leaving the city limits or by creating communities away from the city center. Because there was "no claim or finding that the school district boundary lines were established with the purpose of fostering racial segregation," outlying communities could not be forced into an integration plan to benefit Black children in the city of Detroit. This marks the beginning of the Supreme Court's move away from a race-positive, pro-integration stand, made possible by *Brown* and deliberately toyed with in *Green* and *Swann*, and toward a race-neutral, colorblind approach that benefits White children over Black.

The End of *Brown*: *Parents Involved* and Beyond

After *Milliken v. Bradley*, the Supreme Court heard only a handful of desegregation cases until the 1990s. And by then, they had clearly stepped back from *Green*'s and *Swann*'s possibilities of full enforcement of *Brown* and embraced *Milliken v. Bradley*'s weaker threshold. There are three cases from the 1990s that solidified the Court's colorblind approach: *Board of Education of Oklahoma City Public Schools v. Dowell* (1991), *Freeman v. Pitts* (1992), and *Missouri v. Jenkins* (1995).

Each of these cases centers on a different question, but in each of them the Court issued rulings that made desegregation more difficult. In *Dowell*, the Court ruled that Oklahoma City had met its requirement to obtain "unitary" status, thereby nullifying a decades-old court order to desegregate Black and White students. The Court's language makes clear its transition from positive race-consciousness to negative colorblindness. Rather than insisting that districts eliminate segregation "root and branch" (as *Green* had done) or using Court power to promote busing for integration (as in *Swann*), *Dowell* found that districts had only to ensure that "the vestiges of *de jure* segregation had been eliminated as far as practicable." "Practicality" is a much weaker standard than "root and branch."

Similarly, in *Freeman v. Pitts*, the Supreme Court took a fundamentally American approach to public policy when it applied an incremental strategy to ending court supervision over school districts that had been under a desegregation order. Incrementalism, first clearly identified by Lindblom,[48] is an understanding that policy makers do not start from the roots of a policy problem. Rather, they begin their analysis with what they already know and assume about a policy problem and its possible solutions. From a policy perspective (of course, there are other reasons as well), this is why policy makers in the United States do not switch to a socialist economy or promote sweeping new policies like national healthcare.[49] *Freeman v. Pitts* allowed local school districts to be "partially released" from desegregation orders as they began to meet minimum standards.[50] They did not have to reach the standard of "unitary" status before being forgiven for their segregative sins.

By 1995, in *Missouri v. Jenkins*, Tushnet argues that the Court firmly decided, "We've done enough."[51] In this case, the Supreme Court ruled that the lower court did not have the power to demand a tax increase to fund larger salaries for teachers in an attempt to entice White students to come to Kansas City for their education. This case mirrored *Milliken v. Bradley*, which had said that areas outside of city limits cannot be forced to engage in a city's desegregation attempts.

Through the 1990s, then, the Supreme Court ruled that many school districts had essentially "done enough" to combat their former de jure segregation and allowed them to move to a "unitary" school district, as was the goal established by *Green*.[52] This move was firmly completed in 2007, when the Supreme Court ruled that the school district in Seattle could not use race to promote racial integration.[53] This case, *Parents Involved in Community Schools v. Seattle School District* (*PICS*), firmly marks the Court's move away from the positively race-conscious policies they toyed with in *Brown*, *Green*, and *Swann*, and their full embrace of colorblind individualism. Still structured by a field bounded by race and capitalism, the Supreme Court in *PICS* made it difficult for public schools to leave the lower left portion of figure 3.1. Schools now are both colorblind (in a negative way, in that they ignore how race has structured power, privilege, and resources) and individualistic. The rights of individual students (or their parents) are more important than the rights of the communities they represent. In Stone's language, this is the privileging of the market over the polis.

The Seattle case is relevant to this discussion for two distinct reasons. First, it marks the clear, final end of a national policy promoting racial diversity in K–12 public schools. Although the Court gave itself room to promote race-positive integration until 1974, the cases after that began limiting districts' abilities to implement integration plans. *Milliken*, of course, forbade the requirement that suburban areas participate in desegregation/integration plans. The 1990s cases discussed by Orfield and Eaton allowed districts to obtain "unitary" status, thereby ending their court-ordered desegregation plans.[54] And *PICS*, in 2007, *forbade the use of race for the purpose of racial integration*. School districts can no longer use race to promote integration within their districts, whether they had been subject to a previous desegregation order (*Meredith v. Jefferson County*, decided with *Parents Involved*) or not (like Seattle, the subject of *Parents Involved*).

Second, it is worth noting that the Seattle school district was using students' racial identifications to balance schools within the context of public-school choice. Students were permitted to choose which of the district's twenty-one high schools they would attend. Only when a school had too many requests was race used, and then it was used to promote a racial balance that matched the school district overall (40 percent White and 60 percent nonwhite).

Chief Justice John Roberts's plurality opinion ignores the context in which Seattle designed its voluntary (i.e., not court-ordered) integration plan. Applying strict scrutiny, as is common when a government institution uses race as a classification, Roberts's opinion argues that Seattle (and Jefferson County) engaged in "discriminating among individual students based on race by relying upon racial classifications in making school assignments."[55]

By taking an approach that ignores the landscape created by racial capitalism and its descendent, colorblind individualism, the Court here implies that using race to promote integration is equivalent to using race to maintain segregated Jim Crow schools. In Roberts's argument, there is no difference between pre-1954 laws that required separate schools for Black and White children and Seattle's attempt to maintain racial balance after permitting students to choose whichever high school they would like to attend. This is the culmination of colorblind individualism, and deeply symbolic of the neoliberalism that pervades the country.

Conclusion

The Supreme Court has received, and deservedly so, many accolades for its decision in *Brown v. Board of Education* in 1954. Symbolically, the decision represents a clear break with the past. It is the first time one of the three branches of government at the federal level demanded an end to the apartheid schools that were prevalent across the American South, and might even be seen as the final step in Reconstruction. Southern states had to agree to the Thirteenth, Fourteenth, and Fifteenth Amendments in order to rejoin the union, and we can read *Brown* as the final, if much delayed, step in that process.

Like all public policy, however, *Brown* was written by those with power in the broader American political and social structure. It was also written by people with political goals, who knew the political lay of the land. It is no secret that the decision was delayed so it could be nuanced enough to get every member of the Court to agree in a unanimous decision. This is a political move designed to show a unified Court and minimize backlash, not a policy designed to be as strong as possible to promote equity and break the racial capitalism and colorblind individualism that has always structured the United States.

The vagueness built into *Brown* and *Brown II* (the harm came from segregation itself, even if the original focus was on clear laws that demanded it; district courts were to implement desegregation as quickly as possible while also being "deliberate" in their actions) allowed the Court to move in two different future directions. The later cases *Green* and *Swann* took the view that *Brown* demanded active integration and that children's racial identifications must, of necessity, be part of their school assignments. How else would integration occur?

However, the political backlash proved to be too much for the Court, especially after its membership changed with four Nixon appointees. Although Nixon's two 1970 appointees, Chief Justice Berger and Justice Blackmun, voted with the unanimous Court to approve the district court's busing plan in *Swann*,[56] all four Nixon appointees,[57] along with Eisenhower nominee Justice Potter Stewart, voted to uphold Texas's unequal school financing system in *San Antonio* in 1973. This marks the Court's turn toward more conservative decisions, and away from the way *Brown* was interpreted in both *Green* and *Swann*. The Court has ruled all later school desegregation cases with a much more conservative lens, and made desegregation virtually impossible in *PICS*. Thus, the United States' framework of race and capitalism worked to keep school desegregation policy firmly within its boundaries. While a couple of cases began to challenge that framework, the spiral of policy change ensured that political backlash would bring the policy back to more comfortable ground.

This is the context in which many families across the county continued to try to find the best education possible for their children. As the leader of national school-desegregation policy, the Supreme Court provided the context for public education not only in the American

South but also in the more traditionally liberal North. New York State and its capital city, Albany, may have a strong reputation for supporting liberal Democratic policies and politicians, but they remain within the framework provided by the Supreme Court. That framework minimizes the possibility of real integration, forcing parents into limited choices. We turn now to a discussion of Albany and the context it provided for the charter school movement.

4

An Unequal City

Albany's Political Landscape

Corruption's such an old song that we can sing along in harmony
And nowhere is it stronger than in Albany.
—Lin-Manuel Miranda as Alexander Hamilton in *Hamilton*

Albany has one major-league sport: politics.
—Grondahl, "How 100 Years of the Democratic Rule Has Shaped the City of Albany"

In 1921, a scandal broke out in Albany that changed the city's political course for the next one hundred years, and counting. Then led by the Barnes Republican machine, the city, residents discovered, had spent eighteen thousand dollars on coal that was "delivered without charge to [Republican city officials'] homes."[1] This scandal, reported by the *Albany Times-Union*, still the city's primary daily newspaper, destroyed the Barnes machine that had led Albany since 1899.[2] Democrats took advantage of the scandal, swept the 1921 elections, and have held every major elected office in the city—and most in the county—ever since.

Neither Albany nor New York State was new to scandal in 1921. Both had been controlled by political machines for a century by the time the Albany Republican machine fell apart. New York State, headquartered in Albany since 1797, was led by Martin Van Buren's Regency, a powerhouse of a political machine in the Jacksonian age.[3] New York City, of course, is infamous for its control by Boss Tweed and Tammany Hall. And, naturally, the century-long reigning Democratic party in Albany city and county politics has seen its share of scandals and investigations. But none of them have been quite strong enough to topple Democratic power, entrenched by the O'Connell machine by 1921. Locals offer different dates as to the end of the machine; it may have ended in 1983 when

Mayor Corning died in office, or perhaps in 2004 when an outsider—but still a Democrat—won the Albany County district attorney race. No matter the end date, the O'Connell machine held power for generations, and vestiges of the machine continue to haunt the city to this day.

In order to maintain power, the Democratic machine that took control of the city in 1921 placated homeowners with low property taxes for the next fifty years. This privileging of homeowners over renters that was at the core of the O'Connell machine was laden with racist and class-based overtones that continue to impact city politics and, especially, its public schools today. The Albany Democratic machine kept taxes low for middle-class White homeowners, leaving largely Black and poor immigrant residents without many city services. Although the city had limited alternative taxation opportunities, middle-class White homeowners were targeted with the benefits of low taxes and related minimal services. This means that nonhomeowners, who frequently needed greater public services, had limited opportunities for quality education, well-paying jobs, affordable housing, or other benefits. The prioritization of middle-class White homeowners over other residents created segregated neighborhoods, underfunded schools, and political strife. All of these issues continue to impact Albany, and its schools, today. Chapter 2 established that racial capitalism developed into contemporary understandings of colorblind individualism, and chapter 3 showed how these concepts applied to school desegregation policy. In this chapter, I explain and show how the Democratic machine installed these concepts at the urban level in Albany.

Colorblind Individualism Motivating Policy Design

Politics is a collection of stories and symbols that serve to mask and reify power.[4] The hegemonic status of racial capitalism and its descendent, colorblind individualism, means that the symbols that constitute political power and the stories that support those symbols are easily drawn from racialized tropes that have inherent class importance. These symbols, and their related stories, provide the scaffolding for a racialized, capitalistic hierarchy without having to resort to policies like enslavement or Jim Crow segregation. The law may be neutral, but its effect is not.

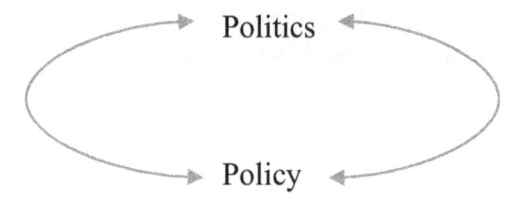

Figure 4.1. The Circular Relationship between Politics and Policy

Because their hegemonic status means that they form the very core of the American polity, symbols of race and capitalism are embedded in the design of public policy at all levels of government. Even when policy appears to be neutral on its face, it is constructed—deliberately or not—within and upon the very structure it is attempting to change or maintain. The policy design movement within public policy scholarship is based on the recognition that political power and stereotypes of different groups form the foundation of every individual piece of legislation.[5]

The impacts of politics, including the core symbols of race and capitalism, do not end when a policy is designed. Not only do politics create policy in a very logical sense, but these policies, upon implementation, serve to further impact, and even create, new politics.[6] The result is a circular relationship in which politics create policy, which creates politics, which then create policy. And the cycle continues.

In this repetitive, circular relationship, politics and policy continue to impact each other. Both are built on and reflective of symbols of race and capitalism. This makes it extremely difficult for a political system to create significant change. In a city like Albany, with a century of one-party rule and deeply ingrained racism and classism, even legislation that attempts to break this cycle serves to repeat it instead.

This includes the role of property taxes, home ownership, and power in municipal politics. The process began with the O'Connell machine's decision to limit taxes while also limiting services. In the language of policy design,[7] the O'Connell machine positioned positively constructed, politically powerful, middle-class, White homeowners as its primary target. This preference for the constructed notion of "taxpayers," which really indicates middle-class homeowners, over other constituents is common in American politics at all levels of government; it is this same construct, for example, that motivated Proposition 13 in California in 1978, preventing the state from raising much-needed money for education and other services by taxing property. For O'Connell, this preference for the middle class was driven by a desire to serve the voters who kept the machine in power. With a high home ownership rate in Albany, low taxes benefited the majority of voters and, by extension, the machine.

Low property taxes, however, did not benefit everyone. Decades after Mayor Corning died and the O'Connell machine's remnants continued to cling to urban power in Albany, property taxes remained high on the agenda. After losing the battle to keep taxes low, Mayor Corning had raised them significantly in 1972; Albany taxes on homes now hover around 3–4 percent of a property's assessed value. The high rates that Albany homeowners pay now ironically have the same political effect as the machine's earlier attempt to keep them low; they make it politically difficult to raise taxes even further in order to support education and other municipal goals. They also continue to keep Albany homeowners, who remain overwhelmingly White, politically powerful as they seek to keep their taxes from increasing further. In the views of many homeowners, higher taxes paid by them would be used to benefit groups that do not own their own homes. And, in the language of colorblind individualism, nonhomeowners are not "taxpayers."

This preference for homeowners and the racism upon which it is based are not lost on current residents. The powerful duality of race and class is also front and center in the minds of communities that do not benefit from either symbol. Aretha, an older Black activist whose family had been active in Albany politics for years, made this argument unprovoked. We were discussing the development of Albany charter schools over coffee in a local café when she said that "it all has to do with taxpayer dollars. To me, and I stand by it, you have the White taxpayer against the Black student because it is all about where they live. They feel that they are entitled, the White taxpayer, they are entitled to determine how the school district is run. . . . [Elected officials] are not representing these folks [indicating darker skin on the back of her hand]; they are only representing the White taxpayer [turning hand to show lighter skin on palm]." Aretha's claim personalizes the scholarly argument that policy design is not only about the stereotypes and political power of target groups. Instead, policy also has the power to inform individuals about how much they are valued (or not) by the polity.[8] Her statement clearly indicates a view that elected representatives are more concerned about White demands than Black ones, at least in Albany.

Cities, states, countries, and other polities all have and show their preferences for some populations over others. They want homeowners who contribute to the tax base; hence the US tax code's traditional benefit for homeowners, who are allowed to deduct their mortgage interest from their federal taxes. At the same time, polities prefer not to have criminals and those in poverty within their boundaries; this is why criminals are imprisoned and communities across the country fight against building low-cost housing. Individuals who do not "contribute" in traditional ways (i.e., middle-class homeowners, a group largely constructed as White) are not as valued. Lilliane, another local Black activist, made this feeling of value—or the lack thereof—central to her understanding of local politics: "It was always go in a sense to take care of who we call the taxpayers. You hear that a lot, right? We're the taxpayers. I beg to differ. Every person that pays rent pays taxes and oftentimes they're paying more for less space, because they're poor, okay. For us to go around talking about 'we the taxpayer,' 'we don't want the taxpayers to leave.' You already telling other people that they don't count."

Aretha and Lilliane have both lived in Albany for decades and served their community through elected offices, volunteer work, activist leadership, and in additional ways. I did not ask any respondent whether they thought that "taxpayer" was code for "White," or whether they felt that their own, Black community was well represented in city or state government. Both brought these up organically.

Aretha and Lilliane show the impact of policy design that focuses on the interests of policy writers over citizens, even when those interests are also anathema to a democratic society that claims the mantles of equality and justice. Policies are built by politics, and these policies continue to influence politics by treating categories of people differently. In Albany, racial capitalism and its cousin, colorblind individualism, served to keep the O'Connell machine in power. The O'Connell machine's privileging of the White middle class has not been forgotten, and this history continues to shape city politics, policy, and power today.

Beginnings and Populations

Like many American cities, Albany was not first occupied by European settlers. The Iroquois lived in the region long before Henry Hudson, sailing for the Dutch East India Company, sailed up the now-eponymous river in 1609. The Dutch established Fort Orange, which would grow into the city of Albany, in 1624, and all Dutch land was transferred to English rule in 1664.[9] These early dates make Albany "the longest continually occupied European settlement in the eastern United States,"[10] and Albany also holds the second-oldest city charter in the country.[11]

Albany continued to grow in both population and regional importance with the completion of the Erie Canal and the construction of railroads.[12] The city included both European immigrants and Black Americans, most of whom were enslaved until New York abolished slavery in 1827. The city was also a significant stop on the Underground Railroad until the Civil War.[13]

Colonized by the Dutch and English, Albany was dominated by their descendants in its early European history.[14] Although Dutch names continue to be found throughout the city's streets, the population began to shift to the Irish as that group immigrated to the United States en masse. And while the city remains tied to its Dutch heritage, celebrating it every May with its annual Tulip Festival and traditional street-scrubbing activities, city politics have long been dominated by the Irish. The Irish population in Albany grew steadily; by 1875, "one in six Albanians was Irish-born,"[15] and every city ward had an Irish neighborhood by the turn of the century.[16]

While the Irish were the primary ethnic group and developed political power, Albany was (and is) a very diverse community. This diversity, centered around White ethnicity and religion for decades, remains visible in the city's celebrations and historic buildings. The Irish population was somewhat challenged, but never quite matched, by German immigrants, whose numbers were about half those of the Irish.[17] There was a large enough German population for several churches and German-language newspapers.[18] Polish immigration increased after 1900,[19] and the Black population increased dramatically with the Second Great Migration after World War II.[20] But, by 1921, it was the Irish who controlled politics in the city.

The Democratic Machine

Although Albany has early roots in what became the United States, a serious discussion of Albany politics really begins in 1921. This is the beginning of the O'Connell machine, led by "Uncle" Dan O'Connell as the Democratic Party chair through his hand-picked mayor, Erastus Corning, for over forty years. While the power, organization, and patronage of the O'Connell machine were similar to machine-style politics common in American cities, the Albany machine was unique for its Catholic-Protestant unity and its sheer longevity. Over a full century later, voters in Albany continue to discuss whether or not specific candidates in Democratic primaries have connections to the machine that took control in 1921. Democrats maintain a stronghold in city politics; with about eleven times as many registered Democrats as Republicans within city limits,[21] the real contest for city elections is the Democratic primary, and many seats go unchallenged by Republicans in general elections. Between the O'Connell machine and its vestiges, the city of Albany "ranks first as the longest run of uninterrupted Democratic rule."[22] The story of the O'Connell machine reads like an overblown crime novel; it involves not only basic political graft, corruption, and direct payment for votes but also the kidnapping of Dan O'Connell's nephew for ransom and rumors that O'Connell ordered a hit against the legendary gangster Jack "Legs" Diamond.

While Dan O'Connell himself only held elected office for two years (he was the city assessor from 1919 to 1921), he built a powerful machine with his brothers and the Corning family, an old name in elite New York circles.[23] O'Connell worked closely with the father of Erastus Corning, who would serve as mayor for eleven terms (1942–1983).[24] O'Connell ran the machine in the background with power that was both absolute and unquestioned. As Albany native and novelist William Kennedy put it,

> [O'Connell] shaped the way everyone around me thought and behaved politically. I believe it was a common Albany syndrome for children to

grow up obsessed with being a Democrat. Your identity was fixed by both religion and politics, but from the political hierarchy came the way of life; the job, the perpetuation of the job, the dole when there was no job, the loan when there was no dole, the security of the neighborhood, the new streetlight, the right to run your bar after hours or to open a card game on the sneak. These things came to you not by right of citizenship. Republicans had no such rights.[25]

Neither O'Connell nor Mayor Corning was shy about the nature of their political relationship. Corning, when asked whether O'Connell was still the boss in Albany, replied simply, "Oh, yes," after he had already served several terms.[26] O'Connell, when challenged by another politician that he should not use the "boss" label, simply reminded him, "But I am the boss."[27] No one in Albany doubted who had power and control.

The O'Connell Machine, Political Power, and Ethnic Communities

The O'Connell machine had much in common with other urban political machines. While strictly Democratic, it had little use for ideology. This lack of ideology made it easy for the O'Connell machine, like the machines in Chicago and Pittsburgh, to "shift from working-class to middle-class policies for white ethnics."[28] This shift from a focus on working-class benefits, like plentiful low-paying jobs, to middle-class benefits, like low taxes, was directly connected to the needs of the machine as an organization. As Erie notes of many Irish machines, "The machine's organizational maintenance needs—building citywide electoral pluralities, securing necessary party financing, placating the business community—introduced a conservative strain into Irish-American urban leadership, resulting in lost opportunities to represent working-class political interests more fully."[29] In Albany in particular, this focus on conservative politics (all while under the Democratic Party banner) created racial divisions and residential segregation that are still seen today. It cannot be overstated that this shift was deliberate, and that it occurred expressly to keep the machine in power.

Although the history of the O'Connell machine is analogous to those of many other urban Irish machines, factors unique to Albany influenced how the machine financed its activities. While some machines taxed to raise money to provide patronage, Albany borrowed money instead. Albany had (and continues to have) limited taxing abilities because its status as the state capital means that a significant amount of property within city limits is state owned and therefore tax exempt.[30] In addition to state-owned property, large swaths of real estate in Albany are held by tax-exempt nonprofit organizations such as hospitals, colleges, and nongovernmental organizations.

With so much real estate that cannot be taxed, the city had two alternatives: either tax homeowners at a high rate to make up for the tax-exempt land, or borrow money to finance municipal activities. The O'Connell machine made a deliberate choice to borrow money, keeping property taxes low for homeowners for decades. With more tax-conscious homeowners, the machine offered low assessments on homes (homes were assessed at 28 percent of market value) and much higher assessments on commercial property (assessed at 64 percent of market value) until the 1970s. The city's low tax revenue was used to support a large number of low-paying jobs, primarily in the city's "parks and public works departments."[31] In this way, the machine kept homeowners happy by keeping their taxes low, but distributed city resources to a greater number of people to continue getting their votes and winning elections. "Uncle Dan" once said that he would rather have fifteen jobs that pay two thousand dollars per year than one job that pays thirty thousand dollars per year to distribute as patronage.[32]

Ethnic Residential Patterns and Black Segregation

Albany is a city of neighborhoods. As of 2023, the official city website listed thirty-four neighborhood groups, though some are more active than others.[33] Although some neighborhoods have changed over time, the importance of neighborhoods in Albany is not new.

In *O Albany!*, William Kennedy offers descriptions and stories of several of the city's oldest neighborhoods, particularly Sheridan Hollow, Arbor Hill, and the South End. All of these neighborhoods are located in downtown Albany, and all have seen similar demographic changes since they were settled by early European immigrants. Sheridan Hollow, for example, was settled by the Irish early in Albany's European history. This area was home to the "Sheridan Avenue gang," "a band of Irish toughs who, by legend, guarded their turf rigorously and let no strangers pass through."[34] As Polish immigration increased in the early part of the twentieth century, that group took greater control over upper Sheridan Avenue. They established a church (St. Casimir's, which also offered a Catholic school to this downtown neighborhood until 2009), but the Irish and Polish populations declined as Blacks moved into the neighborhood in the 1960s.[35]

The Arbor Hill neighborhood underwent similar changes. In the early twentieth century it was a mix of "Dutch, Yankees, Irish, Poles, and Germans, with a few Italians and even fewer blacks."[36] Arbor Hill, once "the center of elegance" in Albany,[37] began to lose value after nearby Washington Park attracted residents to its surrounding streets. Trolleys developed in 1890, but they did not come into the Arbor Hill neighborhood until 1911.[38] Kennedy claims that this neighborhood was "ghettoized" by the 1960s, saying that it "[inherited] from the exploded South End the dubious superlative of being the city's worst slum."[39] A "ghetto," of course, is a constructed way to dismiss neighborhoods with high economic need and, increasingly, significant populations of people of Color.[40]

Along with Arbor Hill, many Blacks settled in the South End, long a neighborhood of poor immigrants, after the Second World War. This neighborhood saw the greatest increase in Black population of all Albany neighborhoods; only 1.5 percent in 1950, the Black population in the South End jumped to 16 percent by 1960.[41] A 1961 study of the South End concluded that the neighborhood had a 35 percent poverty rate, an old housing stock (the vast majority of the housing was at least fifty years old), and a significant amount of housing that lacked running water.[42] Neighborhoods like Sheridan Hollow, Arbor Hill, and the South End, joined today by additional downtown neighborhoods, transitioned from White ethnic to poor Black through multiple, deliberate processes. None of this is a new development, and these issues began even before the redlining that segregated many American cities.

The War on Poverty, the Machine's War on Blacks, and Blacks' War on the Machine

As national immigration diversified, the Irish-heavy machines in many American cities were successfully challenged by more diverse slates of candidates.[43] New York City, for example, saw La Guardia take down Tammany Hall by building a multiethnic voting bloc of Jews, Italians, and a handful of Irish and WASPs.[44] This was possible because of the significant change in both immigration and voting rates among multiple White ethnic groups.[45] The machine in Jersey City was overthrown in a similar fashion.[46]

The O'Connell machine, however, was not subject to a similar challenge. Immigrants from southern and eastern Europe, so challenging to the machines in New York City and Jersey City, had arrived in the Albany region much earlier and were already voting at high rates before they were mobilized in cities to the south. As Albany wavered between Republican and Democratic control from the late 1800s to 1921, both parties had already reached out to all White ethnic groups.[47] Without the significant growth in the sheer number of voters that occurred in New York City and Jersey City, there was simply no one to mobilize to challenge the O'Connell machine. Instead, "Uncle Dan assisted [Al] Smith and [Franklin] Roosevelt by inviting supporters of the defunct Barnes machine into the Democratic party. By the early 1930s a two-to-one Republican registration advantage had been transformed into a two-to-one Democratic lead."[48] Voters were moved from one party to another, but they were simply not available for completely new registration. Where other machines fell due to ethnic diversification, the O'Connell machine only flourished and grew.

Because Albany had a comparatively high home-ownership rate, at 41 percent by 1940,[49] and because O'Connell was successful at converting many former Republicans into the Democratic fold, the machine maintained an aura of middle-class conservatism. The O'Connell machine deliberately offered homeowners a low tax rate, which made it difficult to supply significant patronage to nonhomeowners. When real property moved to a new owner, "it was deliberately overassessed. The local ward leader would then graciously reduce the assessment, earning the new homeowner's gratitude *and* vote."[50] This reassessment, of course, was limited to those who were registered Democrat.[51]

While other Irish-dominated machines were pressured by competing racial and ethnic groups, this did not occur in Albany. Unlike in Chicago, for example, the Albany machine did not need the Black vote or the votes that came with welfare-state benefits.[52] This was the case because both the Black and the Latinx populations in Albany remained fairly small throughout the federal War on Poverty; even by 1970, Albany's population was only 14 percent Black,[53] though it neared 30 percent by 1980.[54] At its peak, then, the O'Connell machine simply had no need to reach out to Black voters, and, while at its apex, it never conducted a voter registration drive in either the South End or Arbor Hill.[55]

Aside from ignoring Black communities at election time, the O'Connell machine largely ignored the federal aid available during the War on Poverty that would have benefited those neighborhoods.[56] Although it remains controversial, the Community Action Program (CAP), part of President Johnson's War on Poverty, offered an influx of federal funds to community agencies with the requirement that those who needed them most had "most feasible participation." This meant that communities in poverty had to participate in order for cities and organizations to receive the federal antipoverty funds. While works by Moynihan (1969) and Murray (1984) are strongly critical of the War on Poverty and especially the Community Action Program, Cazenave argues that "community action programs played an important role in expanding democratic participation and encouraging residents of poor communities to challenge local authorities using tools of social protest."[57]

Many urban mayors, particularly Democrats although also some Republicans, also wanted antipoverty measures to remain within city jurisdiction, rather than being subject to federal oversight.[58] For many of them, this was about maintaining control over patronage, machines, and racial politics. As Cazenave puts it in his study of the Community Action Program, mayors "felt the need to exercise tight control over local War on Poverty programs as a way to maintain political and racial control in their cities." Further, these concerns "reflected the decline of the political machines they relied on for social welfare programs to win favor with the poor." Mayors were also concerned that, without the ability to control CAP spending, "the poor and people of color might use those programs to build political coalitions that challenged their regimes."[59]

The Albany machine's reluctance to give up power created such political difficulties that Albany was the last American city to receive CAP funding.[60] While O'Connell and Mayor Corning had similar concerns as other urban leaders about relinquishing control, they held out longer than any other machine. This was deliberate, as the O'Connell machine wanted to strengthen its own power "by marginalizing the poor out of the decision-making process."[61] This, of course, was in direct contradiction to CAP's requirement of "maximum feasible participation," and explains why the city's applications were rejected multiple times. The Albany machine was so intent on keeping organizers out of the CAP process that "activists took to the streets and submitted legal challenges to the power and legitimacy of the Albany Democratic Party."[62]

Many of these challenging activists were Black, brought to Albany by the Second Great Migration. This influx of people ignored by the machine created a struggle between those who ran and relied on the machine and those who did not.[63] While the O'Connell machine submitted CAP applications that ignored the requirement of including communities in poverty on their boards, activists worked through Trinity Institution in the South End to apply for CAP funding separately.[64]

Elected officials in Albany refused to create a CAP that included a significant number of people in poverty. Although the federal legislation explicitly required participation by multiple groups, Mayor Corning insisted that the Albany County Board of Supervisors (which was overwhelmingly Democrat and had strong ties to the Corning machine) lead the program.[65] The Board of Supervisors developed the Albany Economic Opportunity Commission (Albany EOC), which submitted a CAP proposal to the New York State Office of Economic Opportunity (OEO). This proposal was rejected in 1965 because it did not follow the federal requirement that CAP boards include members of impoverished communities.[66]

Because the O'Connell machine refused to include community residents as participants, nongovernmental agencies also attempted to develop a Community Action Agency (CAA) in order to oversee and distribute CAP funding. Trinity Institution (now known as Trinity

Alliance), along with other groups, created Albany Citizens Against Poverty (ACAP). ACAP suggested individuals to serve on the Board of Supervisor's EOC, but their list was almost completely ignored.[67] Once the EOC submission was rejected, ACAP submitted its own CAP application to OEO. Their submission was also rejected, primarily because they "had no viable means of financial support or social service experience."[68]

Partly fueled by the disagreements over how to frame a CAA to oversee CAP funding, Trinity Institution monitored voting locations in high-poverty, primarily Black neighborhoods in 1965. They were watching for vote buying, a well-known O'Connell machine tactic, and other voting irregularities (the O'Connell machine was also rumored, with some evidence, to watch how people voted).[69] As payback, Mayor Corning cut Trinity's city funding by twenty-three thousand dollars.[70] After another failed county attempt to gain CAP funding, the City of Albany finally received CAP funding when Trinity submitted another application in March 1966. It was approved and funded that May.[71]

CAP funding through Trinity turned out to be a significant point in Albany's history of racial politics. The agency, known as the South End Neighborhood Community Action Project (SENCAP), "organized new and existing neighborhood groups to take civil and political actions attacking the Albany Democratic Party's mix of loyalty, patronage, kickbacks and intimidation."[72] One of SENCAP's first projects was to fund the Brothers, a group of Black men who organized against employment discrimination in the construction trades and were called "militants" by the local press.[73]

The Brothers and related groups were not the only ones to challenge the O'Connell machine. Homeowners also began to revolt in the early 1970s, after Mayor Corning was forced to increase property taxes by a whopping 84 percent.[74] Municipal borrowing could no longer keep the city afloat with its low taxes. Although registered Democrats outnumbered Republicans by an astounding sixteen-to-one margin at that time, the Republican challenger came close to beating Mayor Corning in the November 1973 election.[75] Further, in spite of the development of SENCAP and the influx of federal funding, the O'Connell machine was able to limit "the city's 15,000 blacks to the South End and Arbor Hill ghettos."[76] As in other cities, Albany kept public housing in specific neighborhoods and used freeways as physical barriers.[77] In Albany, however, there was another significant factor: the building of the South Mall government plaza.

While other machine bosses facing funding problems turned to the private sector to "revitalize" their cities, the O'Connell machine was able to maintain control through public financing of Governor Rockefeller's vanity project, the Empire State Plaza.[78] As the story goes, Governor Rockefeller was driving through Albany with Queen Beatrix of the Netherlands and was embarrassed by the city's decaying neighborhoods.[79] As a result, he proposed a large government office project that would wipe out a large part of the South End, one of the city's most "blighted" neighborhoods.

While urban machines seek construction projects to disburse patronage, the situation in Albany was different from similar projects in Chicago or Pittsburgh.[80] In other cities, "Irish bosses were able to make bipartisan redevelopment deals by enlisting powerful local Republican pro-growth interests—bankers, developers, and business owners."[81] In Albany, however, the redevelopment project occurred through Republican governor Nelson Rockefeller with less machine control. The O'Connell machine opposed the South Mall project because it would remove reliable Democratic voters and taxable property would be replaced with state property.[82]

Rockefeller, aware that "a statewide bond referendum of this magnitude benefiting only one locality would likely be defeated,"[83] was stuck. Although Mayor Corning had initially opposed the project, he then suggested that "Albany County, not the state, sell the bonds to build the South Mall" and lease the land back to the state.[84] Construction began in 1965 and took about a decade to complete.[85] Through eminent domain, the project took one hundred acres of South End property,[86] an area then filled with Irish immigrants and other White ethnics.[87]

Residential Segregation

While Albany's population is about 30 percent Black, the majority of the Black population lives in only three of the city's neighborhoods: West Hill, Arbor Hill, and the South End. These three neighborhoods are also home to Albany's highest poverty rates and lowest home-ownership rates. These are also the only Albany neighborhoods that were redlined by the Home Owners' Loan Corporation in 1938.[88] West Hill, Arbor Hill, and the South End were all predominantly poor, White, immigrant neighborhoods when they were redlined. Today, 69 percent of Whites in Albany own their homes, compared to only 20 percent of Blacks. Arbor Hill is one of the lowest-opportunity neighborhoods in the county, and the South End continues to deal with environmental hazards.[89]

When Rockefeller seized land for the Empire State Plaza, about nine thousand people—including an estimated one thousand Blacks—were displaced.[90] Most Whites fled to the suburbs, which were greatly expanding at the time. Blacks, however, were more limited to Albany, and specific Albany neighborhoods, due to racism.[91] While tearing down homes, Rockefeller and Corning built public housing, including placing one project in an industrial area. Meanwhile, many landlords refused to rent to Blacks.[92] Many Whites who fled to outlying neighborhoods and the suburbs sold their homes to landlords. Those who rented to Blacks kept the buildings in disrepair,[93] with rats, roaches, poor sewage, lack of running water, unreliable heat, and other problems. As the Brothers began to organize, one of their demands was that the city enforce building codes.[94] In these three neighborhoods, over one thousand properties are now vacant.[95] As of 2010, 52 percent of the population would have to move to create an integrated city. The surrounding suburbs range from 2 to 6 percent Black.[96]

Albany Today

These historic trends have created a city with a highly educated population with deep pockets of poverty. As home to state government, multiple hospitals, a state university campus, and several smaller private colleges, Albany residents include a large number of highly educated professionals who serve in government, medicine, and higher education. At the same time, the neighborhoods ignored by the O'Connell machine and redlined by banks with federal approval remain stricken with poverty.

Albany today is deeply segregated along both racial and economic lines. I spoke with a local journalist, Todd, who pointed out that "there's tremendous segregation in the city between the haves and the have-nots,

TABLE 4.1. Albany Demographics. Total population numbers are 2022 estimates. Racial estimates are the most updated as of February 2024. Education, income, and poverty rates are for 2018–2022. Source: Except for graduation rates, data are from the US Census.

	Albany	New York State	United States
Population	100,826	19,673,200	333,271,411
Non-Hispanic White	50.6%	54.2%	58.9%
Black	27.9%	17.7%	13.6%
Hispanic or Latinx	9.9%	19.7%	19.1%
Asian	7.1%	9.6%	6.3%
Bachelor's or Higher (ages 25+)	43%	38.8%	34.3%
Median Household Income	$54,736	$81,386	$75,149
Poverty Rate	23.3%	14.3%	11.5%
High School Graduation (four-year rate)	82%[a]	87%[b]	87%[c]

Note:
[a] 2021–22 data; "High School Graduation Rate, 2021–22," Albany City School District Data, https://data.nysed.gov, accessed November 27, 2024.
[b] 2022 data; "NY State Graduation Rate Data: 4 Year Outcome as of August 2022," NY State Data, https://data.nysed.gov, accessed November 27, 2024.
[c] 2019–2020 data; "High School Graduation Rates," Condition of Education, National Center for Education Statistics, https://nces.ed.gov, accessed November 27, 2024.

more so than I think in other cities. That breaks down along a lot of racial lines." These divisions are shown in table 4.1. Compared to New York State and the United States as a whole, Albany has a more dichotomous racial population (about the same percent of Whites as New York State, but twice the proportion of Blacks and fewer Asians or Latinx residents). Quite a significant number of Albany residents hold a bachelor's degree or higher—proportionately, much more than either New York State or the United States. And yet, the median household income and the high school graduation rate are lower, and the poverty rate is higher. This shows a strong division—while the middle class in Albany is educated and comfortable, the averages are brought down by a large number of people in poverty and without a high school diploma.

These divisions, and the segregation they imply, were noted by multiple respondents. Along with the journalist Todd, noted above, I met with a former school board member who opposed charter schools. As we discussed Albany charter schools over coffee, this individual, Brian, pointed out the differences in Albany neighborhoods:

Albany had, again, a very high degree of segregation. The disparity of income in Albany is gigantic. We don't have rich people in Albany. There are no wealthy people in the city of Albany. There is no private sector. We are all a bunch of government workers and university workers, so we have a middle class and then we have people in extreme poverty. If you look at the data neighborhood by neighborhood, it is awful. We have neighborhoods where the median income is like twelve thousand dollars a year for the household. We have a lot of kids, you talk to the teachers at some of the other schools, you ask them, what is the number one problem in your schools? They will tell you, hunger. They haven't even gotten to homework, reading with your kids at night, and stuff like that, that you would like to see. These kids aren't eating. There is no money, there is no jobs, and there are families with generations of no jobs. That is an enabling factor. That disaster has just been happening.

Decades of disinvestment, segregation, and racism created the Albany that provides the context within which today's parents and guardians live. Todd and Brian both mentioned this as a significant problem, and additional respondents discussed the same problems. Children growing up in Albany can be in completely different worlds, just a few miles apart from each other.

Conclusion

The power of the O'Connell machine relied on and reified the racial capitalism and colorblind neoliberalism the infuse the United States. Privileging homeowners over renters served to maintain a class-based racial hierarchy and a segregated city. This segregation follows children into their schools. We turn now to a discussion of public education in the city of Albany, and how that education opened the door for one of the country's largest charter school systems.

5

City Politics, Policy, and Power

How Charter Schools Develop

We failed, in some ways, to serve our community, for far too long.
—District Employee

I think, in the most favorable light, they failed to recognize the level of discontent amongst poor, minority, lower-ward, South End, Arbor Hill parents. I think [the school board] underestimated the vigor with which [charter schools were] going to come in and target those families and go after them.
—Former School Board Member

In 1997, *Forbes* magazine ran a feature article showcasing the "atrocious Giffen Memorial Elementary School in Albany, N.Y." The article labeled Giffen "one of the worst public schools in New York State" while pointing out that the school is "spitting distance" from the capitol building.[1] The article, referenced by many of the community leaders I interviewed, uses the colorblind individualism frame that is common in American politics. Making no mention of race in the text, the article instead includes multiple references to class and includes photographs of Black children and their families. This brief article showcases how the double helix of race and class—the foundation of American DNA—can be used to motivate neoliberal political action. The article uses negative language toward teachers' unions and the state's educational bureaucracy, calling them "educrats," a "public education trust," and a "monopoly." This is classic anti-union language, and the article blames failing public schools squarely on unions. *Forbes*'s primary goal with this publication was to showcase a privately funded voucher program that covered 90 percent of tuition for any Giffen student who wished to leave their public school and enroll in a private school instead. Many of my respondents pointed to this voucher as the beginning of the charter school movement in Albany.

Milton Friedman promoted the idea of educational vouchers in his classic work *Capitalism and Freedom* (1962). Given individual choices in a competitive market economy, he argued, parents would choose the best schools available for their children. This competition, in Friedman's market-dominated analysis, would cause all schools to improve as they competed for students. Those that could not compete would become market failures and shut down. Writing as the nation was still working to desegregate schools after *Brown*, Friedman also predicted that the market would lead to naturally integrated schools. This is a classic economic approach that views racism as an aberration of an otherwise neutral market, ignoring the power of race as a "master category."[2]

Although some American cities continue to use publicly or privately funded vouchers to give children and their families access to private schools, constitutional questions about the separation of church and state make it difficult to provide this on a larger scale, as most private schools in the United States have a religious foundation. This difficulty with vouchers led policy entrepreneurs to develop charter schools as a public, nonreligious alternative. New York passed a law authorizing charter schools in 1998, and ever since, the state has continued to raise the ceiling on the number of charter schools that can operate in New York. By far, Albany has the highest number of charter schools in New York State per capita, and for years the city was a national leader in charter school enrollment.

This chapter explains why and how Albany saw a rapid expansion of charter school options. After showing why two competing theories, disaster capitalism and urban regimes, cannot explain their development in the Albany case, I show that the city's institutional structure paved the perfect path for charter school development. This institutional structure is built on a traditional Catholic school network, an urban political machine with a powerful mayor, and the city's status as the state capital. This is a story of institutions, of entrenched power relationships, and of powerful policy entrepreneurs.

Locating Charter Schools

Since their inception in 1991, charter schools have grown rapidly in cities across the United States. By 2024, charter schools were authorized in forty-six states and Washington, DC, and more than 3.7 million American students attended over seventy-seven hundred charter schools.[3] Not only do most American states authorize the use of charter schools, but they are present in many individual school districts, as well. While only nineteen districts across the country had at least 10 percent of their students in charter schools in the school year beginning 2005, this number increased rapidly (see figure 5.1).

This steady, significant increase in charter school availability in school districts across the country begs an explanation. Why do so many school districts include charter schools as a robust, nontraditional public-school option? When this option is available, why do so many parents choose charter schools? The second question is addressed in chapter 6. I address the first question in this chapter.

Potential Explanation 1: Disaster Capitalism

Naomi Klein coined the phrase "disaster capitalism" to refer to "orchestrated raids on the public sphere in the wake of catastrophic events, combined with the treatment of disasters as exciting market opportunities."[4] The disasters include natural calamities such as hurricanes (particularly Hurricane Katrina in 2005) and tsunamis (such as the one that hit Sri Lanka in 2004), as well as foreign invasions (the 2003 US invasion of Iraq) and military coups (like the one led by Augusto Pinochet in Chile). All of these disasters opened the opportunity for investment and redevelopment in a way that cannot be duplicated otherwise.[5]

In American cities, this "shock doctrine" can sometimes explain why a community is rapidly transformed into a place where charter school networks compete with, or even fully challenge, a traditional public school system. This is exactly what occurred in New Orleans, when the city rebuilt its school system by relying almost exclusively on charter schools after Hurricane Katrina destroyed much of its infrastructure.[6] After Katrina, "policymakers acted with shocking speed and precision to remake the landscape of New Orleans."[7] While some national news reports and

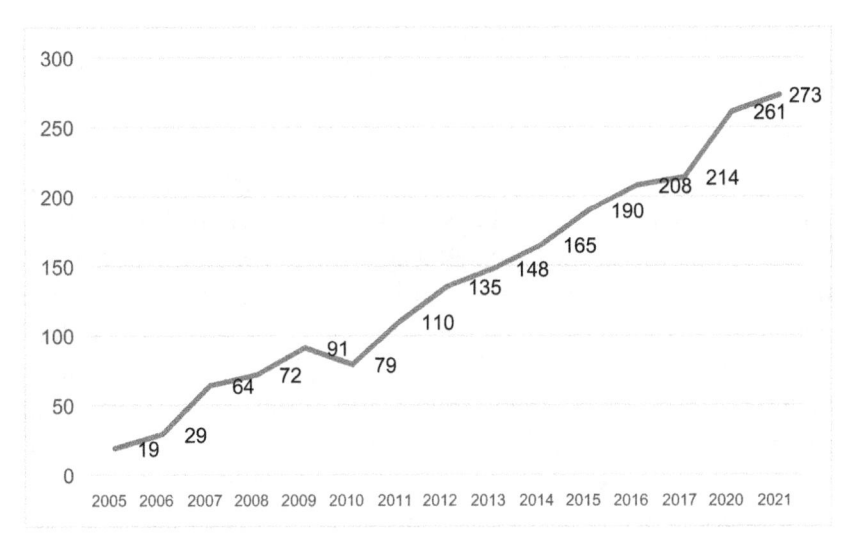

Figure 5.1. Number of Districts with at Least 10 Percent Enrollment. Graph shows the number of districts with at least ten thousand students enrolled in both traditional public and charter schools. Data from annual market share reports produced by the National Alliance for Public Charter Schools.

think-tank studies focus on New Orleans as successfully changing into a charter school city, careful scholarly work comes to very different conclusions. Indeed, the "shock" provided by Hurricane Katrina led to the firing of experienced teachers, especially teachers of Color, the destruction of community, lawsuits, and a significant challenge to democracy.[8]

While other American cities with large percentages of their student bodies in charter schools have been spared such a significant natural disaster, there are other ways to create a crisis. In Chicago, for example, the school system "projects a billion dollar deficit" every year.[9] Taking seriously Rahm Emanuel's 2008 claim (made while he was a member of the House of Representatives) that "you never want a good crisis to go to waste,"[10] Chicago Public Schools shut down many of their public schools and opened charter schools instead, in 2008.[11] Other American cities have a recent history of major crime waves or economic catastrophe. For example, Washington, DC, the largest school district in which over 35 percent of its students are enrolled in charter schools, has a reputation for having high crime rates; in 1989, then-mayor Marion Barry infamously said that "except for the killings, Washington has one of the lowest crime rates in the country."[12] While not the "shock" disaster that Klein predicts will lead to major economic restructuring, high crime rates are associated with high rates of poverty, which open the door to neoliberal investment.

Detroit, Michigan, serves as an additional example of how disaster capitalism might create conditions ripe for charter school development. Detroit, the "ultimate capitalist dystopia,"[13] saw its population decimated from nearly two million people in 1950 to about 630,00 by 2021.[14] This population decline, caused by "the implosion of the automobile industry," left the "city in free-fall,"[15] ripe for "complex financial deals" with Wall Street investors.[16] Unemployment left residents unable to pay their water bills, and the Detroit Water and Sewage Department shut off water supplies to thousands of homes, leading to multiple claims of human rights abuse.[17] While Detroit is not an example of the acute disaster that led to the charterization of New Orleans, its unemployment, deindustrialization, poverty, and crime created a similar opportunity. The crime and poverty that resulted from unemployment led families to prioritize finding a safe school for their children. The belief that charter schools were safer, in Detroit, drove many families to choose them.[18]

In some American cities, then, the concept of "disaster capitalism" can help explain why so many charter schools were built, and why so many families choose them. However, none of this is true for Albany. While winter storms can cause occasional power outages, the city has not seen a major natural disaster. And, like many cities, Albany has its share of crime and unemployment, but nothing like what the cities of Washington and Detroit have experienced. In the context of discussing the development of charter schools in cities like Detroit and New Orleans, one respondent noted that "there is no fundamental reason that Albany, New York, should have among the highest percentage of charter schools in America." Unlike what occurred in many other American cities, the "shock doctrine" cannot explain why Albany developed such a rich network of public charter schools.

Potential Explanation 2: Urban Regime Theory

If we cannot blame Albany's charter school growth on disaster capitalism, is there perhaps another theory that would explain this phenomenon?

Many scholars point to the development and implementation of "urban regimes" to explain policy change in cities. Scholars of education reform in particular also rely on the related concept of "civic capacity."[19]

Many scholars lean on regime theory to understand public-private coalitions and policy implementation. Regime theory builds on the work of Clarence Stone, who argues that Atlanta's coalition of White investors and Black voters and politicians was crucial to the city's focus on and investment in physical redevelopment.[20] Regime theory is fundamentally about coalitions across public and private interests that join together in pursuit of a common goal.[21] In this understanding, a regime is "an informal arrangement by which public bodies and private interests function together in order to be able to make and carry out governing decisions."[22] Urban regime theory has been stretched and modified to apply to multiple cases across the United States and Europe; sometimes, the theory is stretched or redefined dramatically in order to make it fit a particular case study.[23]

Under regime theory, then, coalitions of public and private interests work together to create significant, often positively constructed, urban change. These coalitions can also build "civic capacity," or "the capacity collectively to set goals and effectively pursue them."[24] This civic capacity, like the urban regimes that create it, "relies on cooperation of a wide variety of actors, both inside and outside the educational arena."[25]

While regime theory and civic capacity might be useful for understanding previous attempts at education reform,[26] charter schools provide a fundamentally different type of example. This is the case because charter schools are explicitly not about including the education community in promoting change but about moving away from traditional actors in education politics. Further, if an urban regime requires a public-private partnership that pursues the same goal, that is clearly not present in Albany. Rather than working together, Albany public schools and their charter challengers see each other as stiff competition. Not only do they compete with each other, but they also flatly refuse to work together. For example, one policy entrepreneur of Albany charter schools told me that "not a single person in the district was interested in looking at the [charter] schools." During our meeting, the entrepreneur—hardly a neutral party—boasted about charter school successes while criticizing the Albany public school district. And yet, while he clearly had a specific goal for our meeting, no one from the district ever offered evidence contrary to the entrepreneur's claim that there was no relationship between the two "educating entities": "Instead of having people embracing the alternative, it became this us versus them scenario. Literally nobody was remotely interested in finding out why our school did better than all the other schools. Or why the culture was better, the parents were happier, why 250 parents walked out of a district school and decided to stay in this other school. It was just this constant political barking focused on how much money we were taking from the district, that's how it descended over time."

The pro-charter side was not the only group to indicate that charter schools and public schools did not form a willing coalition. Confirming the distance and negativity between the two groups, a school board member said bluntly, "We don't have anything to do with the charter schools." This board member, Michelle, added that, before she was elected to the Albany City School Board in 2011, there was a "*really* contentious" relationship between the charter schools and the traditional public schools. In her mind, the sheer lack of communication between charters and public schools was an "improvement" over what had occurred before. A former leader of the Albany City School District put this contentious relationship even more starkly in their assessment of the work of the policy entrepreneur quoted above. In their words, the policy entrepreneur is "raping the City of Albany, preying on its inhabitants."

Thus, Albany is not a case of coalition building across public/private divisions to pursue a common goal. Urban regime theory cannot explain how so many charter schools were built in Albany.

State Legislative Foundations

No city can see the development of a large number of charter schools unless its state authorizes their use through legislation. This legislation is present nearly everywhere in the United States. Minnesota authorized the first statewide charter law in 1991, and, as of December 2023, forty-six states and Washington, DC, had legislation authorizing charter schools within their geographic boundaries.[27] New York's charter authorization law came in 1998, and its first three charter schools opened the following year. One of these, New Covenant, was in Albany.

While there is a significant policy diffusion literature at both the state and municipal levels,[28] many of my respondents pointed to different, Albany-specific reasons for the New York State charter school authorization law. Originally passed in 1998 with a statewide cap of one hundred schools, the New York charter law has been amended to allow up to 460 charter schools as of January 2024.[29] Typically known as a Democratic, sometimes progressive state, New York was led by Republican governor George Pataki, with a Democratic-controlled assembly and Republican-controlled state senate, when the legislation passed.

It is not unusual for a Republican governor and Republican-controlled state senate to support neoliberal legislation. The more difficult portion of the process was getting the assembly to agree to the legislation that was decried by teachers' unions and threatened to harm public schools. As explained by multiple respondents, the assembly agreed to pass charter school legislation because their long-awaited raise was tied to the proposal. One school board member, who was not shy about his negative views toward charter schools, implied that the assembly's eventual agreement to charter school legislation was simple political graft: "The way they got it passed through New York State is through simple bribery. It is a fact that you can look up. In New York State the charter school bill was tied to a raise for the state legislators. That's how it got through, under Pataki."

A former member of the New York State Assembly confirmed this view, although he characterized it a bit differently. I met with David in his kitchen not far from my own Albany home. David had opposed charter schools throughout his career, and explained that "the heavily Democrat-controlled assembly didn't like charter schools. The unions didn't like charter schools." This former member of the assembly provided much-needed context, when he indicated that, in 1998, the legislature "had not had a raise in, like, a dozen years." In addition to the promise of a long-overdue raise, the assembly was promised that charter schools "would be innovative, they would be equal opportunity, allowing people to go whether they were on the straight A or just on the borderline so they would reflect the inclusivity of public schools. They would be tuition free. They would be experimental and everybody knew, then as now, there is a lot of failings in education, public education in particular. And they could try things, they could try different hours, a different school year. Uniforms, same sex education." Additionally, the assembly was assured that "you could also unionize" in charter schools.

This, of course, is not what happened. Under New York law, organizers of charter schools do not have to recognize unions. Rather than the experimental education the assembly voted for, many respondents described Albany charter schools as being strict, disciplined, and even robotic. Further, the state law authorized charter schools to hire teachers without the normal credentials that are required for teaching in New York public schools.[30]

Once New York State passed charter school legislation, the playing field was open to anyone who wished to open a charter school within state boundaries. New York is home to multiple large cities, each with its own iteration of urban problems, including public education. And yet, no other city in New York State sees as high a percentage of its students in charter schools as Albany does. While both Buffalo and Rochester (both much larger cities than Albany) show a steady increase in charter school enrollment, Albany remains the leader in charter school enrollment in New York State. (The only exception was in 2015, the year two Albany charter middle schools were closed by the state.) New York City, home to the Harlem Children's Zone and other charter school experiments, is so large that it did not reach 10 percent charter enrollment until 2016.

Therefore, the question remains: Why did Albany become the charter school leader in New York State? What factors led to such focused energy on this small city?

Factors Leading to the Creation of Charter Schools

Most academic research on charter schools focuses on how well they perform. Another set of literature investigates why parents choose charter schools, and a focused group of scholars are interested in charter schools' effects on segregation. However, there is little work explaining why some cities see a much greater development of charter schools than other cities.

On the basis of the handful of studies that seek to explain why some cities develop more charter schools than others,[31] we know that, in a state that authorizes charter schools, districts that have larger Black

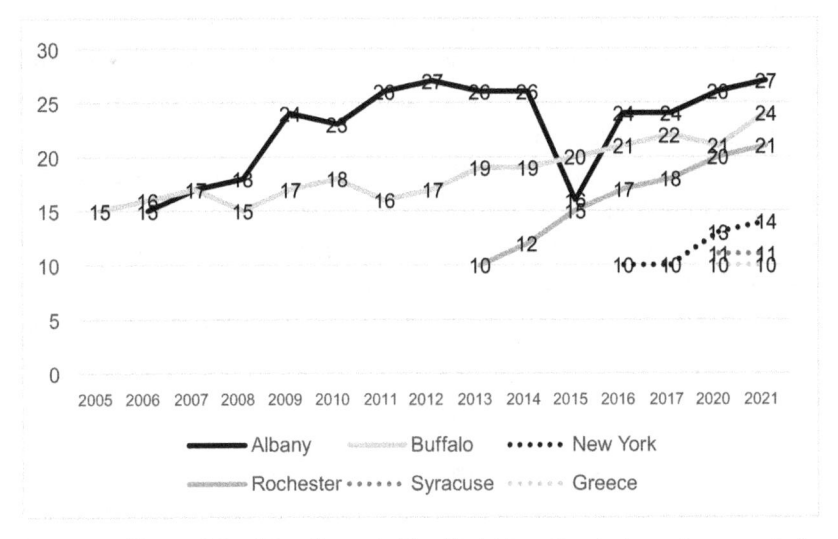

Figure 5.2. Charter School Enrollment in New York State. Graph shows the percent of students enrolled in charter schools in New York State school districts that have at least ten thousand students enrolled in both traditional public and charter schools, and at least 10 percent of their students in charter schools. Data from annual market share reports produced by the National Alliance for Public Charter Schools.

student populations,[32] coexist in communities with large percentages of adults who have a college degree,[33] have "high fractions of students enrolled in private schools,"[34] high drop-out rates,[35] low test scores,[36] significant local income inequality,[37] a per-pupil spending rate that is lower than their state average,[38] a high rate of unionized teachers,[39] and an appointed superintendent,[40] and are located near other districts with charter schools are more likely to develop charter schools than areas without these characteristics.[41] Broadly, these studies suggest that local demographic factors are crucial to understanding why charter schools develop. They also suggest that, "once a state adopts charter school legislation, political and institutional factors are more important than educational needs in predicting the number of charter schools."[42] Albany has many of the demographic characteristics associated with the development of charter schools.

However, while previous research can suggest potential independent variables leading to charter school development and growth, all of the publications referenced above are quantitative studies. These studies are important in providing a foundation of knowledge, but they do not permit an in-depth consideration of *how* or *why* demographic or institutional factors lead to charter school saturation in a given community. To do that requires focused qualitative work based on an individual district.

Building on previous work, then, in the remainder of this chapter I explain why Albany developed so many charter schools in a relatively quick time frame. In this case, the city's historic reliance on private Catholic schools for education, its historic political machine, and its status as the state capital worked together to create the foundation for charter schools. In this chapter, I first explain the role of the "policy entrepreneur" and then show how these entrepreneurs created an explosion of charter schools in Albany.

Central to this discussion is the role of meaning. Neither politics nor political actions have inherent meaning; rather, what they mean and why they matter are constructed by those who commit and are affected by political actions. In the development of Albany charter schools, there are two central figures that develop meaning; these are policy entrepreneurs and political institutions. In other words, this story is much deeper than demographic factors, test scores, or teachers' unions. All of these concepts matter, but they matter only in the context of a public school system constructed as failing and parents and caregivers who rightfully demand justice for their children.

Policy Entrepreneurs

While he was not the first to discuss the concept of "policy entrepreneurs," the term is most associated with Kingdon's "multiple streams" framework.[43] In his seminal *Agendas, Alternatives, and Public Policies*, Kingdon argues that public policy develops in three separate "streams": problems, policies, and politics. Each of these streams flows independently through the broader political structure (what Mintrom refers to as the "policy milieu"),[44] and whether or not a public policy is placed on the agenda and then implemented depends greatly on when and how these streams come together. When the streams join, they open a "policy window," at which point a talented policy entrepreneur can place the policy on the formal agenda for a vote by the legislative body.

While Kingdon's study, originally published in 1984, focuses on US federal policy, scholars have applied the framework to other countries and individual American states.[45] Indeed, the multiple-streams approach is widely used in a variety of settings.[46] In each of these studies, scholars use Kingdon's multiple-streams framework to apply the streams of "(1) problem recognition, (2) the formation and refining of policy proposals, and (3) politics."[47] Each of these "streams" flows independently. This theory fundamentally challenges a traditional policy process model that assumes an orderly development of problems, then potential solutions, then implementation. Instead, Kingdon stresses that potential policy solutions are being developed separately from the recognition of specific problems, so that the solutions are readily available when the problem is recognized and the politics are friendly.

When these streams come together—that is, when a problem is recognized, a policy solution is available, and the politics are right—the streams join together and open a "policy window." This policy window is opened by a policy entrepreneur who recognizes that the problem, policy, and politics streams are aligned and the time is right to promote a specific idea or plan. Fundamentally, policy entrepreneurs are "advocates for the proposals or for the prominence of an idea."[48] They may come from government, academia, lobbying organizations, or other institutions, but they are defined by their willingness to invest in an idea by committing time and resources to promote it. Frequently, the name of the policy entrepreneur can be easily linked with the policy itself; a classic example is the linkage between Ralph Nader and seatbelt laws.

While Kingdon's ideas promoted wide scholarship, not all of his theoretical components were fully defined. In *Policy Entrepreneurs and School Choice* (2000), Mintrom uses school choice as a case study to develop a more theoretically rich definition of "policy entrepreneurs." Mintrom argues that scholars should consider policy entrepreneurs as analogous to entrepreneurs in the marketplace, primarily by considering the introduction of "innovation." In Mintrom's description, innovations "represent changes that are deliberately designed to lead or force people to break out of particular routine behaviors and come to new understandings of their environment."[49] In this understanding, a policy entrepreneur is someone who promotes change at the root, rather than the branch.[50] (While Mintrom stresses that incremental changes are sometimes the result of innovation, large-scale changes almost always require the work of a policy entrepreneur.)

For Mintrom, the work of the policy entrepreneur occurs in a given "policy milieu." Particularly in discussions of school-choice policy, this milieu includes, among other things, "the institutional structures governing policymaking, current policy settings, and the behaviors and expectations of other groups and individuals around them."[51] In other words, the policy milieu is a set of political and social institutions, actors, and norms.

The second primary addition Mintrom made to the concept of policy entrepreneurs is the focus on meaning and frames. Policy problems, Mintrom avers, are socially constructed and frequently reliant on symbols.[52] Further, if policy problems are socially constructed, that lends a significant amount of power to the individual who can utilize language to show the desired construction.[53] It is this language that becomes the focal point for policy entrepreneurs. Policy entrepreneurs, who act as innovators much the way economic entrepreneurs do in the marketplace, link Kingdon's problem and policy streams. This does not necessarily occur simply because a given problem would best be solved by a particular solution, but because the entrepreneur is promoting a specific idea and needs a problem to which it can be linked. The entrepreneur uses language that will promote their desired policy within the given institutionally structured policy milieu.

Further, policy entrepreneurs who promote a specific policy are adept at using available frames. The concept of "framing," while in wide use in political science, sociology, and related fields, is most frequently attributed to the work of Erving Goffman. In *Frame Analysis: An Essay on the Organization of Experience*, Goffman argues that a "frame" identifies "definitions of situations that are built up in accordance with principles of organization which govern events—at least social ones—and our subjective involvement in them."[54] Crucially, frames are *subjective*. Their subjectivity requires someone adept at using language and symbols to convince others that they are, indeed, important.

This is exactly where policy entrepreneurs shine. Mintrom argues that policy entrepreneurs "[make] others aware of a policy problem and [convince] them to interpret that problem in particular ways."[55] The role of policy entrepreneur in this understanding is significantly more powerful than in Kingdon's presentation. For Kingdon, the policy entrepreneur is crucial in bringing together the problem and policy streams when the politics are friendly. The entrepreneur opens the "policy window," permitting a legislative vote and eventual implementation of the policy. Mintrom, however, views the policy entrepreneur as almost *creating* the very problem itself. The policy entrepreneur reads the social milieu, picks up on important or interesting facts, develops or becomes attached to a particular idea, and shows that this idea will solve a constructed policy problem. The entrepreneur places both the problem and the related policy solution on the systemic and formal agendas, acting in a classic "second face"- of-power way.[56]

The Role of Institutions

The concept of "new institutionalism" argues that institutions are not only solid buildings and formal governing organizations but a relatively stable set of norms and social constructions. Institutions provide "rules, routines, and standard operating procedures" to political life.[57] At its core, the new institutionalism is more about challenging other approaches to political science (especially the "social context of politics" and the assumption that individuals make thoughtful, rational decisions) than about offering a new, if still somewhat disjointed, epistemology.[58] Fundamentally, the new institutionalism argues not only that institutions are shaped by political life but also that institutions *shape political life*. In that sense, it is similar to Lowi's classic argument that not only do politics create policies but policies create politics.[59]

Political institutions are thus autonomous political actors. They shape political life by providing meaning, frequently through the use of symbols.[60] Institutions shape political preferences that *develop within the political structure*. As March and Olsen put it, "Preferences and meanings develop in politics, as in the rest of life, through a combination of education, indoctrination, and experience."[61]

It is fundamentally the role of the policy entrepreneur to read these institutions (what Mintrom refers to as the "policy milieu"), identify their meaning, recognize the interests that they created, and offer a contextual solution to political desires. The development of charter schools in Albany relied on the city's institutional and historical structure, both of which created meaning about public schools and school choice. A small group of local policy entrepreneurs then offered charter schools as the policy solution to these interests, and the boom began.

There are three fundamental institutions in the development of charter schools in Albany. These are a historic political machine led by a strong mayor; a robust network of Catholic and other private schools that made alternatives to traditional public schools very much the norm for multiple populations within the city; and the city's status as the state capital. After seeing charter-authorization legislation through the state legislature in 1998, policy entrepreneurs turned to the city of Albany to begin building. They targeted Albany deliberately, attaching meaning to the already-present institutions and offering a policy solution that they characterized as a positive move for civil rights, equality, and justice.

Institutional Factor 1: The Political Machine

As explained in the previous chapter, a traditional Irish political machine dominated the city of Albany for decades. In *Rainbow's End: Irish-Americans and the Dilemmas of Urban Machine Politics, 1840–1985* (1990), Steven Erie recognizes Albany as one of the six "classic Irish-American machines" across the country. As with most machines, the Albany machine "organized the electorate in order to control the tangible benefits of public office—patronage, services, contracts, and franchises."[62] The Albany machine lasted far longer than most others; it "reached [its] zenith in the 1960s,"[63] and, many argue, finally died when outsider Democrat David Soares was elected district attorney in 2004.[64] Albany mayors have a history of longevity; with a term of over forty years (1942–1983), Mayor Erastus Corning was one of the longest-serving mayors in the United States, and Mayor Gerald "Jerry" Jennings served from 1994 to 2013. The entire process of charter school development, and the beginning of its contraction, occurred under Mayor Jennings.[65]

Although urban political machines built their power and structure by providing patronage to working-class White ethnic groups, those that survived the loss of resources caused by the Great Depression were forced to cater to the middle-class homeowners.[66] Indeed, the postwar strength of the Albany machine (along with those in Chicago and Pittsburgh) "is attributable to [its] ability to shift from working-class to middle-class policies for white ethnics while piggybacking welfare-state programs for blacks and Hispanics."[67] This desire to keep homeowners happy meant that the O'Connell machine in Albany kept taxes low. Homeowners were so happy with this arrangement that, between 1921 and 1969, the O'Connell machine "routinely won city elections with between 70 and 86 percent of the vote."[68] Homeowners finally revolted when the city's finances were so bad that O'Connell "[increased] real-estate taxes by 84 percent."[69] Although Democrats outnumbered Republicans by a factor of sixteen to one, the Republican challenger nearly won the 1973 mayoral election.[70]

The historical machine's control of tangible benefits was directly, and deliberately, related to public education. The low taxes, noted by Erie, that kept homeowners happy also meant that there was little funding available for public schools. Until 1971, the machine controlled the city's appointed school board, its budget, and its employees.[71]

Local activists and elected officials noted the same arrangement that Erie discusses. Multiple respondents pointed to a traditional arrangement between a previously dependent school district and the mayor's office. Until 1971, when the Albany City School District became independent from the city, the mayor-led machine used schools as a form of patronage. As explained by one respondent, an anticharter district employee, "There was a time when . . . [the mayor] was essentially the superintendent of the school district." Not only was the mayor in charge of the city's schools, but "previously, essentially, the majority of the school board was controlled by the Democratic machine in the City of Albany." The machine's control over the schools allowed it to use teaching jobs as patronage.

This view was confirmed by another interview with a former school board member. This individual, Melinda, had served on the Albany City School Board during the early rapid growth of charter schools in the city, and strongly opposed them. As she put it, "Before [independence], Mayor Corning controlled the schools. And that's why our schools were political, very, very political. Teaching jobs were patronage jobs."

Because schools were used as patronage, there were few quality controls. Teaching was not seen as a profession, and neither were public schools thought to be either good or efficient. This was, in many respects, a deliberate outcome of a machine-controlled school system. Indeed, multiple respondents argued that Albany homeowners had an unwritten deal with the Democratic Party: homeowners would not demand greater investment in public education, and in return the party would keep property taxes low. Because public schools were largely populated by lower- and working-class students while the middle and upper classes chose private schools, many people saw this as a win-win situation.

Melinda continued her discussion about the historic role of Albany mayors and the public/private school divide. Because of the agreement to keep taxes and education spending low, "the education mindset for middle-class families was private schools. This was an Irish Catholic population with an Irish Catholic political machine. All your kids went to Catholic schools in the city of Albany. The public schools were largely the dumping ground. It's where the poorer families went." Steven Erie confirms that "one-half of all students were enrolled in Catholic parochial schools," causing the O'Connell machine to keep public school spending low. This arrangement "won the endorsement of Irish, Italian, and Polish middle-class voters—and the powerful Catholic church."[72]

But it was not only the Catholic community and institutions that benefited from private Catholic schools. Asa is a local Black activist, whose children were growing up while Albany public schools remained under machine control. Although her children were grown, Asa's work with a national civil rights organization kept her in tune with the state of public education. As she put it, children of Color "are not being educated in our public school systems." In her language, this is the case because "people don't see the worth and the value in people of Color."

Asa's own children had experienced similar difficulties in public schools. While attending a public elementary school, her son "felt he was being picked on and targeted," and his teachers "would call for the slightest thing." Her daughter, who was slightly older, also wanted to move to a different school because "every day she was being bullied, she was getting beat up or taunted or something." With charter schools not yet an option, Asa pulled her children from public schools and placed them in Catholic schools, even though her family was not Catholic. As Asa tells the story, once parents from her Baptist church community saw her children excelling in Catholic schools, other Black parents followed her lead.

The Albany political machine thus established low-performing, underfunded public schools in exchange for support from middle-class White ethnic voters. Although this ended when the school board became independent, with elected board members, in 1971, the idea of a dominant party ideology with a strong mayor remained. Even without firm control over either the traditional schools or the charter schools that began developing after 1998, Albany's mayor provided public support for charter school growth.

Not only did the Albany machine deliberately create underfunded schools for its poor children and children of Color, but Albany's still-not-quite-yet-dead political machine provided crucial symbolic support for charter school development. Technically, the mayor has no official role in the city's charter schools. In fact, one of the most frequent arguments against charter schools is that neither the school board nor city residents have a voice when groups or individuals apply for a charter.[73] However, multiple respondents, both those who support charters and those who do not, argued that Mayor Jennings played a significant role in their local development. One respondent noted that, although politics are now largely built on slick advertising campaigns, Jennings was "the old-fashioned retail": "He's a very tactile, detailed mayor, he knows every block. You call him up on his radio show and he knows who your neighbor is, it's spooky. [He is a] show up at every funeral, show up at every wedding kind of politician. He very much controls everything in the city."

The mayor's traditional machine approach, coupled with some animosity toward the school district (unlike previous mayors, he had no control over it, and the superintendent's salary is larger than the mayor's), made him less likely to support the city's schools. Tania, a former member of the Albany City School Board, pointed out that Mayor "Jennings appeared at ribbon cuttings for most if not all of the charter schools. He spoke in favor of it as an alternative on his radio show; he was constantly very negative about the school board and the school district."

This lack of support for the city's public schools fed into a palpable, if technically unnecessary, symbolic support for charter schools. Another former school board member, Theo, argued that "the mayor of Albany actively supported the growth of charter schools in Albany." Mayor Jennings offered symbolic support for charter schools by attending application hearings and ribbon cuttings for new schools, as well as more tangible support by leasing city-owned land to Albany's first charter school, New Covenant, for one dollar. These symbolic and financial gestures were appreciated by the policy entrepreneurs, especially because the strongest state-level charter supporters were Republicans and Albany is an overwhelmingly Democratic city.

Although he had no official power over whether or not a new charter school would open, Mayor Jennings did retain much of the power that was traditional to the Albany mayor's office. In this case, Jennings's most important role occurred when charter school applicants needed a building approved. As one of the primary policy entrepreneurs told me, "All of the buildings we've done the city has to approve, which in this city means the mayor personally approves; even though there's a process, all the decisions are actually made by the mayor. You have to go through the process and meet all the requirements, but if you've met all the requirements and he doesn't like it . . ." The Democratic machine, historical use of schools as patronage, and strong mayor fed an institutional structure ripe for significant change.

The idea that public schools were left to wither under the Democratic machine was echoed by activists who promoted charter schools in the city of Albany. Under the political machine, this extended to the way public schools treated their students' parents. As Asa, an activist, explained, public schools "don't have the key to the parents' hearts, and they don't understand how to include them and involve them." Asa took her children out of Albany public schools while they were still under the control of the machine.

The Albany political machine cannot be underestimated as an institution that created norms, expectations, and political desires. The deliberate decisions to keep (predominantly White) homeowners happy by keeping their property taxes low even though it meant minimal investment in public schools logically led to unhappy parents. Even after the machine no longer controlled the schools, the mayor retained symbolic power, and his endorsement of charter schools, through actions like approving building permits and attending ribbon-cutting ceremonies, provided evidence for the entrenched idea that Albany public schools continued to be "dumping grounds."

Institutional Factor 2: The Catholic School Network

Along with a strong political machine, Albany was (and still is) home to a large number of private schools. Private schools were central to the machine's ability to use the school system as patronage. Without having private schools available, it is likely that citizens would have demanded stronger public schools long before they did. Patronage, poor public schools, and private schools all worked together. Theo, the former board member discussed earlier, said that "the existence of so many private schools took away the pressure that those families would have otherwise exerted to make the public schools better. So it was pretty easy for the machine to get away with treating the schools as a patronage mill, because who was going to fight them on it?"

Using public schools as patronage allowed party officials to avoid making real demands on them, it kept voters happy by keeping property taxes low, and it kept Catholic school enrollment high as Catholic schools offered one of the few viable alternatives for many families. Former school board member Theo went so far as to call this deliberate on the part of the diocese: "There was no well-organized effort to address [failing schools]. . . . There was an unwritten deal, I think, between the machine and the Catholic Church." As White families fled the patronage-laden public schools for better academic programs in the Catholic (and other private) schools, public schools were left with larger populations of students from minority backgrounds and with a high rate of poverty. A former district employee, Sharon, said that "if you were White Irish Catholic, you went to the Catholic schools. The public schools were reserved for poor Whites, Jews, and Blacks." Indeed, around the time that the school board became elected rather than appointed in 1971, half of Albany's children attended Catholic schools.[74]

This historic trend of having a significant percentage of the city's population in private schools laid an institutional foundation that was crucial to the later development of charter schools. Catholic schools were attended not only by White Irish and Italian Catholics, but the diocese also operated schools in the city's Black neighborhoods. With a segregated population, placing schools in the city's downtown neighborhoods virtually guaranteed a high Black student body. At the time of its closing in 2009, for example, St. Casimir's was 89 percent Black and 5 percent Latinx. This enrollment reflected the school's neighborhood; 2010 Census data show that the surrounding census tract was 9 percent White, 76 percent Black, and 10 percent Hispanic.[75]

Further, the Catholic schools in Albany, like those across the country, were previously able to provide a significant amount of tuition support. As Aretha, a local Black leader, put it, "Years ago the Catholic Church was much more charitable. If you had a large family, because there were a lot of Catholics that didn't believe in birth control, [you] could go to the school and say, 'I don't have enough money, I can't pay all five of them,' you know what I mean. So they would cut a deal . . . 'We will have you pay for two or three.'"

Later, the voucher program discussed earlier in this chapter made Catholic schools more affordable and accessible. This tuition assistance made it easier for families in the city's higher-poverty neighborhoods to choose Catholic schools. Certainly, not every family made this choice, and not every family could afford to do so even if they wished. However, the very availability of that option was part of the local educational landscape. Both while Catholic schools provided the primary alternative and after the growth of charter schools, Aretha explained, "the word 'choice' becomes paramount." Having a choice is a symbol of freedom in the United States, and this was not lost on parents who did not wish to send their children to public schools.

This also means that, when charter schools began to develop in 1999, the city's parents of Color were already comfortable with alternatives to public education. There was no need to convince parents that they could leave the public schools to get a better education. Indeed, many of them had been doing that for years. As Asa told me, "A lot of people my age, a lot of them went through the Catholic school system as opposed to the public school system." Catholic schools were a popular choice for the Black population, in spite of the fact that the vast majority were not Catholic.

Indeed, the large number of Catholic schools in the city provided one factor leading to the significant rate of charter school development. Not only were citizens used to the idea of nonpublic education, but many students of Color had been able to attend Catholic schools on scholarships or vouchers. There is a clear relationship between the two types of schools; as the Albany charter school network grew, the Catholic schools began to close. While Catholic school enrollment is shrinking nationally, there is evidence that the availability of a free alternative is a significant factor in the closing of Albany's Catholic schools in particular.[76] The number of Catholic schools in Albany decreased 64 percent from 2000 to 2010; this is double the drop across New York State for the same time period.[77]

Community members mentioned several times that those who are unable to pay for private school tuition enroll in charter schools instead. As Asa told me, "In the olden days I would have put my children in Catholic schools. But now the Catholic schools are shrinking. . . . And then the charter schools came along. . . . The charter schools replaced the Catholic schools for us." Aretha, another Black political leader, confirmed this when she said that everybody in her family went to parochial school. Her own children, who grew up before charter schools opened, also went to Catholic schools. Aretha made the connection between Catholic schools and the sense of having a choice very clearly: "Again, choice, again something that I am familiar with. I chose to put my kids in parochial school. It was in the history of my family and we did it."

Nor was the pro-charter community the only group to suggest that the development of charter schools in Albany caused a concomitant decline in Catholic schools. A former school board member who opposed charter schools, Dorothy, stated, "I believe that as the charter schools started to gain force, that the Catholic schools started to shut down because for a long time, they ministered to the poor in the inner city. Their elementary schools had a lot of scholarship students." Sharon, a former district employee, was more succinct when she simply stated that "the diocesan schools were always a choice other than the public schools." The previously strong Catholic school network fed an educational culture that supported choice. As charter schools began to open and Catholic schools closed, the free charter option was a significant draw—especially for the inner-city poor.

As an institution, then, the strong Catholic school network in Albany created the viewpoint that there were legitimate alternatives to public schools. Because of their wide availability before the development of charter schools, parents had a political interest in nontraditional education. This large network also fed the idea that Albany public schools were failing, for why else would there be so many alternatives?

Institutional Factor 3: The Capital City

Capital cities in American states are not always the largest or most important cities. For example, Albany is a fraction of the size of New York City, Springfield pales in comparison to Chicago, and Sacramento is easily overshadowed by Los Angeles. There are other cases in which the capital city is the largest in the state, such as Boston, Little Rock, and Denver. However, regardless of their comparative size, capital cities are able to gather attention and media focus because they serve as the seat of state government. Indeed, state capitals are well represented among American cities with high charter school attendance rates. Of the fifty American state capital cities, since the 2006–2007 academic year eighteen of them have had at least 10 percent of their students enrolled in charter schools. (See table A.3 in the appendix for full information.)

Are there specific institutional factors that lead to greater charter school enrollment in capital cities? There is little literature available that explains what might cause a capital city to look different from other cities in a given state. If being the seat of state government allows greater policy innovation, whether in education policy or other fields, *why* does that occur?

This research begins to answer that question. In addition to its historical institutional structure, many respondents argued that policy entrepreneurs deliberately targeted Albany because, as the seat of the state capital, Albany has symbolic importance. More importantly, legislators and lobbyists from around the state routinely spend time in the state capital. This allows a policy entrepreneur to showcase their work, and encourage other local elected officials to implement the policy within their own geographic jurisdiction. In this way, a policy entrepreneur who chooses a capital city for implementation can be more confident of policy growth. While other upstate cities in New York are larger than Albany, none has the constant flow of elected officials and legislators that the state capital does.

This argument came up multiple times. Rick, an anticharter community advocate, said that "one of the reasons I think it happened in

Albany, is Albany is the capital city. These guys had a point to prove, that charter schools are the answer to what they saw as broken public schools. Where else would you do it but in the capital city? If it happens in the capital city, then people sit up and watch it." Theo, the former school board member, agreed: "[The policy entrepreneur] targeted Albany very deliberately. If you want to demonstrate an idea, where better to do it than the state capital?"

Coupled with its status as the state capital is Albany's comparatively small size. This made it easier to implement enough charter schools to create real, significant educational change with a reasonable capital investment. New York City and other upstate cities are much larger, with greater student populations. As Michelle, a former school board member with a more moderate view on charters than some, argued,

> Albany is the capital of New York. It is a small enough population . . . with one hundred thousand people or ten thousand kids. New York City is too many, there's no way. Buffalo, all the big five,[78] it's too many to really start to say we can actually go into this [with enough of an] investment. [In Albany] you can actually make a huge difference, a huge change. Based on the fact that it was the capital of New York, and the size, it was looked at as an example.

Because of Albany's manageable size and political importance, many respondents argued that policy entrepreneurs wanted to use the city as an example to show that schools of choice were better than traditional public schools. The underlying argument of several anticharter respondents was that entrepreneurs wanted to turn Albany into something like New Orleans, with near-total charter school enrollment, or even cause the closure of all public schools in favor of complete reliance on charter schools. In response to a question about why Albany had so many charter schools when other cities in New York did not, Sharon, the anticharter former school district employee, replied,

> I believe [the policy entrepreneur] wanted to charterize the district. And he picked . . . the capital of the state. Albany is not so big, we are not one of the big five. It was just right, just right. Where is the tipping point? Where is the tipping point? There are ten thousand kids now, there were

ten thousand kids at that time, [with] fifteen schools. Okay, now the school district has twenty-six schools. It makes no sense. It makes no sense. There is no rational logic to it, there is no logic to it. . . . You really just want to bust the system, get it to its breaking point and then charterize the whole school system.

The policy entrepreneurs I spoke with validated the arguments made by their political opponents. As the state capital, Albany is frequently visited by elected officials and other politicians from all over the state. The hope of one entrepreneur was that, when politicians come to Albany on state business, they would be surrounded by well-performing schools rather than failing schools: "My theory is that we did it in the shadow of the capitol. Then all the light bulbs would pop over everybody's head, and the district would say, this is a lot better. Then people would want to come and study it, and figure out what we were doing right, and then they'd replicate in their schools." An elected official, Jane, argued that Albany was "by design . . . the experiment for the state."

Conclusions: Creating Meaning in Albany

Scholars have not ignored the important question of why and how charter schools develop. Those who focus on multicity studies identify institutional and demographic factors as common independent variables, but these overviews cannot focus on the development of meaning that is so important to a critical study of public policy. And while some scholars focus on the growth of charter schools in individual cities, these cities are usually either quite large (such as Lipman's Chicago) or uniquely struck by disaster capitalism (such as Buras's and Harris's New Orleans). While these studies are important, they cannot explain the vast majority of cities with significant populations of charter school students.

Fundamentally, public policy should be understood as a constructed solution to a constructed problem. The importance of the work of policy entrepreneurs who read a city's policy milieu, have intimate knowledge of its institutions and its history, and shape a solution to their understanding of a problem cannot be overstated. In Albany, policy entrepreneurs relied on the city's historic political machine with its strong mayor and traditionally weak public schools, its population's familiarity and ease with nonpublic schools, and its status as the state capital to create a network of charter schools so large that, for years, it directly challenged the city's traditional school structure.

Just as studies of charter schools in Chicago and New Orleans cannot serve as models for understanding charter school development in other cities, the three primary institutional factors in Albany (the political machine; the historic reliance on Catholic schools; its status as the state capital) will not be identical in other cities. However, this chapter provides an exploratory beginning to understanding why smaller cities are likely to gravitate toward charter schools. Scholars seeking to understand similar development in other cities without clear disaster capitalism or unified urban regimes should study their city's institutions (in both the old and the "new" sense) to glean how policy entrepreneurs construct problems and solutions.

Of course, Albany would not have seen such significant charter school development without the concomitant demand from parents and guardians. The second step to understanding the development of charter schools in Albany (or in any city) is to ask why parents are drawn to them, and why they enroll their children in them. We turn to that question in the next chapter.

6

Why Parents Choose

The Limits of Public Education

MR. PREZ: Get here early. I'll let you in, and you can shower.
DUKIE: My dirty clothes?
MR. PREZ: Put 'em in this bag, leave 'em in the locker. I'll bring 'em home and wash 'em."
—Season 4, Episode 6 of *The Wire*

> We secretly run a laundry operation, we actually don't advertise it to parents. What we found is a healthy percentage of kids, or an unhealthy percentage of kids, were coming to school rather dirtily clothed. We were secretly changing the kids out, laundering the clothes, redressing the kids. We didn't want everybody to be sending their dry cleaning to school, and we also didn't want to embarrass the parents. But we couldn't stand by and have kids going around and walking in disgustingly vile clothes.
> —Policy Entrepreneur, Personal Interview

The Wire, an HBO television show that aired from 2002 to 2008, received popular accolades for its disturbing portrayal of life in decaying inner-city Baltimore. David Simon, the show's creator and producer, has said that *The Wire* is "really about the American city, and about how we live together. It's about how institutions have an effect on individuals, and how, whether you're a cop, a longshoreman, a drug dealer, a politician, a judge [or] lawyer, you are ultimately compromised and must contend with whatever institution you've committed to."[1] Of course, there is a fundamental difference between the fictional television show and the students whose laundry Albany charter schools will wash; Dukie, in the show, is a neglected child of addicts stuck in a public school. Albany charter school students, as shown by those whose parents met with me for an interview, have families who are carefully looking out for their best interests. And yet, the common denominator of schools that will do a student's laundry is striking.

As explained in the previous chapter, charter schools developed in Albany because policy entrepreneurs were able to frame policy problems and solutions to fit the city's institutions. Albany's history as a city with a strong Democratic machine, its traditionally strong Catholic school network, and its status as the state capital all worked together to create an environment that was ripe for charter school development. However, the previous chapter showed only one side of the equation. Like other neoliberal policies, charter schools rely on both supply and demand to remain a robust option in any given city. While policy entrepreneurs were able to supply the charter schools, parents and guardians had to supply the "demand" to keep them in business.

In this chapter, I evaluate how Albany charter school leaders, including the policy entrepreneurs whose actions were crucial to building a large charter school network in the city, successfully targeted a population that wanted a nontraditional option. As Catholic schools began shuttering and even those that remained had less money available for scholarships, private schools were not an option for many families in Albany. This was particularly true for families of Color in working-class neighborhoods. Targeting this group, and not the middle-class parents who were largely happy with their options (or could afford private schools if they preferred) was deliberate. The American double helix creates a strong overlap between race and class, and the city of Albany remains largely stuck in a Black/White dichotomy. Charter school leaders tapped into a desire among the city's economically disadvantaged Black neighborhoods to find the best options possible for their children. Further, charter school leaders capitalized on desires for private school–like amenities and, as a consequence of building a strong charter school network, manipulated parents into supporting an antidemocratic policy.

The idea of "target groups" comes from the policy design literature, and is most closely associated with Schneider and Ingram's argument that policymakers use public policy to assign benefits or burdens to positively or negatively constructed social groups.[2] In this case, I argue that there was an analogous process occurring at a more micro level;

once the state of New York had passed legislation to authorize charter schools, local charter school leaders designed their schools to deliberately target specific populations to encourage them to leave traditional schools and enroll their children in charter schools instead. In targeting working-class families of Color, these charter school leaders removed a significant block of people who challenged the public schools from the race-conscious, justice-oriented Left. All of this occurred through color-blind policies that never explicitly mentioned a desire to remove active Black parents from public school communities, but that was the clear, and utterly predictable, result.

Choosing Schools

The demand side of school-choice theory argues that allowing parents to choose a school will empower them politically because it provides them with economic agency. Frequently, there is an underlying assumption that parents will select the best school for their child by evaluating a school's academic program and related variables. In the marketplace model, parents who choose to leave a public school for a private or charter school are putting pressure on public schools to improve so that they will not continue to lose students and be forced to close. In that way, as motivated parents leave failing public schools for better options, the failing schools are forced to improve and, therefore, all students receive a better education. The ideology behind this argument is strictly neoliberal because it assumes that political empowerment derives from market-based choice.[3]

However, research has shown that choosing a school is not as simple as evaluating test scores, graduation rates, class sizes, or other academic measurements. Parents include many other variables, such as a school's location, transportation, uniform policy, start time, and other practical issues as they consider leaving a traditional school for a charter school (or other option). Too many studies ignore the broader, contextual environment in which parents and students live. This environment is colored by practical issues such as location and transportation, as well as less tangible but still very real problems like racism and classism. Further, there are always two forces at work; Ellison and Aloe note that there are "push" factors encouraging parents to leave their assigned public schools, and there are "pull" factors that cause them to select specific schools over others.[4]

On the "push" side, Ellison and Aloe note that parents choose to leave "schools they perceive to be failing institutions plagued by issues of disorder and unsafety, poor material conditions and low academic achievement, and pathologizing racial discourses."[5] They further note that participants in the multiple qualitative studies they reviewed "view their local public schools as failing institutions that, on one hand, lack the necessary resources to provide an adequate education to their children and that, on the other hand, compensate for structural deficiencies by implementing reductive school curricula and disciplinary practices that marginalize poor students of color."[6] Thus, parents are driven to leave public schools because they are institutions that fail to educate their children, are unsafe, and focus too much on discipline. Although many of these factors are replicated in Albany parents who choose to leave the public school system, Ellison and Aloe stress that parents' first decision is to leave a public school, not necessarily to choose a different option. As we shall see in this chapter, parents in Albany do not always fit that model. Although some have experience with public schools and deliberately left them for multiple reasons, others were either inexperienced with their district school or, most surprisingly, had been happy with their public option and left it anyway.

Although it seems a logical assumption that the strongest "pull" factor is a robust academic program, evidence for the pull of academic factors is mixed. Early studies of school choice were divided on the role of academics in pulling a family to a specific school; Martinez and Thomas found that academics were important,[7] while the Carnegie Report argued that academics made up only a small portion of the factors pulling families to specific schools.[8] In addition to academic programs or offerings, research indicates that parents choose a school because it is convenient,[9] because its values match those of the family,[10] or because it is perceived as being a safe environment.[11] Broadly, "pulling" parents into specific schools are perceptions that these schools "have a positive institutional culture, small class sizes that allow students to receive more individualized attention, and challenging curriculum and special programs that will prepare students for university education."[12] Ellison and Aloe also find that parents are drawn to schools that seem to provide a "family"; the same phenomenon occurred among Albany parents who choose a specific school.

While economic theory assumes that parents will evaluate all available evidence and select the best school for their child, this assumption "erases the complexity of the lived experiences of parents in urban communities."[13] Economic assumptions ignore the many variables that lead families to choose a specific school for their child. More problematically, multiple studies have found that parents of higher income are more likely to select a school based on academics, while those of lower income are less likely to do so.[14] As Schneider, Teske, and Marschall put it, "Lower socioeconomic status and minority parents are more likely to value schools that perform the bedrock function of providing a safe environment and the fundamentals of education. They desire such fundamentals to increase the likelihood that their children can pass the gatekeeping points on the path to economic success. An emphasis on values, including diversity, is perhaps a luxury that middle-class and white parents can better afford."[15]

Given the strong overlap between racial identification and income, this division between factors that draw middle-class and working-class families leaves open the possibility that students of Color will end up in schools with lower academic standards. If this occurs, it will only exacerbate problems of racial hierarchy and segregation.

As I explain in the following discussion, parents have diverse reasons for selecting specific schools. Frequently, they place their reasons within a broader logic. It should be noted that, in some cases, parents also show a lack of knowledge of comparable options; for example, they may say that they chose a charter school because it provided free after-school services, even when their neighborhood district school provided a similar free service. Nevertheless, parents' reasons are legitimate within their own worldview, and lack of information should be interpreted as evidence of how well charter school advertising campaigns work. In this chapter, I focus on why parents choose charter schools. My discussion is framed by those who chose a magnet school or chose to stay in their assigned neighborhood school, as making the choice to stay should also be considered a choice.[16] Because of their deep interconnectedness and intrinsic importance in the American polity, I address issues related to race and neoliberalism separately in the following chapter.

Although most parents identified several clear reasons for choosing a specific school, that was not always the case. Occasionally, there was no clear reason given for moving to a charter school. This was true of Tracy, a White mother of two who chose charter schools:

> My oldest just went to [a neighborhood elementary school]. I really liked it, actually. They had the separate, the classrooms were separate, so it wasn't like they were in with all the bigger kids. Like the pre-K, they were coddled . . . as they should be. Their classrooms were separate. They had class doors, so it wasn't like they were constantly in the mainstream.
> . . . But the teachers were good . . . and they listened to me. The teachers did listen to me when I was there, and I said, "Don't put my daughter at just the regular standards." Because [our neighborhood] is a lower economic, like the kids do function at a lower level. But my child wasn't like that. The only reason why, like I said, I sent [her] there was again, the hours. We had to bring her to and from. But she was in the before- and after-school program, which was free. So that was another thing that benefited us. The Boys & Girls Club was a free program. So we did that, and . . . they were really hands-on with my daughter. I did like it there.

Tracy's discussion is unusual. She was happy with her local elementary school, even while she acknowledged that, because it was located in a neighborhood with lower economic power, the other children "function at a lower level." This is a recognition of the race and class hierarchies by which her child was surrounded. Tracy's family was not wealthy, and they took advantage of the free after-school program available at the neighborhood elementary school. And yet, she moved her child to a charter school when it became an option. Tracy's story was echoed by a handful of other parents, but it was not the norm. Most parents provided clear reasons for why they chose their charter or other school, including reasons for leaving their traditional school and factors drawing them to their own school of choice. We turn now to a discussion of those factors.

Factors That Lead to School Choice in Albany

Previous literature divides reasons for school choice into "push" factors that cause a family to leave a specific school, and "pull" factors that draw a family to enroll in a different school.[17] However, these variables frequently overlap with each other. For example, while a variable like longer class time seems like a "pull" factor drawing parents into charter (or other) schools, that should be interpreted along with the "push" factor of traditional schools that do not offer that longer day. Therefore, rather than dividing variables into "push" and "pull," I discuss these factors as mirrors of each other. In the remaining portion of this chapter, I explain the multiple variables that draw families to choose specific schools in Albany. These variables include practical attributes like having more time in school, a school's location, and its perceived safety, as well as attributes that are more commonly associated with private schools, such as single-sex education and school uniforms. Parents also discuss the importance of how their social networks view different schools, and some mention academic programs. Contrary to most expectations, however, academics provides only one small part of the many reasons why parents enroll in a given school.

Class Time: Longer Days and Academic Years

According to my interviews with charter school leaders, shortly after they began building schools in Albany, they moved from "the theory of illumination," in which they wanted to showcase a different and, in their minds, better way to run educational institutions, to "the theory of market pressure," in which they hoped that enough families would leave district schools that the district would be forced to change its practices in order to compete for students. Part of the impetus for providing this market pressure was to offer parents practical reasons to leave district schools, including having their children in school for longer periods of time. As one policy entrepreneur told me, "We had substantially longer school days by a couple hours. We had longer school years, depending on the school, twenty, twenty-five days longer. Four of our schools went to year-round schooling, and so kids were never out of school more than three weeks. That's a different approach."

The creation of this opportunity clearly spoke to working parents with limited childcare options. Indeed, the most common reason by far that parents offered for sending their child to a charter school was the extended school day. The longer school day available in charter schools not only provided additional instruction time but provided greater flexibility for working parents. A related common reason for choosing charter schools was their longer school year. In the same way that a longer school day allows working parents greater flexibility, the longer school year also cuts down on days when parents need to find and pay for alternative childcare.

Extended School Day

Charter schools in Albany have much longer school days than the traditional public schools. While each one sets its own schedule, they typically start earlier and end later in the day than district schools. This is partly the case because charter schools, under New York law, are not required to recognize or negotiate with teachers' unions. Therefore, demanding longer days from teachers does not necessitate that teachers are paid more, as a union would likely demand.

When parents explained to me that a significant reason for choosing a charter school was the longer school day, that was almost always placed within the context of avoiding the need to pay for childcare before or after school. This was true in spite of the fact that many Albany elementary schools, especially those in the same neighborhoods as the city's charter schools, provide free after-school care.

The need for childcare was most clearly stated by Katelyn, a married White mother employed as a social worker who has two children in a charter elementary school. In the United States, with limited free childcare options, Katelyn felt pulled between her need to earn an income and her need to care for her children. As she told me,

> And for parents like me, who work? Who [can] pay all this money for childcare? No. Nobody. And you know their extended school days? You know, I'm working 8:00 to 4:30 . . . And my kids are coming to that age where they can start to get off the bus and be home, [but] they're not there yet. So you know, that was another big thing. Other schools start at 8:30. And they get out at 3:00. What am I going to do with that? So then I have to work. This is where I'm pulling in the whole "parents have to work multiple jobs" if you work in the human services. I have to have three jobs so I can pay my bills and then, I have to pay for childcare. So

how do I do this? You know this is where parents get so stressed out and so torn. How can you be a parent and how can you work?

The need for childcare stretched across racial lines, and was a causal factor in school choice for multiple people of less economically advantaged backgrounds. Billie, a Black woman with grandchildren in charter schools who had encouraged her daughter to take advantage of the charter alternative, placed part of her reasoning in the context of available childcare. While some Albany neighborhood schools offer after-school childcare to pre-K students, not all of them do. Billie and her daughter found that lack difficult and frustrating: "If you got a four-year-old at pre-K . . . there's no after school for them. So what do you do with a four-year-old, when you work until 5:00? You know but charter schools, now has kindergarten. My grandson don't come home until quarter to 5:00. Which make him have a longer day. And I think that's needed for everybody."

Another family with elementary-aged children had a similar view. Tracy, a White mother who works three jobs, placed the longer school day and available transportation together. As she explained, both of these variables allowed her more time to work. She explained it this way:

> When we were looking into schools for my oldest, we wanted something that was close to home, but something that would be [easy] for busing. We looked for busing because of our work schedules. Me and my husband were trying to figure out the best thing. Because obviously, if she takes the bus, then we won't have to worry about transportation and stuff like that. [With our neighborhood public school], time was not good for us. School starting at 9:05, you know, most parents . . . I worked nights, my husband worked days, but I would work overtime. It just didn't work for us. . . . So the school day program, that's another reason why we chose [our charter school]. Their school day initially had started, when my oldest started, was at 7:30, and it went to 4:00. Now, it goes 7:45 to 3:45. The time is good. You can drop off your kids anywhere between 6:45 and 7:30, or 7:45, whatever. They serve breakfast. Unfortunately now, it's hard because they do take the bus, and they're one of the first on the bus, so they get on the bus at 6:20. So it's a long day for them. But my main thing, like I said, was the school schedule.

Related to the longer school day, the busing schedule also provides parents with additional time to get to and from work while their children are not yet home. While riding the bus adds additional time to the child's school day (which is also true for those who attend traditional Albany schools), charter school buses are adding that time onto a day that is already longer. Tracy relied not only on the longer school day but also on the provided transportation that tacked on additional time during which she knew her children were being cared for:

> TRACY: Again, the transportation thing was a big thing. The busing gives us an extra half an hour, you know. Like last year, they were on the bus for almost an hour, which is a long time.
> RYANE: Each way?
> TRACY: Yeah, because they got on at 6:20, and they got home last year at like, 4:45. This year, they got home about 4:20, 4:15, so it's a little bit better. But you know, like I said, that's the only thing right now in hindsight, where I'm like, I kind of feel bad, but at the same time, I'm like, "Well, if they miss the bus, I can always bring them. It's not like I can't do that." Or my husband can. But yeah, that's kind of where I stand with that.

Another parent, Natalie, is a single Black mother working two jobs. Natalie's daughter went to a traditional neighborhood school for a year before moving to a charter elementary school. Like Tracy, who stated earlier in this chapter that she was happy with her district school before moving her child to a charter school, Natalie did not feel "pushed" out of her district school. She was happy there, but chose a charter school explicitly because of the longer days it provided: "She gets out of school later. I had to rush from work to get her out of public at 3:15. Whereas, the bus can drop her at my mom's house at 5:00 and when I get off work I can pick her up and go home. So, later days."

Extended School Year

Albany charter schools not only have longer individual school days, but their students also attend school more than the state-mandated 180 days that public schools are open. This works the same way as the longer school days; it means fewer days when parents have to arrange for childcare or, in the summertime, send their children to camp. Katelyn, the White mother with children at an elementary charter school, told me, "On average charter schools keep them in school between three and ten weeks longer. Given the time frame, and public schools' [time frame], for that mom who's working three jobs, that's a big deal. There's no question any mom who has to work three jobs to pay for her [child]care, hands down, will choose a charter school over a public school any day."

While parents who chose a charter school clearly appreciated and relied on the longer school days that made their work schedules easier, parents who did not choose charter schools also recognized that this was one reason why some parents would make that decision. Brenda, a White mother of two who works in sales and marketing and sends her children to a traditional neighborhood school, argued that charter schools "tailor their product to a particular market." When I asked what she meant by that, Brenda explained that "some of them [charter schools] have longer days, [and] they don't have as many breaks and that appeals if you're a single parent." Mindful of contemporary colorblind norms, Brenda was hesitant to discuss empirically verifiable overlaps between race and economics. Although it took her some time to make a race-related argument, she eventually said, "I feel like it seems like mostly African American and Hispanic students are the ones that end up in charter schools and so I'm guessing they're offering things that appeal to that to the, that demographic. . . . One of the things I think is that those longer days, you do not need to, you know, pay for the childcare." Another White mother, whose children had attended a magnet school, viewed charter schools' longer hours in a very negative way. While Brenda had referred to this as a "marketing" process that was logical for a private organization, Kathleen focused on the longer school day as a much more nefarious way to bring families to charter schools: "I find it, you know, it [a charter school] preys on low socioeconomic families who need childcare and so they go for the longer day because they need the childcare."

The need for parents to have reliable, safe childcare while they were at work was, therefore, a clear theme. The policy entrepreneurs made their schools' days and years longer to appeal to a working-class demographic.

This appeal succeeded immensely, as seen in the comments from parents who were drawn to that benefit. Further, it was recognized by noncharter parents as either appealing to a need or "preying on" charter families.

Location

In addition to the longer school days and longer school year, many parents stated that they chose a charter school because of its location. Albany charter schools are deliberately placed in areas with high poverty rates; there are no charter school options in middle-class neighborhoods.

For example, Layla, who had two children in an Albany charter school when we spoke, was quite clear about how important location was to her. When I asked her to name the most important benefits of sending her children to that school, her first response was, "They're close. They're close to my house."

Katelyn had a similar reaction. In discussing how she chose her children's charter school, she provided a broader context. However, it was clear that location was also important to her: "So [my child] had went to pre-K through [a community organization], and they started handing out flyers about schools. My sister-in-law had previously put her kids in [a specific charter school] and had a wonderful experience with them. So I started looking around and you know, poking on websites, and given the location of the school in relation to my house, I thought it was most appropriate to try to get them through there. They were uniformed, which was something that I was looking for, so we ended up putting in our applications and they were accepted."

Tracy, with two children in an Albany charter school, had a similar reaction as Katelyn. Tracy places school location along with the importance of having access to a school bus. Both of these, for her family, would allow her and her husband to continue working at their present jobs: "So basically, us looking into schools, we didn't really have much of a choice for pre-K, and they didn't have the option at [the charter school we eventually chose]. When we were looking into schools for my oldest, we wanted something that was close to home, but something that would be . . . for busing. We looked for busing because of our work schedules."

Other families, particularly those who chose Albany magnet schools, considered location for their "backup" choices. Albany magnet schools require parents to complete an application form to enter a lottery to gain a spot. Parents can place up to three schools on that list, and location was important for their second choices. Several short snippets show how common this was:

> JENNIFER: Actually, the school that we're closest to was actually [a specific school]. So that was our backup because that's the closest school.
> BRENDA: We've considered [a specific] magnet because it's closer now to where we live.
> AMY: [A specific magnet school] is actually the closest to us and that's probably our backup or second choice.
> STEPHANIE: We liked [a specific magnet school]. We liked [another magnet school], but we didn't like [it] enough to list it because we figured we live so close to [our preferred school].

Private School Attributes

A second common reason for choosing a charter school is that they mimic many attributes of private schools, but without charging a private school tuition. These attributes include things that are not normally found in public schools, particularly uniforms and single-gender education. There is an underlying assumption among many Americans that private institutions—of all kinds—are inherently better than their public counterparts. Although most associated with Reagan's claim that "government is the problem" and the Right's current disdain for "government schools," this element of neoliberalism cuts across party lines.

This preference for private over public is strong in Americans' views of primary and secondary education. As of 2017, the most recent year they asked the question, Gallup found significant preferences for private schools, whether religious or secular. Although the data had shifted a bit over time, the trend did not change dramatically from 2012 to 2017. Overall, just 5 percent of respondents thought that public schools were doing an "excellent" job at providing education, compared to 21 percent for both parochial and independent private schools. Considering those who thought each type of school was performing at an "excellent" or "good" level, public schools came in at 44 percent support, parochial schools at 63 percent, and independent private schools at 71 percent.[18]

There are multiple possible reasons why Americans are so disenchanted with their public schools. One possibility, of course, is that private schools are simply better. However, empirical evidence does not support this argument. Although private schools tend to have higher test scores and other common metrics, controlling for income generally washes away these benefits.[19] A more likely explanation for Americans' preference for all things private over public is the general distrust of government that Reagan actively promoted. Such distrust is reinforced every time an outsider runs for office, proudly proclaiming their lack of insider status. Donald Trump, for example, clearly ran his 2016 campaign as an alternative to traditional Washington politics. In the aggregate, Americans broadly believe that private systems are better than public ones. Leaders of Albany charter schools were able to use this preference to further manipulate parents into selecting charter schools by giving them private-like attributes.

First, however, it is instructive to hear from Tracy, a White mother of charter school students whose eldest child would age out of their elementary charter school a few years after we met. I asked her what she planned to do once her child was too old for the charter school they attended at the time:

> TRACY: I was thinking about [local private schools] for my oldest. My youngest . . . I don't know. Like I said, academically . . . both of them have it, but behaviorally, my oldest would be much better at that kind of environment.
>
> RYANE: Right. So you're deciding, then, between either a different charter school, or [a private school]?
>
> TRACY: Yeah.
>
> RYANE: Why?
>
> TRACY: Because . . . I feel like the public schools from K to 6, is good in the city. I feel like middle school is when I start to question because the kids are older, they're fiercer, they're more aggressive. If I were to have to put them in public school, I would go to [one specific district middle school over another].

RYANE: Okay. Why would you do that?

TRACY: I feel like it's more organized. I feel like it's more of a private school, more smaller than, I don't know. I worked at child protective for six years, and just going into the different schools . . . just seeing different . . . like if Livingston was still around, I would never, oh my God . . . I feel like my children would succeed better at [the preferred middle school].

RYANE: Okay. Is that something that you would think about? Putting them in a public school for middle?

TRACY: Possibly. But I don't know. I think I'd rather go private.

RYANE: Okay.

TRACY: [I have] to see if I can get financial aid or scholarships. You know, my heart races because I don't know. And it scares me. It's not that I'm trying to hide them from anything. I just feel like, I just want them academically to succeed well, like well beyond, but I also want them to be in a very structured . . . I don't feel like the public school system holds up to charter, or even private school, or anything like that because I feel like the standards are different.

Tracy's discussion makes a clear distinction between public and private schools, especially at the middle school level. Not only does she think that "the standards are different" in charter and private schools, but she thinks that the children in public middle schools are "fierce" and "aggressive." This is a clear example of how colorblind individualism has impacted public views of political institutions, especially public schools. The public is inherently bad—it is "the problem," in Reagan's words. Decades of segregation and disinvestment, particularly in Albany public schools, have pushed people away from public institutions and toward private, or quasi-private, ones instead.

Uniforms

One common marker of many American private schools is that they require their students to wear a standardized uniform. Like most American public schools, Albany schools do not require school uniforms. Many parents desired school uniforms for the ease of getting dressed in the morning and avoiding perceived bullying over expensive items like sneakers. These were some of Tracy's motivations:

> TRACY: I like the uniforms, too. That's another thing. Uniformity. A lot of parents are against it, but I feel like it's beneficial because not one kid is looked at differently. Because you all got the same stuff on.... You know, when you have the girl with the Jordans, or you might have the kid with the Ugg boot. But, honestly, if that's the only thing you have to worry about, that's okay. I feel like that is a huge piece, is the uniforms. It's huge.
> RYANE: Is that part of what drew you? Is that part of why you wanted a charter school?
> TRACY: Yeah. That's a lot of the reason, yes.... I feel like it helps all the kids to see that, you know, and they provide you with two shirts, so yes, you may have a kid that has dirty shirts or whatever, but again, the school's very helpful. They'll help you.

Because each charter school is independently chartered and managed, they all have their own uniform policy. While Tracy, above, noted that some students at her children's elementary charter school wore expensive shoe brands, other schools require a full uniform, including specific shoes. Billie, whose grandchild attended a different elementary charter school, focused on the role of identical (or near-identical) shoes: "I like that every kid looks the same. They have the same shoes, they all got on the same outfit. So there's nobody to bully nothing about sneakers or anything."

Billie was not the only one to be concerned about bullying. Katelyn, a White mother with two children at an elementary charter school, was concerned about both bullying and expectations, and found uniforms to be helpful for both:

> I liked the uniformity. There is too much bullying going on now with kids. Everybody is looking at oh, you don't have the right sneakers, you don't have the right clothes, so that was something that was important. I didn't want to struggle in the morning. When I go to work, I have a standard that I am supposed to be upholding. I have a dress code that needs to be adhered to, so I don't think it's a bad thing to start to instill into my children early, that this is something that is expected of you. You get up,

and you have to wear your belt, you have to tuck in your shirt. My kids do very well with expectations and knowing what's coming so that was something that I wanted to standardize for them across the board . . . at home and at school.

Here, again, we see the impact of broader neoliberalism in school choice. While Katelyn wanted to prepare her children for future jobs with uniform standards or dress codes, not all positions require that. This focus on uniforms confirms that "schools produce workers."[20]

Catie, a Black mother with a child at a different elementary charter school, was also happy with the uniforms. When I asked her if she liked them, she said,

> Yeah, I do. I do, until it's time to get ready to go someplace and I didn't realize he grew out of his clothes long ago. . . . But I do like having uniforms. [My son] knows exactly what he needs to put on each and every time. And I feel it kind of frees his mind for, you know, learning. Learning in school. So I feel like in that sense it just kind of helps, you know, that that's one less thing you gotta worry about. Plus you don't have to worry about, "Oh I seen [a child] with those jeans on the other day." The messed-up shoes and things of that nature, you know, we don't have any of that. We don't have those issues because if they'd seen how [my son] dress on his own they would. He will put on any shirt, any pair of pants.

Uniforms, a common private school denominator, were very popular with charter school parents. They liked them for three distinct reasons: (1) they prevented bullying of children whose families could not afford designer fashion; (2) they eased the morning routine, since there was never a question about what a student would wear to school; and (3) they allowed students to ignore nonessential issues like clothing and shoes, and focus on their schoolwork instead. Although this benefit was not as clearly identified, uniforms also prepare students for the workforce.

Single-Sex Education

The second part of some Albany charter schools that mimics a private school is the availability of single-sex education. While most Albany charter schools enroll both boys and girls, there are single-sex options in elementary and high school, and there were two single-sex middle schools (one for boys and one for girls) until 2015. While a handful of public schools nationwide have attempted single-sex education, no traditional Albany schools offer this option.

While many parents discussed the draw of single-sex education, few belabored it, and none discussed it in as in-depth a manner as was common for discussions of uniforms. Those who chose a single-sex charter school simply stated that it was a factor that they thought would serve their children well; similarly, those who chose coeducational charter (or district) schools also thought their children would be happier and more successful in that environment. Only a small handful of parents had single-sex education as a priority, and came to charter schools specifically for that reason.

An example of a parent who prioritized single-sex education is Janie, a Black mother with three children. Her oldest child was an adult, and had gone through the district's traditional high school. Her second child had attended an all-girls charter high school and was a college student at the time of our meeting, while her youngest was in a coeducational charter middle school after having attended a single-sex charter elementary school.[21] Janie's oldest daughter was in high school before a single-sex charter school was available, but she said that, even for her oldest, she "really wanted to do a Catholic school at that point, or [another] all-girls [school]."[22] She toured single-sex private schools, but relented when her daughter wanted to go to the coeducational district high school.

By the time Janie's middle child was ready for high school, however, there was a single-sex charter high school available. Again, Janie wanted a single-sex education for her daughter and considered her options. "And then that's when the charter school opened up, the all-girls, so I thought I'd give it a chance because . . . it's an all-girls school." The same was true for her youngest child; when I asked Janie what made her choose her son's single-sex charter elementary school, she said, "Well it was pretty much the fact that it was an all-boys school." Although Janie explained the draw of single-sex education more than other respondents, those who chose single-sex schools had similar reactions.

Part of what draws parents to charter schools is their ability to mimic private schools. This is particularly true with the uniforms required by

Albany charter schools, and the single-sex education available at some of them. Adding these elements provided an additional draw for a population that has felt left out of public systems, reinforcing the idea that private options are inherently better.

Social Networks and School Choice

Many parents in all types of schools indicated that they were motivated to select a specific school because they had friends or family members there, or because someone in the community encouraged them to consider a particular school. This was especially common for both charter schools and magnet schools. This mirrors other research showing that parents' social networks influence which schools they consider, evaluate, and choose.[23]

For example, Janie, who was drawn to single-sex education, was also strongly persuaded by a member of her community to try a charter school. As she said, "I chose [this school] because . . . actually one of our members at [her place of work], worked over there. And the lovely things he spoke so highly of the program and he was a big, big, big participant of, and advocate for [this school]." Other charter parents, including those who did not choose a single-sex environment, had similar reasons. Natalie, a Black mother of two young children, placed her older child in a charter school for kindergarten, although she had been pleased with the same child's prekindergarten program in a neighborhood school. I asked Natalie why she chose that charter school, and she said, "Well, I was going to like a mom's group every Saturday, where they teach the parents what are the developments of their kids and what needs the kids have in school, and it was suggested for me to sign her up to go to [this particular school] when she was in kindergarten."

Natalie's story is unusual in that not only had her oldest child attended a neighborhood school, but both Natalie and her child had been happy with that school. The primary reason she moved her child to a charter school was that a member of her social network suggested it.

Parents who chose a district magnet school had similar reasons as those who chose a charter school, particularly those who chose the city's most competitive magnet school. Karen, a middle-class, married, White mother of three, enrolled her child in a prekindergarten program in her neighborhood elementary school, but then moved her to a magnet school beginning in kindergarten. When I asked why she made that move, Karen was very clear: "Most of our neighborhood friends were going there. Especially the ones who had kids that were a year or two older rather than going into neighborhood school." Karen had a similar reason for not considering a charter school for her children; as she said, "Most of the people in our social circle weren't going to those schools. So there wasn't really a strong draw."

Similar relationships exist with parents who choose a private school. Chad and Sarah, White parents of one child who began at a district magnet school, were unhappy with the environment he was in. When they wanted to remove him from his magnet school, they considered their neighborhood school, but were concerned that they would be disappointed again. As Chad put it, "How many strikes out do we get and disrupt his life?" Instead of risking another "strike," Chad and Sarah put their child in a private Catholic school. They made this choice because, as Chad explained, "We knew some families that had moved there, so we had personal insight as to what was going on in the school. And we didn't want to take a blind faith leap again."

Parent Involvement

Parents at both charter and magnet schools stated that they appreciated the parent involvement in their school community. This was both a draw for parents and a reason to stay in their schools of choice. The implication was always that their child's school had better parent involvement than other types of schools, particularly traditional neighborhood schools.

For example, Natalie, who moved her children from a public pre-K program to a charter school primarily to take advantage of the longer school day, was pleased that her children's charter school worked hard to create an involved community of parents.

> NATALIE: They have family day. It's education for the parents, where the kids can go in their classroom and be supervised while the parents can be engaged in a workshop.
> RYANE: What kind of workshops?

NATALIE: The one that I liked last year that they had was a workshop on how to save money for the college tuition. They also have performances, dance performances. So, I like the fact it's on Saturdays, from 9:00 to 11:00, where you don't have to rush from work to get somewhere or get out of work early to be somewhere. A lot of people show up. Pretty much the whole school shows up for this family day. It's, I think it's very family oriented. We had a Harvest Party one Saturday, slash Picture Day. So it was nice.

Katelyn, a White mother with two children in a different elementary charter school, also praised the parent involvement. In her view, the school made parent involvement an expectation, and the school and parents formed a partnership:

There is a lot of involvement with parents. They are constantly doing things, they're sending out flyers about parent advisory meetings, they have an expectation that parents volunteer two hours per month, they like to get them in, and if not, at least two hours per year. They like to have them come in once a year, at least, to volunteer. They are very involved with their parents—they envision it as a partnership. It's not just your children that you drop off to school so that they can be educated and come home. They expect parents to be involved actively with their children at school and at home. That's pretty much how it's described, is a partnership.

For some parents, this high expectation of involvement can be overwhelming. Billie, who enrolled her youngest child in Albany's first charter school when it opened in 1999 and later encouraged her grown daughter to enroll her children (Billie's grandchildren) in charter schools, was critical of parents who were not able to put in the time the school required. As she explained it, part of the reason why she liked charter schools was the parent involvement. Billie told a story about another mother who could not put in the same amount of time: "I think to some parents it's too much parent involvement. 'Cause one lady left while my girls were at New Covenant [Albany's first charter school] and said, 'You all get on my nerves. I'm in school and I can't keep coming to these meetings.' Everybody looked at her, you know, but it's your children. So she took her kids out of New Covenant and put them back down at [a traditional neighborhood elementary school] because it was too much parent involvement."

A policy entrepreneur mentioned a similar issue with their frequent parental contact. Albany charter schools, particularly those that were established fairly early, were especially active in ensuring that students enrolled in their programs attended school every day. As the entrepreneur put it, "Our whole theory was if we could just get them into the school building we could just take it from there." To ensure that children would attend, the school provided alarm clocks when necessary and called parents and extended family members of students who were not present at the start of the day. This communication continued for other issues; every time a student had a disciplinary problem, the school called a parent or guardian. This became frustrating to some parents:

> The only time in the first year I had a parent come to a board meeting was to ask whether we could just give her a summary at the end of the week of her child's misdeeds, rather than calling every time something happened. We'd call because our theory was parent engagement. If we had a problem, the kid might be misbehaving because something was happening at home. We couldn't be saying one thing and then they go home and the parent say, "Oh that was stupid. I can't believe the teacher made you do that." There had to be a synchronizing of expectations. When anything we consider to be an infraction to happen, we would call the parent. The mother came, because in one week the kid had like twelve things came up, so she got twelve phone calls. She's just like, can't you just give me a summary at the end of the week. I almost broke down laughing, like, "Can't you help us figure out what the problem is?" I composed myself, I'm saying "No, we are not changing our policy."

The desire for parent involvement was also clear among parents who chose a magnet school. For example, Bethany, who moved her children from a private religious school where she was unhappy, wanted to enroll her children in a magnet school. For her, the draw was not the particular curriculum available at the four magnet elementary schools in Albany, but more the fact that parents had to choose them deliberately:

BETHANY: I wanted a magnet school because I felt like the magnet schools, by the nature of them, were parents who were more involved in their kid's education.
RYANE: What would make you think that?
BETHANY: Because you have to fill out the form. I mean, the rest of it, for any other school, you just go. But I felt like that little bit of effort of having to fill out the form, it was more of a self-selected group. A lot of people aren't just going to fill out the form.

Directly related to maintaining active parent involvement is a parent's ability to be in direct contact with their children's teachers. Multiple parents of charter school students explained that they were comfortable texting their child's teacher during the day, and felt that their chosen charter school excelled at communication. Tracy, with two children in an elementary charter school, explained it very clearly: "Like I said, the hours are good, they're always available. If you need to speak to any of the staff, like I said, they're always available. Email communication, Facebook." Tracy came back to the school's stronger communication later in our discussion:

> I really feel like they've been receptive to everything. Whenever there's a question, it's answered. Whenever there's a problem, it's solved. It's not like there's ongoing issues, so I really don't feel like there's been anything challenging. Like I said, with my own child, the behaviors, it's new to me. But they've been resilient. They've been on top of it. They're keeping involved. Her teacher's like, "I'm not telling you to get you upset or anything." She said, "I'm telling you to let you know where she's at today. But I'll handle it. That's what my job is."
>
> It's good to know that. And like I said, the parent liaison, she'll call you back within twenty-four hours. I mean, she's just on her job. They all know you, so I don't feel like anything has been kept from me that hasn't been. But again, I'm a very active parent, so it may be different for somebody else.

This support of communication efforts differed from the experience of those who remained in district schools, and even from that of many of those who chose a private school. Few parents complained about communication from the district or a teacher; instead, it simply did not come up as something that parents praised. There were exceptions, of course, including Bethany, who appreciated her child's magnet school teacher's communication and compared it very favorably to the private religious school she had experienced first: "I liked that they were available and responsive and a lot of times, I felt like, 'Oh, I shouldn't be bothering them, I shouldn't be nagging them,' and I did it anyway, and I always started with, 'I know you have a lot of other students to deal with, but here's what I need from you.' And for the most part I felt like they were responsive, which was much different than [the private religious school]."

Communication can even be part of why a parent leaves the traditional public school system for a charter school. Layla, a divorced Black mother with two children, had toured her traditional neighborhood school several years before we spoke, when her oldest child was entering first grade. There were many things that she and her son's father did not like, including what they considered to be a "chaotic . . . atmosphere." Layla and her former husband enrolled both of their children in a charter school instead, saying that "it goes back to the way that the teachers communicated with the parents."

Parent involvement and the related concept of easy communication with teachers drew many parents to both charter and district magnet schools.

Safety

Multiple studies show that parents who select a school for their child consider the school's safety as an important part of their decision, especially in "depressed cities with high proportions of charter schools."[24] The same was true in Albany, and parents of all types (charter; magnet; neighborhood; private) indicated a concern about their children's physical safety while at school.[25] This came up in multiple forms; parents were worried about large-scale school shootings (parent interviews occurred five to six years after the Sandy Hook massacre), localized violence (there was a large, well-publicized fight at the city's only public high school in the midst of parent interviews; a few students were hospitalized with stab wounds and the school shut down the following day), gang violence, and bullying. In keeping with the interpretivist approach, I did not ask any parents if they were concerned about their children's safety, and yet most of them brought it up organically.

One example of a concern for safety came from Bethany, a White mother of two whose children had attended a private school, a magnet school, a city middle school, and the city's only traditional public high school. While in high school, her oldest son, who was primarily enrolled in college-preparatory courses, took a shop class that had a long-term substitute while the assigned teacher was on medical leave. Bethany's son was frustrated that the substitute did not demand any work, and the class became a free period. Bethany explained the problem like this:

> So the substitute didn't do anything and [my son] told me and I called. The principal must have said something to the substitute, who let out a string of expletives about "The MF who told on me and ratted me out." And then the rest of the kids in the class were like, "Who told? Who called? Who called [the principal]? And now we gotta do fucking work." So ... we switched him to another section that was not quite as hostile. In the end I don't think they figured out ... who had told, but if you're afraid ...

Although Bethany did not indicate that her child ever experienced direct physical threats, it was clear that both she and her child were concerned that other students would figure out that the college-bound student who did not normally take vocational courses was the instigator. This, of course, is also laden with racial and class hierarchies. Bethany's is a middle-class White family, and these students frequently excel in the high school's Advanced Placement and International Baccalaureate programs. Students in the vocational courses are less likely to be either middle-class or White. It is fair to interpret this story as a White kid afraid of the poorer students of Color in his class.

Similarly, Dorothy is a White mother with two children who were originally enrolled in a private school. They spent only a year at that school, then attended a magnet school, and a district middle school. When the older child was ready for high school, she went to a second private school; at the time that we spoke, Dorothy's younger child was still enrolled in a district middle school.

Dorothy and her partner left the first private school quickly because of safety concerns. This school has children in a large range of ages in each classroom, which made Dorothy uncomfortable while her oldest child was still in kindergarten: "Okay, bottom line is the reason we were out of there is that we didn't feel my daughter was safe. There were a lot of issues with the classrooms with older kids and the school didn't do anything to the extent that around April, we're like, 'Okay, we don't want to send her there like one more day.' We barely lasted the first year and we just took her out at the end of the year."

Dorothy's concerns about safety continued. While she did not mention having any safety concerns while her children were in a district magnet elementary school (which was the Whitest and most economically privileged school in Albany), these concerns returned in middle school. Albany middle schools are majority Black with high economic need. As Dorothy explained, "There were a lot of fights, there were a lot of discipline issues, and she was really coming home stressed." Dorothy's daughter chose to stay with Albany schools because of her close friend network, but Dorothy made it clear that she was willing to remove her child at any time.

While in middle school, Dorothy's child also attended the high school each afternoon to take advanced courses. Her child was at the high school the day a fight broke out and one student was stabbed. Like many local parents, Dorothy was quite shaken by this event:

DOROTHY: And that big thing at Albany High last week.
RYANE: With the fight, yeah.
DOROTHY: Actually I was pretty annoyed at the principal's response. [My daughter] was there that day. She came for class. There was a fire alarm and they went outside and then the fight started. And they went back to class, and then the principal got on the PA and said, "You can go to class or you can go home." Like, why would you give them the choice? Because a lot of the kids already took off, so she was like, "Do the right thing, blah blah blah." So everybody went. Everybody took off, right? And then I think there was more fights, and [my daughter] called me a little panicked. I was like, "Just stay in the class with the teacher, it's probably your safest bet." And I was in [a nearby city], so I'm like, "Okay, I'm leaving now, I'll pick you up."

But then everybody left, so she went out and then they evacuated the hallway 'cause somebody pepper sprayed. So, now they're like, "Okay, you have to leave. We're evacuating the school." She's running outside and there's all these police cars and she's walking along.

RYANE: That poor girl.

DOROTHY: And luckily a friend was picking up her son and she saw her and she's like, "Come on, I'll take you home." And... normally I'm like, "No, thank you, it's okay," but today I'm like, "Yes. Please."

These experiences had a significant impact on how Dorothy views the role of schools in American society broadly and in the Albany community specifically. In response to my question about what she thought was the most important thing school should provide for her children, she said, "Well, I mean, safety is number one. If I don't feel my kids are safe, they're not going there. And that has been, for example, a reason why I never would consider, say, [a local suburban] High School, with all their drug problems. I would not want my kids going there."

Ted, a White father of one elementary-aged child, had a similar reaction as Dorothy. While Ted and his partner were happy with their child's neighborhood school and never felt a reason to look for other options, he did voice broad concerns about safety. When I asked him the same question I asked Dorothy (What is the most important thing a school can provide for a child?), his response was very clearly shaped by the 2012 shooting that occurred at Sandy Hook Elementary School in Newtown, Connecticut. That event made Ted nervous about an upcoming primary election, because, at that time, many public schools served as polling locations: "Okay well safety is a big thing, when we had, when the shooting happened in Connecticut I'll never forget dropping him off at school and I was like . . . [cannot vocalize his thoughts]. The result of that was we had elections, the primary came up, it was in school, I kind of raised hell, a few people were annoyed at me but the school was open and the kids were in school and I said anybody can walk in. Knock on wood it's never happened here in Albany but you know, there's copycats." In response to a follow-up question about what a school should provide to a child, Ted came back to safety: "I mean safety is a big thing, and the child wants to feel that they're safe and we get problems with the bullying and that's part of the safety where you don't want them to be picked on or beat up."

Layla, a Black mother, chose a single-sex charter school for both of her children. Her older child had only attended single-sex charter schools, but her daughter attended kindergarten at a district magnet school before Layla moved her to a charter school for first grade. While Layla did not mention any specific safety concerns, she did indicate that a sense of safety was a significant reason for continuing with her chosen charter schools:

> My personal decision is because I feel safe when I drop my children off knowing that I have an expectation for them to stay safe and be educated to the best of the ability of the school structure that I have faith in. Which would be, you know, the charter school system at this time. And I have confidence that that decision, you know, is the right one because I feel comfortable and safe bringing them to that establishment to receive, you know, the teachers of . . . you know, the teacher or the structure of the environment that I'm placing them in.

Safety concerns were also discussed in terms of a child's broader environment. Ronnie, a Black father from Schenectady, a city about twenty miles away from Albany, pulled his young son out of his public school and sent him to an Albany charter school. Ronnie had to drive his son back and forth every day for the first year, although busing was offered after that. Ronnie was pleased with his son's school, but he was frustrated that charter schools weren't available in his own city. In his words, political and community leaders in Schenectady were more concerned about the city's opioid epidemic than about improving the schools. In Ronnie's mind, however, these two issues were intricately connected:

> My focus is, honestly right now what I want to try to focus on, is trying to see about getting a charter school opened up in Schenectady. That's really where I want to be is, How can we make what's happening in Albany happen in Schenectady? Why can't what's happening in Albany happen in Schenectady? You know, like everybody's so focused on the opiate epidemic, on the drug epidemic. You know, we could stop it by breaking the cycle and that's saving the children. If you get them educated,

you can present it in the school system, you know, and like I, that's just my honest belief system. I mean, I'm a product of the drug epidemic, you know, both my parents use, I used, my son doesn't ever want to use, you know what I'm saying because he sees his father in a different way, you know what I mean?

Ronnie's own experiences with illegal drugs, coupled with the city's focus on addressing the opioid epidemic, was enough to make him drive almost an hour, round-trip, morning and night to keep his son out of that environment. As with many other parents, safety was paramount for Ronnie.

Academics

The fundamental assumption behind schools of choice is that parents will choose a school that will serve their child best. As a response, the theory goes, all schools with have to compete for enrollment, and that will cause all schools to improve. Although survey data show that parents who choose charter schools claim to do so primarily for academic reasons, that was not high on the list of responses from Albany parents. Many parents did say that part of their motivation was related to academics, but the other reasons already discussed—more time in school, uniforms, single-sex education, safety, etc.—took clear priority. This challenges the theoretical assumption that academic needs will drive school choice.

Parents of magnet school students (and sometimes neighborhood school students, who did not have to make an affirmative choice) also discussed academics both at their own schools and at charter schools, as they perceived them. Although most charter school parents enthusiastically discussed their children's academic progress in the schools they chose, noncharter choosers had a much different understanding of what education looked like in charter schools.

As an example of how academics are placed second to other factors, consider the words of Tracy, a mother with two children at a charter school. Although she indicated that academics were important to her, this discussion was framed by the importance of transportation and start time:

Me and my husband were trying to figure out the best thing. Because obviously, if she takes the bus, then we won't have to worry about transportation and stuff like that. We actually applied [to two charter schools]. She was accepted into both, but ultimately our choice was [the one farther away], more so because of the bus transportation because that was our kind of main thing. We looked at both and they both had pretty equal academics. Our standards are pretty high as parents for our kids. I'm not just saying that. Both of our children are very intelligent. They're like at a different level.

Academics was important. Not picking a city school, again our neighboring schools, we had [two magnet and two neighborhood schools nearby]. Again, time was not good for us. School starting at 9:05, you know, most parents . . . I worked nights, my husband worked days, but I would work overtime. It just didn't work for us. . . .

So the school day program, that's another reason why we chose [our charter school]. Their school day initially had started, when my oldest started, was at 7:30, and it went to 4:00. Now, it goes 7:45 to 3:45. The time is good. You can drop off your kids anywhere between 6:45 and 7:30, or 7:45, whatever. They serve breakfast.

I include this longer excerpt from Tracy to show how she discusses academics. The first part of her response focused on transportation. She followed that up with a discussion of academics, but then came back to the more practical element of school start time. While it is clear that Tracy and her husband wanted a strong academic program for their children, at no point did she state or imply that she left Albany public schools because charter schools would have stronger academics. For her family, the primary motivator was finding a school day long enough to permit Tracy and her husband to be home when their children were home.

Layla, a Black mother with two children in charter schools, placed a much stronger emphasis on academics than Tracy did. Although Layla's older child had started in a charter school, her younger child attended kindergarten at a traditional Albany neighborhood school. She was not happy with her child's district school, which prompted her to move her younger child to a charter school for first grade. Layla discussed her focus on academics after explaining why she was not happy with her daughter's kindergarten year. Again, I provide a longer quotation to show where academics is placed in a broader context:

> LAYLA: I didn't like the public school system at all. I never really did, for my children's choice. But I guess lack of planning on my end, she never got picked for any lotteries for the charter schools that I had wanted her to get into for kindergarten. So by default she had to go to the public school for the kindergarten.
>
> RYANE: Okay. What didn't you like about the public school that she went to?
>
> LAYLA: Everything from the stress through their parking to the way staff communicates to you, to the larger class ratio compared to the charter school structure and classroom sizes. There's a huge difference ... because instruction is very important and the instruction of the public school is truly only to keep the standard of the nation for the record of the state, not the individual child, and I feel it's geared towards the charter school with it. With obviously the individual emphasis on the exams. I'm not saying they don't stress the children on exams, but they give more attention individually to the child, you know, teaching.
>
> RYANE: Okay. And how would you describe her school?
>
> LAYLA: I guess good would be my description but it's a well school, well kept. Familiar staff, like they keep the staff, you know, in their places, like everybody seems to stay on their, you know, stay in their post. I don't know if that's what they call it at the school, you know, staying where they're supposed to be in the school and you know they communicate very well so when they give teachers directions from what I see in the morning and the afternoon. You know, for dismissal or pick up or things like this. It just seems that everybody just flows to the schedule.

While Layla affirms that academics is important to her, her dislike of her daughter's kindergarten year was related not to the academic structure or offerings but to communication. She does mention class size, but does not link class size to academic achievement. Her next statement critiquing public schools is vague and unclear, though she then moves into a discussion of standardized tests. However, charter school students in New York State take the same standardized state exams that all public-school students take. Finally, when asked to describe her younger child's charter school, she focuses on order and communication, not academics. As with Tracy, Layla's focus on academics is secondary to other needs.

Janie, with two children who had graduated and one who had attended a charter elementary school and was enrolled in a charter middle school when we spoke, had similarly conflicting statements about academics in her child's charter schools. She had mentioned earlier that her primary reason for choosing a charter school was single-sex education, and that she had been encouraged to try a charter school by someone she knew through her work with a community organization. When I asked her to compare charter schools to more traditional public schools, she was contradictory; she began by stating that there were no significant differences, then focused on stronger academics in the charter schools:

> RYANE: Do you notice any particular differences between the traditional public schools and the charter schools? Since you now have children that have encompassed all of these, how would you view them differently?
>
> JANIE: Probably, I don't think there's that much of a difference. I think more is required of the students in charter schools, is what I'm finding as far as grade levels in order to pass and so, I'm thinking the curriculum is a little bit more harder in a charter school than probably a public school. At least, that's my perception of it.

Later, however, when I asked Janie to describe her son's charter school, she was much less positive. Janie wished to move her son back to a traditional public school, but allowed him to stay in his charter school because he wanted to stay in the familiar environment. In Janie's interpretation, while her son's charter school required more academically, it did not provide students with the resources to meet those demands. Janie thought a traditional public school would be stronger that way:

> RYANE: How would you describe the charter schools, particularly the one your son is in now?
>
> JANIE: Honestly, because of him, he is still there. I think if it was left up to me I would pull him.

RYANE: Why does he want to stay?
JANIE: I think it's out of fear, because it's all that he's ever known.
RYANE: And why would you consider taking him out?
JANIE: I think a public school with him in particular, because he struggles with, for instance, ELA [English Language Arts], with the charter school there's really no . . . there was no after-school help for him.
RYANE: Mm-hmm . . .
JANIE: Testing, I would get the tests back with what he did but not what the actually test was so I couldn't understand or couldn't show him how or where he went wrong so that he can correct it, even though it may not count for . . . I know with [his charter school] the passing grade level is higher than most schools, and um, there was just no real help to help, to me, extra work or whatever to get him that one point.
RYANE: Okay.
JANIE: There's no summer school, which I have a really big issue with. Honestly, so he should be in a different grade but because there's no summer school . . .

Thus, while Janie thinks charter schools demand more academically than traditional public schools, she does not think they provide what her son needs to meet those demands.

Ronnie, the father from Schenectady who drove his child to Albany for a charter school for a year until the school was able to provide transportation, clearly focused his choice on academics. Unlike most of the parents who had experience with Albany schools, Ronnie was very critical of what his son had experienced in his public schools in Schenectady:

At the end of the day, Schenectady city school district really does not provide sufficient, um, education for children. You know what I mean? If they're not doing well, they say that they're bad students and then they push them to the wayside and just focus on children that's willing to accept the information and push them forward.

So, um, I wanted my son to have a better education. I needed him with me in order to do so because I knew she [his son's mother] was not going to take him out of public school and put him in a charter school and I needed him to be with me so I can get him into a better school. And that's exactly what I did. I took him over the summer, enrolled him in the charter school and told her like, listen, he needs to live with me in order to go to this charter school because they didn't have buses at the time and that was the truth. And then they got buses and the rest was history. So he's been living with me ever since and I got physical custody of him and so, I mean, that's really how everything ended up, you know, formulatin' to where we're at today.

Billie, a Black grandmother with grandchildren in charter schools, also placed significant focus on academics. However, her argument was not that the charter schools provided better academic preparation, as the literature predicts. Rather, she liked charter schools because she found that they provided more remedial education: "We chose [the charter school] because they teach kids at their level. That's what charter schools do. They teach kids at the kids' level and then bring them up to where they're supposed to be."

Similarly, Katelyn, a White mother with two children in charter schools, was pleased with their academic progress. She was especially happy that one of her children was reading by the end of kindergarten: "I like their academic standards. My children were both reading fresh out of kindergarten. Unheard of. I wasn't reading out of kindergarten, and I mean my daughter was fluently reading books out of kindergarten. My son was a little bit slower to catch on but . . ." However, while Katelyn was happy with her children's academic progress, she had no experience with Albany public schools to compare that experience. Her children had started their education with a charter school because she was drawn to the uniforms and the longer school day. She did not leave Albany schools for better academics.

Those who declined to choose a charter school in Albany also had particular views of the academic programs in charter schools, though they tended to be much more negative. Sometimes, this negativity was an understanding that the academic programs in charter schools were perhaps *too* strong. Stephanie, a married White attorney who had applied for magnet lottery spots for her son to begin kindergarten when we met, considered a charter school for him. However, the longer school day—a clear attraction for many charter school parents—seemed too overwhelming to her:

> STEPHANIE: Ultimately, I decided it was just way too much school.
> RYANE: What do you mean?
> STEPHANIE: I mean it, it's sort of silly to me as like a selling point, but like [my son] would get nine hours of instruction. Wow. Nine hours, you know, like that is a lot of instruction instead of paying for aftercare where he can just bounce a ball or run around. Like he'd be learning. Initially that sounded really great to me. But then I was like, I don't even work nine hours a day. Like the idea of like being taught nine hours a day. Like just a little intense.

While the longer day draws in parents who have difficulty paying for childcare, for Stephanie, childcare was not a financial burden. Being in a financial position to send her child to school for a traditional-length school day meant that she was not interested in the long days offered by charter schools.

Kathleen, a White mother of two children who chose an Albany magnet school, was much more strident in her disdain for charter schools and the type of education she thought they provided:

> RYANE: As you look at your options and think about a different school or figure out what the options would be, have you ever thought about a charter school?
> KATHLEEN: No. I am really against charter schools. I think their philosophy is not about the child, it's about teaching to a test. I think it's about union busting. I think it sucks funds off of public education and it weakens public education. I think it makes an already hard job harder for our public education to do because it's spreading thin resources even thinner. I don't think that the arts are supported in the charter schools, at least the ones around here. In other places they actually have charter schools that do actually have interesting other educational focuses and themes and things like that. And you know in other areas there might be an arts-dedicated charter school. But around here, it's very much about a regimented teach to the test and that is not what I'm interested in for my child's education at all.

> I just find it horrifying. I find it inappropriate. I find it, you know, it preys on low socioeconomic families who need childcare and so they go for the longer day because they need the childcare.

Similarly, Karen, a White mother of three children who had attended magnet and neighborhood schools, along with the city's only traditional high school, did not consider a charter school any of the multiple times that she considered moving one of her children. To Karen, there was simply no academic draw to a charter school. After explaining her philosophical disagreement with how charter schools are funded, Karen explained that she saw no reason to leave the public school system:

> They [charter schools] weren't offering anything that was different or special from standard elementary school. . . . They didn't have a Montessori, they didn't have a dual language or a multilanguage. They didn't have a multicultural or, you know, even some of the other charter schools that I've seen around the country that have sort of yoga and meditation, you know, peacefulness kind of theme. There wasn't anything that was very different. None of the charter schools seem to offer anything special other than a standardized curriculum with a longer day and a longer year which, after a couple of years when I sort of investigated that a little bit, turned out to not even be true. So I was always sort of questioning whether what they were offering was really anything better and I didn't find it to be.

No parent claimed a lack of interest in academic preparation. However, that was not enough, on its own, to draw students to a charter school. Charter parents who mentioned academics framed it with more important variables, like transportation and the length of the school day. Parents who chose a magnet school, or to stay in the traditional district school, did not think charter schools would provide stronger academics.

Discipline and Structure

A final variable drawing parents to charter schools, though not to neighborhood or magnet schools, was a combination of discipline and structure in the Albany charter schools' approach. Many noncharter choosers also recognized this discipline and structure, and avoided charter schools for that very reason. Sometimes the desire for discipline and structure was simply stated as a given without much context. When asked about the most important thing a school could provide for her child, Layla, a Black mother with two children in charter schools, responded, "A sound routine structure would be first and foremost."

Other charter choosers had similar views. Janie, whose youngest child was then in a charter middle school, said that she liked that his charter school focused on "teaching them to be leaders and taking responsibility for their actions. It was more structured." Ronnie, who spent a year driving his son from Schenectady to an Albany charter school, mentioned that he did so partly because of the school's structure. By fourth grade, his son had different teachers for many of his classes, rather than staying with one group the way elementary classes typically work. Ronnie appreciated this very much, because he thought it taught his son structure: "It's like they're in middle school already, so they go from period to period. So they'll leave one classroom, go to another classroom through each period of the day. And I like the set-up because it teaches them structure and discipline because, all right, you got a certain amount of time to do this. Okay, your time here is done. You're going over to 4C. You know, I really enjoyed the structure that they have."

Conclusion

Supporters of the neoliberal approach to education with its focus on school choice frequently argue that parents will (1) have access to adequate information to make a good choice; (2) use that information in a predictable way; and (3) choose the school that will provide their children with the best possible education. Frequently, this "best possible education" is assumed to be based on a strong academic foundation.

However, research has shown that many parents do not have access to adequate information. Even when they do, their school choice is not based primarily on a school's academic program. Rather, practical issues like the length of the school day and year and a school's ability to provide transportation take precedence. Beyond these practical issues, other important variables show that many parents are looking for a private school experience without having to pay private school tuition. The focus on uniforms and single-sex education made this abundantly clear.

Neoliberal theorists are not completely wrong in their prediction that parents will consider academic programs when choosing a school for their child. However, the perceived strength of a school's academic program was not the top factor for any of the thirty-two parents I spoke with. Academics are almost an assumption; parents take for granted that a school of choice will provide a strong academic program. This allows them to focus on the practical concerns that shape their daily lives.

This chapter has focused primarily on how parents make decisions about charter schools. In keeping with the American foundation of colorblind individualism, which is built on a structure of capitalism and racism, parents also have very different understandings of the roles of both race and the market in the broader school universe. We turn to those topics now.

7

Divided by Choice

Race, Class, and Inequality

Albany is a split city. A White portion and a Black portion.
In terms of race and economics, it's very segregated. . . . It's
really a tale of two cities when it comes to education.
—Policy Entrepreneur, Personal Interview

There are many factors that push families away from their neighborhood schools and pull them into a school of choice. Unlike the predictions of those who most strongly support school choice, most of these variables were not directly related to academics. Practical issues, especially the length of the school day and academic year, were much more important.

These factors were all framed by a specific context. In Albany, charter schools heavily target families of Color with high economic need. This, along with charter schools' physical locations, means that Albany charter schools are predominantly (80 percent or higher) Black and Latinx.[1] This composition of the student bodies was not lost on those who chose charter schools, nor on those who deliberately did not choose them. A policy entrepreneur I met with noted this when he said that "in the Black community [charters] are viewed as Black schools. I think in the White community they're also viewed as Black schools."

In this chapter, I examine how Albany parents—both those who chose charter schools and those who did not—understand race and class dynamics in the city and its educational offerings. In keeping with colorblind individualism, very few White parents mentioned race as a reason to avoid or enroll in charter schools. Instead, they used coded language to "politely" discuss racial issues without having to acknowledge the proverbial elephant in the room. Many Black parents used similar language, though some used language that promoted race consciousness.

These examples, discussed in this chapter, show where the national hegemonic colorblind language is being challenged.

As detailed in chapters 1 and 2, race and capitalism are intertwined in a double helix and provide the basic DNA of the United States. These two concepts, while remaining tightly connected to each other, have each developed over time. Thus the "colorblind individualism" that now forms the American core is only the modern incarnation of the racial capitalism that allowed the young nation to flourish on Black backs. As Derrick Bell once put it, "Racism is not disappearing, it's adapting."[2]

This adaptation explains why most Americans have learned to use nonracial, colorblind language in public. No matter what they might say to their close friends and family members, the days of being comfortable using racial epithets in public are largely gone. This is part of why the 2016 Trump presidential campaign was so startling to so many people. While his most vociferous supporters were happy to hear their hidden racism finally expressed publicly, many of his opponents thought that the two elections of Barack Obama meant that the United States had finally forged ahead of its racist past. Racism, however, is structural. The change in public norms that Trump so violently violated was only a measure of outward-facing individualistic racism.

Although out-facing racism declined significantly after the civil rights movement, American structures were framed by racial capitalism. The policies of the civil rights movement made adjustments, but did not fundamentally rebirth a nation built as a slavocracy. The DNA was never replaced. Individual racism is more hidden now than in the past, but structural racism still provides the genetic structure of the American experiment.

This leads to two different, but complementary, conclusions about structural racism and individual racism. First, structural racism does not disappear with policy change. It is at the core of American founding documents and institutions, and cannot be extracted like a gene splice. Second, the successes of the civil rights movement mean that, Trumpism notwithstanding, most individuals will continue to hide their racist views. Instead of racist Trump-like rhetoric, most racist views are coded and hidden, but designed to communicate and maintain the racial hierarchy. This hierarchy is separate from individual racism: while some users of this communication are deliberately promoting their racism, others may well be fully unaware of the power of their language in maintaining the hierarchy. This is due to the power of the racial concept, of its hegemonic status, and as American DNA.

This process occurs in three primary ways: through coded language,[3] the promotion of colorblind ideology,[4] and dog whistles.[5] Frequently, these uses of language promote colorblind ideologies that ignore race at best, or encourage the further indoctrination of the racial hierarchy at worst. By carefully examining how colorblind and coded language is built, I show that these tools of language are frequently used to hide more traditional racist ideas.

Racial "code words" provide a way to invoke racist themes without directly challenging the newer American norm of racial equality.[6] They can also be a fundamental part of *rearticulation*, defined by Omi and Winant as "a practice of discursive reorganization or reinterpretation of ideological themes and interests already present in subjects' consciousness, such that these elements obtain new meanings or coherence."[7] Rearticulation can work in both directions; language might be used for empowerment, as when themes from the civil rights movement were rearticulated to support Black Power and Black nationalism rather than assimilationism.[8] However, language can also be rearticulated in the opposite direction. For example, when people quote Martin Luther King Jr.'s desire for everyone to be "judged not by the color of their skin but by the content of their character" without context,[9] this language becomes supportive of the dismantling of affirmative action programs rather than a call for racial justice. This is a rearticulation of King's meaning, without a change of his words.

This type of rearticulation was clear in the 2023 Supreme Court decision, known as *Students for Fair Admissions*, that virtually ended the use of affirmative action in public and private college admissions. Writing for the majority, Chief Justice John Roberts was critical of universities that have "concluded, wrongly, that the touchstone of an individual's identity is . . . the color of their skin."[10] Justice Thomas, in his concurring opinion, argued that the 2023 decision "sees the universities' admissions policies for what they are: rudderless, race-based preferences." Justice Thomas, long an opponent of affirmative action policies, deliberately invoked the national mythology when he said that affirmative action "policies fly in the face of our colorblind Constitution."[11] This decision shows that the Supreme Court has fully rearticulated Martin Luther King Jr.'s call for racial empowerment into colorblind ideology that limits opportunities for people of Color. Once a call to stop racial discrimination, colorblind arguments are now a way to uphold current racial structure.

Rearticulation is fundamentally about power. When civil rights movement language was rearticulated to support Black Power over assimilationism, it promoted self-determination for those who used it in their pursuit of racial justice. When conservatives quote Martin Luther King Jr. in their quest to dismantle racial-justice programs, they do so to maintain the current racial hierarchy. Social and political backlash to the civil rights movement rearticulated the goal of racial justice into a framework supportive of maintaining the racial order. This occurred as the racial state moved from a position of racial dominance to one of racial hegemony, and is characterized by the use of nonracialized language to promote and support racist ideas and structures. This process occurred largely through colorblind ideology. In this ideology, the civil rights movement readjusted American politics so that it fit the language of the country's founding documents. With the end of slavery and legal, formal segregation, the argument goes, individuals truly were created equal. Without laws that required or even permitted separation and differential treatment based on race, the state can no longer be blamed for different achievement levels. And this "achievement" is distinctly neoliberal; it is measured in terms of wealth, income, and levels of education obtained.

If differences remain between White and Black Americans—including clearly documented differences such as educational attainment, income, and wealth—then, under hegemonic colorblindness, the cause can no longer be found in laws that required different treatment. The civil rights movement removed the possibility of attributing innate, genetic differences to socially defined groups; few people will argue that Whites are inherently smarter than Blacks, for example.[12] Without the possibility of insisting on genetic differences and without laws permitting different treatment of racially defined groups, the ideology continues, differences between racial groups must be due to culture. This way, "culture" becomes the politically correct way of making racist claims. These claims have been fully rearticulated to be not directly racist, but they still allow individuals to make racist statements. That racism is now simply hidden in colorblind language.

The challenge is that using colorblind language makes it very difficult to discuss race, racial issues, and racial problems. There is a broad American assumption that we must "avoid race as the surest way to get past racial problems."[13] Along with this assumption is the contemporary American penchant for avoiding discussions of race altogether, with a preference instead for colorblind discussions that lead to "a public blindness surrounding all things connected to race."[14] While Omi and Winant are critical of all things colorblind, Haney López notes that "some conservatives have converted colorblindness into an ideology that facilitates and also protects dog whistling."[15] A "dog whistle," "coded talk centered on race,"[16] is different from colorblindness in that it is much more deliberate. While many people use colorblind language without reflection, and some use it with a true belief that they are promoting racial justice and equity, the dog whistle belies the racist truth that is hiding just beneath the surface. All of this language works to maintain racial hierarchy and power, whether this is the users' intention or not.

Both racism and capitalism are embedded throughout American politics, including both major political parties, and the language conveying these ideas is evident at all levels of society. Modern racism does not have to be overt in the Trumpian style to be powerful. Rather, "The 'racism' in dog whistle racism does not refer to individual bias, it refers to a willingness to manipulate racial animus in pursuit of power."[17] While Haney López places more blame on the Republican Party than on the Democrats, and he focuses on elite actions over those of everyday people, the same processes are seen in Albany. These are largely Democratic voters, and the parents I interviewed were not political elites. Dog whistles and coded racism are not limited to political leaders; they are embedded in American institutions and political discourse.

The dog whistling that Haney López discusses was clear in Albany conversations. "Dog whistles" include (1) "thinly veiled references to nonwhites"; (2) "[emphasis on] the lack of any direct reference to a racial group"; and (3) claims of playing the race card. While not all respondents used all three parts of Haney López's framework, the "thinly veiled references to nonwhites" were nearly ubiquitous. Careful not to make more directly racist claims, only some people went far enough to include step 2. And the third, while rare, was used by respondents who worked to maintain both racism and their own innocence from it.

Most of this chapter is dedicated to understanding how colorblind language hides racism and not only permits but promotes the maintenance of the racial hierarchy. First, however, I show that structural racism remains embedded in Albany schools of all types. This provides the context for later discussions of colorblindness and dog whistles that serve to reinforce the hierarchy.

Racism in Albany Schools

Multiple respondents claimed that they or their children were victims of racism in Albany public schools, and that racism was part of the reason why they chose something different. Most of these were charter families, although the group does include one parent who used open enrollment to move her child from a predominantly Black elementary school to one that was 50 percent White. Respondents who made claims of racism included Blacks with Black children and Whites with multiracial or Black children.

The strongest claim of racism came from Billie, an older Black woman whose own children had gone through different Albany public and charter schools and who was now helping to raise a grandchild. Billie is a community activist, and we met while she was working the desk at a volunteer position. Billie enrolled one of her children in the district's first charter school, which closed after eleven years for failing to meet its charter's goals. I asked her why she chose to leave her district school and enroll in an unknown charter school instead:

> RYANE: What made you decide to try New Covenant Charter School?
> BILLIE: Well because our children aren't always treated good.
> RYANE: Okay. When you say "ours," do you mean racially?
> BILLIE: Racially. Yes. They're not treated good, they're not taught well. And, how can I put it, they were, like, undereducated. Okay. So I put [my son] in New Covenant. And then he went to Junior High ... and he had to go to Livingston. ... Over here at Livingston, it was hell. You know? And the kids get locked out, until the bell rang and they suspended them for being late. I mean you know dumb, dumb stuff

to bring them down, to step on their self-esteem. So I didn't like that at all.

This discussion came early in my meeting with Billie. She paints a vivid picture of a school district that deliberately mistreated Black children and set them up to fail. Billie continues with a discussion of her daughter, now grown. In this discussion, Billie, like a few other parents, conjures up images of prison—not only the sheer cruelty that she describes but the sense that students must "do their time" at the school, just as a prisoner must "do time." Billie's description of her daughter's high school years was poignant:

> BILLIE: My daughter . . . was at Albany High. She did four years at Albany High.
> RYANE: Was she happy there? And were you happy?
> BILLIE: It was all right. It started changing after a while. Okay. So much so that her senior year, I was just in the office every day and they said, "You can't come here every day." I said, "Why? My school taxes are paid." You know, why?

Although we continue with Billie's discussion below, it is worth taking a moment to review her invocation of neoliberalism in this brief passage. Similarly to Kathleen, discussed later in this chapter, Billie implies here that the fact that she had paid her taxes entitled her to some sort of compensation. For Kathleen, the expectation was the power to choose which school her children attend. For Billie, the expectation was to sit in a school building office to watch over the school's operations. Billie and Kathleen are from very different backgrounds; Billie is an older Black activist from a downtown neighborhood, while Kathleen is an upper-middle-class White professional in a gentrified neighborhood. The fact that both of them so strongly implied that paying taxes entitled them to their chosen actions shows the hegemony of neoliberalism.

My conversation with Billie continued:

> BILLIE: And the things I heard the teachers saying like if they didn't see me sitting in the corner. . . .
> RYANE: You'd go in the classroom?

BILLIE: No, I would be sitting in the office and they come in and the things that they'd be saying and the receptionist will keep giving her the eye, you know, giving her the eye to let her know that I was over there, you know, and she kept on talking anyway and she was talking about this Black kid. "One more time he's late I can't wait to suspend him" and blah blah blah. You know it was that kind of attitude. And then my daughter was in her last year and she was sitting in the cafeteria and a girl walked across and punched her in her face. So she got up and she hit the girl back but my daughter is the one that got suspended.

RYANE: And not the other?

BILLIE: Not the other girl. Okay. And they made a mistake, which they don't do any more, of letting me see the tape. And you see the girl walking across the cafeteria and punch my daughter in her face. But the principal told me if she had laid there and been battered, then he would suspend the other girl. . . . So she got suspended. And when they suspend them, they suspend them for five or six weeks. That's a long time to be suspended. And I got so tired of fighting suspensions. But she came back. [And] they put her on a . . . academic something. Okay. To make sure that she caught up with her work and so she can graduate. Never get in trouble in the whole four years. Except for that. . . . But she came back. She completed that assignment. And she had a biology teacher that decided that he was going to fail her anyway even if she did all the work she did. I talked to [the superintendent]. And he said, "It must have been an academic thing." I said, "No sir." She finished everything. She did her time. And what that teacher told me straight to my face, because [my daughter] was kind of heavy. "I don't like fat girls." So he failed her so she wouldn't walk across the stage to graduate. I mean it was cruel things like that. . . . So now [my daughter] has a son [and] she put the son in [a district school] for pre-K. They have a room at the front of the school where they put the kids in when they're disruptive in the classroom. The room is dark. It's their time-out room. It's their time-out room. I'm serious. The room is dark. It has very dim lighting so you could barely see. And that's where some of the bad kids, especially the little Black boys, sit all day long. When I dropped my grandson off at [that school], there was kids, little boys, that refused to go to school.

One little boy was crying so damn hard, he was a little Hispanic boy. "Mommy, please don't send me back in there, please." She was dragging him to the school door. Then a man got up with two kids that he dropped off before. Okay. And they would run away.

RYANE: Away from the school?

BILLIE: Away from the school. Soon as he put them to the door, they would run away.... You know, it was terrible.

RYANE: Was [your grandson] unhappy there?

BILLIE: Yes, yes. A teacher told me one day when I picked up, he just had on a T-shirt, it was wintertime, no hat, no gloves. [She said,] "Well I got kids here that dress themselves." I said, "You also got some four-year-olds who do more physical labor in the morning than you do all day." And she just looked at me. You know? This little boy, how's he gonna keep up with the hat and the gloves?

RYANE: Yeah, they need help for a while.

BILLIE: Yes they do. They need help for a while. And it got so bad that he kept saying, "Grandma, she won't let me go to the bathroom. She won't let me go to the bathroom." I said, "So when you keep askin' her and you gotta go real bad," because he was starting to pee on himself, "you go over there to a corner and pull your winker out and go potty." Well he did it one day. "Because my grandma told me to do it. You don't let me go to the bathroom. My grandmother told me to do it." And [the teacher] was pissed. You know, she wrote him up for it, but you won't let him go to the bathroom. In pre-K, the bathroom's in the classroom. They only got to walk a few steps. But we took him out of there and we put him in [a charter school] and he's doing a lot better.

While Billie's experiences were unique, partly due to the sheer length of time she had sent children and grandchildren to Albany schools, her views of the district are important for understanding the broader charter school movement. Billie's stories, spanning two generations, are all framed by race. Her experiences include having a daughter who, in her view, was suspended because someone else physically assaulted her, then missed her own graduation due to a teacher's prejudice against heavy Black girls. This daughter's son was cold in the winter because his teacher would not help him with his hat, gloves, or coat, and he got in trouble for urinating in a classroom after his teacher refused to allow him to use the restroom.

While there are other stories of racism, discussed below, that corroborate Billie's overall experiences, none are as detailed or as cruel as hers. Indeed, some individuals, upon hearing her stories, might be tempted to dismiss them, and to assume that she is claiming racism where it does not exist. And yet, there is no one who can understand racism more clearly than its own victims. An individual outside of these relationships cannot dismiss Billie's claims because they were not there. The interpretive method encourages scholars to understand relationships from an individual's point of view, and Billie's point of view is clear: her family was a constant victim of racism, and this did not change until they left Albany public schools.

Billie's view, if not the sheer cruelty of her experience, was mirrored by Gloria. Gloria is a White/Puerto Rican mother of two multiracial children in charter schools. An experience in a neighborhood school related to her children's racial identity encouraged Gloria to seek their education elsewhere:

> GLORIA: He did go to pre-K [at a district elementary] school. We had a major issue with one of the teachers. Got so bad to where he didn't want to go to school anymore.
> RYANE: Really? Do you know what happened?
> GLORIA: I don't know. Honestly, if you want my honest opinion, I feel like [his teacher] didn't like biracial children, to be honest. I met with the head of the UPK [universal pre-kindergarten] program. There happened to be a slot in the other classroom. He went there, and perfect the rest of the year. No issues. I don't know, but that's what happened.

Gloria provides another example of an individual whose interpretation of their own experience may differ from that of an outsider. Although she could not clearly identify what had made her child so unhappy in his first pre-kindergarten classroom, she believed it was racial. This belief caused her to enroll her children in a different school in the future.

Later in our conversation, Gloria mentioned that there are few White students in her children's charter school. She explained this lack of White interest in charter schools in a distinctly racial way. While this example of racism is not from district officials, it does suggest a broader racist environment in district schools:

> RYANE: You mentioned a comparatively smaller number of White children at that school. Why do you think that is?
> GLORIA: You want me to be honest with you, right?
> RYANE: Absolutely.
> GLORIA: I honestly think that a lot of White families don't consider charter, because that's the ghetto school. They're not going to send their kids, and they think down [on charter schools].

Gloria's hunch, that more White parents do not choose charter schools because they are viewed as being "ghetto schools," is borne out in later interviews.

A final example of racism in the Albany district schools came from Clara. Clara, an educated White mother with a Black child, utilized the district's open-enrollment policy to move her child to a middle-class school when her young child was struck by a heavy boot thrown by another student. Clara shared with me a conversation she had with a friend, a Black parent with a child in the school her daughter first attended. The friend's child had an experience with feeling physically threatened, similar to Clara's child's experience. Clara encouraged her friend to bring this up with the school, and the friend did not believe that anyone would listen to her:

> CLARA: I suggested [to my friend,] "You should go in." And she said, "I can't go in." And she said, "They listened to you because you're White. They're not going to listen to me because I'm Black."
> RYANE: Was she another parent?
> CLARA: Another parent. Yup. And that concerns me about that school too, because it is . . . I was the minority and I'm concerned that the parents don't have a voice at that school. Because here I am, an educated White woman who doesn't even feel welcome in that school,

but then you have a refugee from Somalia, you know what I'm saying? Who feels very uncomfortable at that school.

Of course, traditional district schools were not the only ones with racist actions or symbols. Ronnie, the father from a nearby city who enrolled his son in an Albany charter school even though it required a significant drive each way for the first year, was extremely happy with his choice. Ronnie was positive that his son's charter school was much more academically challenging than his first school had been, and he was proud of how much his son had achieved since enrolling there.

And yet, Ronnie was deeply concerned about the symbolism of one of the school's practices. The school had taped lines on the floor for the children to stand on. Ronnie, who had spent time in prison, thought that these lines were too similar to what he saw while incarcerated. In his view, the school—the best option he had for his son—was preparing him for a life of prison. This came up when I asked Ronnie if there was anything he would change about the school he chose for his son: "Take them damn lines off the floor. You know, in the prison system, right? They put these lines on the floor, right? So the inmates could walk on the lines and if you step out of the lines, right, you get disciplined for it. And I'm not talking about some light discipline, right? I'm talking about strict disciplined for it. And um, when I seen them on the, in the school, which they did this year, I was like kind of traumatized by them because like, what the hell is those lines?"

These stories, crossing generations, schools, race, and class, provide strong evidence of a racist public school system. While not everyone experiences racist institutions in the same way, these stories explain why some people wanted to find alternative educational options for their children. However, the racism in Albany public schools was not only institutional. Multiple parents used language that perpetuated racism. We move now to these discussions.

Individualized Racism

There are three different ways to discuss race and to make racist statements. The first is *colorblindness*. This is an attempt to avoid mention of race altogether, and it frequently comes with an assumption that any differences in racial "achievement" are due to inherent, individual, or cultural factors. However, colorblind language has become so ubiquitous that it is, sometimes, also used in genuinely nonracist, or even antiracist, discussions. Second, those who wish to make more directly racist claims but are aware that they need to keep their language neutral in order to be socially acceptable, use coded language. This is a way to make clear, direct racist statements without actually mentioning race. Third, some people become so comfortable with their racism (or so unaware of it) that their language becomes fully racist. This is the trajectory of language; it goes from colorblind to coded to racist. Each level is a bit less concerned about social acceptability than the one before, and each is more directly racist than what came before it. The rest of this chapter focuses on how parents—primarily White, middle-class parents—use language that perpetuates racism. All of these parents would deny being racist if asked directly.

Colorblindness

There is a strong American penchant to deny the ability to see color. Statements such as "I don't see color" or "we're all the same under our skin" are common. Colorblindness is the opposite of race consciousness. A colorblind approach claims that race has no power, and should not have any power. A race-consciousness approach understands that, even though it is a social construct, race remains a powerful tool.[18]

Scholars and activists have been extremely critical of the colorblind movement. Claims to be colorblind are frequently used to cover up racist actions or statements, and colorblindness blinds individuals to differences that are perpetuated by the American racial hierarchy. However, this criticism is not maintained throughout the country. Many Americans remain unaware that colorblind ideology can blind them to racial problems, and they view being "colorblind" as equivalent to being race neutral.

And yet, some Albany parents used colorblind language in a very different way. Although scholars and activists are right to challenge colorblind claims when they are used to explain away the need for programs like affirmative action, parents also use colorblind language as a way to promote diversity and integration. One example of this came from Tracy, a White mother whose children have a Black father:

> TRACY: I try to teach my children not to see color of people's skin. I'd rather just have them learn about them as a person. They've experienced, just in the past couple years, my oldest would get, "You're White. You're White." And she's like, "No, I'm not."
> RYANE: This is at school?
> TRACY: Yeah. On the bus, you know? But when I like go to the school, they're like, [saying hi to my child]. And it makes me feel good because I'm like, "Okay, they're doing okay." Like I said, my youngest can hold her own and I don't think she really cares. I mean, she likes the friends and all that, but like again, the kids don't look at color, but they're mostly around Black children, which is just . . . and I'm okay with that. Like, I have White friends, but most . . . Like I said, my church, my school, my area, I'm in a predominantly Black neighborhood.

In this discussion, Tracy is trying to project a colorblind ideology and trying to teach this ideology to her biracial children. This is the type of approach that many colorblind adherents think they are presenting. In this approach, race really doesn't matter. Tracy and her children are *not* fully blind to race, and Tracy can acknowledge that her children have a different racial identification than some other children. Her goal, however, is not to ignore race completely but to argue that her children should be friends with everyone. This is the nonracist element of the colorblind movement. We should note that it remains very far from racial consciousness; under that approach, Tracy's children would project pride in their mixed-race heritage.

However, not all colorblind language remains as neutral as Tracy's did. A similar discussion using colorblind language came from Janie, a Black mother whose youngest child was enrolled in a charter school: "I was brought up in, I don't know the right way to put it, my mother always taught me to be colorblind, so I had friends of all nationalities and all religions. And to me we're all equal, and I want to instill that in him, that one is no better than the other. We are all on the same playing field, what you do to excel is what makes you a better person or whatever."

At first glance, Janie's language looks very similar to Tracy's. It is tempting to assume that Janie is just as truly racially neutral as Tracy is. However, in Janie's case, her colorblind language was hiding a more racist orientation. Janie's language quickly devolved into coded language, providing evidence for the argument that colorblindness is often a first step toward coded racism, as Bonilla-Silva argues.[19]

Coded Racism

Picking up from Janie's colorblind claim, above, we can see that colorblindness can be used to code, or hide, racist claims. While Janie's claim above clearly argues that everyone is, and should be, equal, she did not think that Albany High School would be a valid option for her child. At the time that we met, Janie was not very happy with her child's charter middle school and was considering a private or charter high school for his future. I asked her if she would consider Albany High School, the city's only traditional public high school. Her reaction was reminiscent of that of other parents who avoid Albany High because of its large population of students of Color and high rates of poverty:

> JANIE: I'm not sure with his personality that he would do well in . . . Albany High or anything like that. He's a very soft-spoken child. . . . It might be, it would be a major eye-opener for him.
> RYANE: Okay.
> JANIE: Honestly.
> RYANE: Is it how large Albany High is?
> JANIE: The large, yeah, the different areas that the kids come from. . . . I—I just, I don't know how to, [my son is] just a homebody. He's a . . . he's a boy but he's a homebody. He doesn't know anything about the different areas that kids come from and, uh, I don't know the right word to use for that which, you know where I'm going with that.

Thus, Janie now implies that her initial colorblind statement ("no one is better than the other") was providing coverage for a more traditionally racist approach to the city's public schools. Janie does not want her child at Albany High because it would be "a major eye-opener for him." When I tried to clarify whether Janie was concerned about the high school's sheer size, she quickly moved instead to "the different areas that the kids come from." In a segregated city, "different areas" refers to neighborhoods of Color that are plagued by poverty. She clarifies this by stating that her child is "a homebody," someone who is not aware of or not prepared for all of these "different areas" in the city.

It is also clear from her language that Janie was not comfortable with the discussion we were having. Most people include hesitations or repetitions in their spoken language that they would not include in writing. However, other parts of Janie's interview do not include as much hesitation as shown in the passage above. Janie stops and starts, changes track, and does not complete all of her thoughts. As Bonilla-Silva argues, spoken language like this frequently indicates lack of confidence or unease with the conversation.[20]

After hesitating, Janie firmly codified her language with her final statement, "You know where I'm going with that." It is not unusual for a parent to be concerned about Albany High's student body. The fact that Janie made this statement to me—a middle-class, White mother—suggested that she shared concerns that she assumed I might also have. This statement also came with a very pointed look. She did not have to say that she did not want her child around students of Color from difficult economic backgrounds; the code words communicated her concerns clearly.

A similar example comes from Tabitha, a professional Black mother of two who moved her children from a neighborhood school to a charter school, partly because they would be surrounded by more Black students. However, while Tabitha appreciated that the predominantly Black student body made her children more comfortable around their family members, she wanted to ensure that this did not go too far. She worked to ensure that her children, especially the older one, knew that he was "not the typical African American kid . . . growing up in the typical ghetto, you know, project type environment. And I want him to think that he's not the African American that's seen on TV, he's a young man that happens to be African American who lives in this part of town."

Tabitha's reference to "typical" children in a "typical" ghetto gives pause. It is possible that she meant to refer to "stereotypical" people and places, but that is not the word she used. Nowhere in her discussion did she evaluate or critique these "typical" understandings, suggesting that she agreed with them. Tabitha and Janie both provide examples of how coded language can convey racist meanings without using clearly racist words.

This approach was common among other respondents, as well. Ofelia,[21] a Latina immigrant, has two children, both of whom attended an Albany magnet school at the elementary level. But when it came time for her oldest child to enter middle school, she enrolled him in a charter school at his teacher's recommendation.

Ofelia's son's charter school, like all Albany charter schools, is predominantly Black. Ofelia recognized and mentioned this in our discussion, when she exclaimed that "there are a lot of Black kids" at her son's school. She followed this up by saying, "I don't care about race. Rather, it's who they hang out with. That's my only fear. Because there are a lot of kids that you can get wrapped up with and the kids are sometimes... My son... calls me racist. I'm not racist. What happens is that their upbringing is very different. They are very different. Sometimes the way they're being raised scares me."

While Ofelia was careful to acknowledge that race doesn't matter ("I don't care about race"), she focused instead on how her son's classmates—whom she had already identified as being primarily Black—are "different" and "scary." This is a classic colorblind move; she used culture ("their upbringing is very different") and othering ("they are very different") to explain her lack of comfort with her child's Black classmates. The problem is with their culture, not with race itself. This mirrors the dog-whistle politics that Haney López says serves as code for racism; it is also similar to the "racism without racists" that Bonilla-Silva identifies.

Janie and Ofelia provide examples of how coded language allows individuals to make racist claims without using a racial epithet or clear language. Since polite American society now forbids clearly racist statements, most people have moved these types of claims into coded language. Using this language permits them to deny any possible claims of racism that may come from someone else.

Albany clearly followed this pattern. Discussions of how families chose their children's schools were laden with coded language... and a few respondents became so comfortable that they eventually dropped their coding altogether. This provides evidence for the argument that coded language is simply providing a cover for the racist truth that lies beneath. This is the first step that Haney López says is part of dog whistles.[22] Using coded language provides an "out"—it allows people to make gently racist statements without risking being called out for their racism. If others are troubled by the conversation and point out the racism built within, it is easier to walk back a coded statement than a clearly racist claim. Coded language allows people to "test the waters" with their racism, checking to see if their conversation partner (or partners) is troubled by it. If so, they know to stop. And if not, they may freely continue with these claims.

Sometimes, coded language stays coded. For example, Bethany moved her children from a private religious school to a magnet elementary school. They then attended a district middle school and the high school. Her views on Albany High School were mixed. Bethany's interpretation was that Albany High was largely "geared toward" students who needed to be pushed to attend college. She did not see her children as part of that population:

RYANE: What about Albany High? Have you been happy there?
BETHANY: Mostly. I feel like, and I've felt like this for a long time, the schools are geared towards kids who are not necessarily going to college. They want kids to see themselves as going to college. They want kids to envision themselves as having a strong high school career and being able to go to college.
RYANE: Okay.
BETHANY: And my kids are not in that . . . My kids are welcome to go to college if they want to and they have access to it and it's definitely a possibility and they need to make that choice. They both are likely very college bound. But they don't need to be pushed in that direction. Do you understand what I mean?
RYANE: Right.
BETHANY: So what that means is that there is, for example, a class called College and Career Prep, which [was] newly required when my older son entered ninth grade and he really didn't need that class. A total waste of time. . . . They're serving the least common denominator and one of my problems actually with [their magnet elementary school] along the way, is that neither of them have been challenged as much as they needed to be, and my older son

especially. He's in eleventh grade right now, he's taking AP chemistry, and this is the first time in his whole career where he's had a hard time. So our kids were going to succeed no matter where they went, and the question is just really what framework are we going to keep them in? So they say that Albany High is really two different schools.
RYANE: I've heard that, yeah.
BETHANY: And so, it wasn't an issue.

This discussion with Bethany shows two different things. First, she viewed many Albany High students as needing to be pushed to consider college, but also thought of her own children as distinctly different from that population. For her, classes that encourage students to think about college are "a total waste of time." This is a way of making a thinly veiled reference to Albany's students of Color. Bethany clarifies her intent when she follows this up with a statement that Albany High is "really two different schools." This is a common refrain among those in the Albany community, and refers to significant internal racial segregation. While Albany High is majority Black with significant White and Latinx populations, courses geared toward high-achieving students (such as Advanced Placement courses and the International Baccalaureate program) are largely understood to be designed for the middle-class families who could easily leave the public schools if they wished to do so. These courses have much larger White enrollments than Albany High as a whole,[23] leading to the claim that Albany High is really two schools—a mediocre holding ground for students of Color from working-class backgrounds, and a top-notch, academically challenging environment for middle-class, mostly White kids.

What is striking about Bethany's claim, then, is not that she recognizes the "two schools" situation of Albany High School. The unusual part is the positive way she views that separation. Generally, those speaking of Albany High's "two schools" are critical of the segregation inherent in that organization. For Bethany, the "two schools" means that attending Albany High, for her kids, "wasn't an issue." It "wasn't an issue" because, while they are in the same building as large numbers of students of Color and those from more difficult economic backgrounds than her own, Bethany's children were separated enough from those populations that she felt secure in having them attend the school.

While Bethany's description of Albany High remains deeply coded and, therefore, not yet clearly racialized, Lexie's conversation was different. Lexie is also a married White mother, but she and her family live in a less economically secure area in Albany. Her neighborhood elementary school is one of the city's most segregated, with low test scores and a negative academic reputation. Lexie was anxious to keep her children out of that school:

> LEXIE: They told me my home school was [a predominantly Black elementary school]. There was no way I was sending my kids there at all. I was literally in tears and not going to send my kid to school. . . . I'm just as close [to a more integrated, less economically needy elementary school], or [a third elementary school, with a very strong reputation]. There, of course, was no room.
> RYANE: No room . . .
> LEXIE: In the schools. [A separate elementary school] accepted over the phone, so that was great. I thought, "For this west in the city, that should be great." The teachers were great. The administration at the time, not so much. . . . When there were more violent kids in the school—
> RYANE: At [the school your children attended]?
> LEXIE: Everyone gets bused over. That was a problem. I enrolled my girls in karate and then I started looking at alternatives, having no family in the area, and not knowing anything about the school system.

Lexie's early discussion, therefore, stressed her desperation to avoid an elementary school with a large number of students of Color from lower socioeconomic backgrounds. Lexie used open enrollment to enroll her children in a different elementary school, located in a western part of the city. "Western" Albany is interchangeable with "uptown," as opposed to "downtown." Downtown neighborhoods have higher populations of people of Color and higher rates of poverty than uptown neighborhoods. The school Lexie selected is in a very middle-class but aging neighborhood. Once threatened with closure for low enrollment, it now relies on families from other parts of the city to use open enrollment to keep its doors open. Lexie was critical of the number of "downtown" students being bused to her children's "uptown" school. In her view, these children were so violent that she felt compelled to enroll her own children in martial arts courses. Again, note that Lexie never mentions race explicitly. Instead, she focuses on neighborhoods.

Lexie eventually moved her children to a magnet elementary school, where they completed their grammar school education. While they were in their last year of elementary school, her children were able to "shadow" students for a day at their future middle school to see what it was like. Lexie remained critical of the middle school, starting with what her children were exposed to on their shadow day,

> LEXIE: Now they're at [a middle school] and they have a new principal. She's trying to make changes. Some of the kids are not being helpful in the changes because they don't see that there was problems. A lot of the stuff with the middle school, once the elementary school kids shadowed, the language, the disrespect to each other and the teachers, horrible. That's what the kids came back with.
>
> RYANE: Came back to [their elementary school]?
>
> LEXIE: Yeah. To their parents, to everyone. That was just absolutely horrible because my daughter still tells me, the older one, "You chose to bring me up in the city." I said, "In the city we use all of our syllables and proper diction. . . ." She tends to want to slang a bit the way some of her friends are talking. I'm like, "No. Hella no, no, no. We're not saying that."

In this section, Lexie villainizes her children's middle school friends for their disrespect and nonstandard English conversations. These are classic examples of coded racism. Language, especially, remains one of the strongest ways that middle- and upper-class Whites maintain status and privilege over Black Americans. While African American Vernacular English (AAVE) has its own grammatical rules and maintains an internal structure, many Whites simply view it as "less than" standard English. With her criticism of violent elementary students, "disrespect," and language, Lexie was pushing her claims beyond the more coded issues that Bethany employed. Recall that Bethany made a simple statement about Albany High being split into two schools, and then stopped. Lexie continues to push the boundaries of what might be acceptable in conversation.

Lexie continued her discussion about Albany schools by focusing on a fight that occurred at Albany High School shortly before we met. This was a particularly large fight that occurred off school grounds and led to a student being stabbed. The school shut down the following day. Lexie was not the only respondent to bring up this incident, but her view of it was interesting: "I know that there's good opportunities in Albany High, but it's the entire city in one place. I wasn't surprised to see that fight that happened weeks back, because I see the cops at every corner every time school dismisses."

Lexie continues her engagement of coded racism by pointing out that Albany High includes "the entire city in one place." This implies that there are certain areas of the city—and in a segregated city, that means people of Color—that create a violent environment for everyone else. While she remained on the coded side of racism, never explicitly claiming that her children were better than others or that Black children were not equivalent to her own, she skillfully coded these sentiments.

Other respondents were less adept at keeping their language coded. A middle-ground level of coding is provided by Gloria, who identifies as White and Puerto Rican and whose child has a Black father. Gloria's views of Albany and its schools were similar to those that Lexie provided. She began by discussing her neighborhood as being preferable to other city neighborhoods, and this quickly developed into a discussion about Albany's middle and high schools.

> GLORIA: I just choose not to live where some of my friends are. That's all.
>
> RYANE: What do you mean by that?
>
> GLORIA: It's just neighborhood. I wouldn't live in [a specific downtown neighborhood]. That's not a choice for me. I like quiet, and it's not quiet. I have another friend that has three children that lives in Schenectady on [a specific] Street. You couldn't pay me to live there. Like I said, there are places I'm comfortable going, but I'm not going to live there. I like quiet. I like to be away from people, and I don't like surprises. I don't want you to be able to come knock on my door, you know what I mean?
>
> RYANE: Right. Do you like your neighborhood?

GLORIA: Yeah, yeah. Everybody pretty much leaves you alone, and the only thing we've ever had problems with is whenever it comes to a time when people are ordering stuff for Christmas, packages are always getting stolen, but that's like anywhere you live.
RYANE: Yeah.
GLORIA: I feel like they're like, "Oh, that's a nice neighborhood. We'll ride through here," you know what I mean? It is what it is. It is what it is. That's not . . . I don't have to worry about if my son plays on the lawn, is somebody going to drive by and shoot him or whatever.

Although Gloria framed her preference for her own neighborhood around quiet and a lack of "surprises," she finished that discussion with a much less coded statement. Preferring a "quiet" neighborhood is frequently a coded way of saying that one would rather have a middle-class, or a White-dominated, neighborhood. While perhaps not necessarily coded on its own, the opposite of a "quiet" neighborhood would be loud and crowded. This brings up images of cities, and especially inner-city neighborhoods, that have larger Black populations. While Gloria would likely argue that her preference for a "quiet" neighborhood is not about race, her final statement challenges that. Her assumption that a non-"quiet" neighborhood could lead to her son being shot betrays her view that other neighborhoods are potentially (or even inherently) violent and dangerous.

Gloria's understanding of neighborhoods different from her own spilled over into her view of Albany schools. Her son's charter school did not include grades beyond the elementary level, so I asked her whether she would consider an Albany district school after that:

RYANE: Would you ever consider an Albany middle school or Albany High?
GLORIA: Never.
RYANE: Why is that?
GLORIA: My kid is not being walked home with the police. My kid is not going to get caught in the middle of a street rumble. This is not the Watts Riots. I do not want my child to learn about sex and pills and heroin from a peer. That's going to be mommy's job. Frankly,

they disgust me. They have to close McDonald's because of the high school kids.[24]

By now, Gloria is comfortable enough with me to share that the students at Albany High School "disgust" her. Her assumption is that her child would be caught in violence and turn to drugs if he was surrounded by this population. Gloria continues:

> GLORIA: Now don't get me wrong. I know people that have come out of Albany High that I went to college with, but they say that they won't send their kids there now. It's even changed since they've come out of the high [school]. Honestly, I think a lot of that is because those kids don't own that school. They don't take pride in it, and there's not really a lot of inclusion. A lot of those kids that are out there fighting and punching people and telling the cops where to go and destroying people's property.
> RYANE: At Albany High?
> GLORIA: Yeah. I realize that . . . there's exceptions . . . Like I said, I worked a lot with kids. The ones that kind of aren't watched and aren't held accountable are the ones that are fighting in the streets on the way home. Just like the middle schools, horrible reputation for the middle schools. I think since I came in '99, [one of them has] always been on the news, never for anything good either. Always something negative. . . . Everybody kind of comes in and does their time. If I wanted my kid to go to prison, then I would send them to prison.

As we saw from other parents earlier in this chapter, Gloria compares Albany public schools to a prison. Unlike those who mentioned "doing time" or using other prison-adjacent language, Gloria makes the comparison direct.

Gloria acknowledges that some Albany High School students do well, but assumes (and admits that she has no firsthand knowledge) that most have simply given up. She states that the few students who do well succeed because their parents have "different expectations." This is Gloria's coded way of saying that parents of Color, especially those who experience poverty or economic hardship, do not expect much from their children. Because of that, the children fail. She completes her statements about Albany High School (which, by now, has grown to include her views of Albany's middle schools) by comparing it to a prison. There is no doubt that this is a barely coded way of saying that these schools are majority Black and violent; this is the (accurate, though deeply problematic) reputation of American prisons.

Bridging the Gap: Coded Racism Hides Racism

Continuing evidence of coded racism came from Chad and Sarah, a middle-class White couple with one young child. Chad and Sarah provide the first clear example of coded language that can break down to become more traditionally racist, providing evidence that others who code their language more carefully or consistently are hiding racist beliefs and views. Chad and Sarah had originally enrolled their child in a magnet school, but took him out of that school because its population predominantly consisted of students of Color.

Chad and Sarah treated the interview as though they were teaching me about how Albany schools worked; they explained the deadline for entering into magnet lotteries, provided geographic details on where each school was located, and explained the themes of each magnet school.[25] Their approach also gave them the confidence that came from having specialized knowledge. While I found this interview difficult at the time, it did reveal different information than those that focused more on replying to my prepared questions. Chad and Sarah began by coding their racist language, but that coding had dissolved before the end of our conversation. Their experience with Albany city schools was with a magnet school their only child attended for three and a half years (pre-K through half of second grade) before they moved him to a private school.

Chad and Sarah brought up their son's magnet school's racial composition early in our conversation, and unprompted by me:

> SARAH: This past year we found out that the [magnet] school [where he first enrolled] . . . is now 90 percent minority non-Caucasian, so it's the feeder school for . . .

CHAD: We knew that when he applied.
SARAH: Well, I didn't know it was 90 percent.

Although Sarah continued her discussion at this point (we pick that up below), it is worth pausing for a moment to consider her discussion of her child's magnet school. Most schools in Albany are under 50 percent White, making them majority minority.[26] And yet, her response to her husband's reminder that they always knew the school was predominantly non-White is striking. It implies that Sarah would be comfortable with a majority-minority school, but that her comfort level ends somewhere before it hits 90 percent. Sarah continued her discussion:

> But it's the feeder school for families migrating to the United States. So, many of the students, I don't know at other schools, but at that school, are ENL students, which is now English with New Learners. . . . So, there's so much focus on most of the children in the class in each grade, can't follow the lesson because they don't understand English. So they're very below grade level, but they're still in that class or they're getting extra help. Where they're being pulled from the grade to go with an ENL instructor to learn English.
>
> So, in our case, our child is very academically driven. Gifted, if you might say. So, he'd finish his work, and he'd want to read a book, and he would get in trouble. They'd be, "What are you doing?" [He'd say,] "Well, I'm done."

Chad and Sarah came back to their discussion of ENL students later, and lumped them together with students who had special needs. In their view, the school focused too much on these two populations, leaving their own child to fend for himself:

> This past September, they added three . . . specific special ed classes. Like, say one class is crisis intervention, one class is . . . [trails off]. Those children are all segregated from regular ed classes. But yet, if they, say, run AWOL through the school, the whole school is on lockdown 'cause there's a special needs student, you know, in a situation. They added a mindfulness room, which is a padded room.[27] They offer lots of programming for ENL students and families. So we're basically like, well . . . it's fantastic

you're offering all of that for ENL families, 'cause they need that. I understand. They just came from all these countries, it's a lot . . . Thank you for giving them the resources. What are you doing for these children over here? That are meeting the grades, that are doing the work, that are following the rules? Well, they're kind of just like quiet, pushed in the corner. Like, thanks for doing a good job, we have to focus on this kid 'cause he's stealing, or he's missing school, or he's failing. We don't care about you. So to speak.

In the early part of our conversation, Chad and Sarah explained that they were unaware that their school was 90 percent students of Color. They followed that up by explaining that the school had many immigrant children who did not speak English, then negatively compared those immigrant children to their own child's "gifted" status. At the same time, children with special needs also took attention away from their own child. The strong implication, also common in coded racism, was that children of Color were keeping their child from progressing at his natural rate.

Chad and Sarah bridge their use of coded racism to more directly racist claims by discussing discipline. Sarah pointed out that "there's huge discipline problems in the school," another frequent complaint with strong ties to coded racism. Shortly thereafter, Chad and Sarah stopped using coded language altogether. The problem, they finally told me, was that "minority" students take priority:

CHAD: It's basically nonminority students are marginalized at the school. Even when we, first, the very first day, we noticed on a sheet they had markings next to all the students.
SARAH: M and NM . . .
CHAD: MM, MF, NMF, and NMM.
SARAH: We're like, "what's NM," and they're like, "Not Minority."
CHAD: Nonminority male, nonminority female, minority male, minority female.
RYANE: Okay.
CHAD: And so, [our child] was one of only two students that was nonminority in his class, and that pretty much stayed that way for three and a half years he was there. . . . The teachers are definitely not part

of the problem. They are saints to be able to continue to deal with the situation.

By this point in our discussion, Chad and Sarah had given in to their frustrations and were sharing their views freely. They remove all codes as they clearly state that "nonminority students are marginalized at the school." This is followed up with a reminder that this is not the teachers' fault. The implication, then, is that fault for discipline problems lies with the "minority" children themselves, or with their parents. Chad and Sarah followed this implication by providing examples of both children and parents who had, to use their earlier language, "disciplinary" problems. Although, in keeping with colorblind norms and coded racism, they did not clarify the racial background of the individuals they discuss below, the context made it clear that these were not White children or parents.

Sarah begins by sharing her experience while volunteering for the school's book fair. Book fairs are common in elementary schools, and allow children to shop for books and accessories from Scholastic in person rather than through flyers that teachers send home. The books and small items (such as erasers, pencils, and posters) are displayed so children can see them, pick out their favorites, and purchase them right away. Sarah had been volunteering at one of these book fairs when one student stole items on display, but was not punished for his behavior. Instead, in her view, his actions were rewarded:

SARAH: And, at the end of the day, for behaving during the day, the principal brought that child back to the book fair and purchased things for him to take home.
RYANE: In addition to the stolen material?
SARAH: In addition to the stolen property, and the stolen property was never paid for. Because he comes from a hard life [spoken sarcastically, as if in quotes], I was told.[28]

Sarah, who volunteered frequently in the building, continued with additional examples of theft and violence that she either experienced or witnessed at her child's magnet school. She blamed the school's focus on positive reinforcement over punishment, while other "kids have, you know, feared for their lives."

It was clear that Chad and Sarah blamed not only the school's focus on positive reinforcement but also the parents of children they accused of theft and violence. Both of them made this clear:

> CHAD: The parents at [the magnet school] were terrible. I mean obviously, it's, children learn from their parents, but like even something as simple as dropping off kids at [school] was like taking your own life at risk, because it's a one-way road, and parents would stop their car in the middle and get out and leave their car there. And no one could drive down the one-way road.
>
> SARAH: You're just stuck in a flow of traffic and you can't back up, 'cause there's cars, and you can't drive forward, and then the people would come out of the building and they'd be like [slapping her chest], "What is your problem?"
>
> CHAD: Running over, practically running over children. Trying to barrel back up the road, turn around, go the wrong way through the one-way street . . .
>
> SARAH: Throw seven or eight kids in a van with no buckles and take off ninety out of the school lot. I'd call the police, the police would do nothing. "Well, what do you want me to do, arrest parents?" That's what I got from the Albany police.

By this point, Chad and Sarah have established that they pulled their son from this magnet school because it was primarily composed of students of Color and students with special needs, and that these two groups took too many resources and had too many disciplinary problems. They follow that by sharing that they had called the police on parents who did not drive courteously. (Sarah provided no evidence that she actually witnessed children leaving without seatbelts. She seemed to assumed that the population that drove their families away from the magnet school would not use them. And her statement that families were driving ninety miles an hour down a narrow city street was clearly an exaggeration.)

Aside from trying to have parents arrested, there are clear racial dynamics in calling the police department on parents during school pick-up and drop-off. Like many cities, Albany has seen racial friction between the police department and the Black community. Calling the police on Black parents is an act of White privilege at best and an attempt to perpetuate racial animus at worst.

Chad and Sarah's racism quickly devolved into pity. They felt bad for children of Color whose parents did not take care of them. They said this multiple times in a brief discussion at the end of our meeting:

> CHAD: I remember the very first year, I'll never forget the one comment from a teacher, I remember kids were, like, running around the halls, like it was the end of the year. I'm like, "Ahhh, they're probably crazy 'cause it's summer vacation," and I said, "They want to get out of here." And he said, "No, they want to stay." I said, "What do you mean?" He said, "The kids wanna stay because this is the only place where they actually feel loved and get any attention." This was faculty saying it.
>
> RYANE: At [the magnet school]?
>
> CHAD: Yeah. They said because they actually are getting their nutrition, they're getting, even if they act out, they're doing it usually because of, they basically want the attention or just don't have . . . they don't care about anything anymore. Whenever we'd volunteer for classrooms, it was . . . it broke your heart because I remember going into, like, I would be [in a room where] these kids did not know me. . . . And they were, like, hugging me, and they were so happy to see you, and have someone there and read and it broke your heart. 'Cause these kids are so . . . they're like sponges dying to absorb attention and love.
>
> SARAH: Affection, right.
>
> CHAD: And, they are, you just . . . you can't give them enough. It's like, looking at someone that's starving, and no amount of food's enough to make them satiated.
>
> SARAH: But, they don't have . . . like, a lot of them don't have, like, the basics. Know what I mean? Like, they don't have a coat. Or they're walking to school like eighteen blocks without a winter hat. You know, it's stuff like that. You can only do so much, though, too.

These children, the students of Color whom Chad and Sarah blamed for the school's perceived discipline problems, the students whom they pitied, were taking resources that, in their view, rightfully belonged to their own child.

> CHAD: And it's like, [our son's] grammar, and his penmanship, those are all above where he needs to be, but they have so much work to take care of the other kids that... and I don't blame them, I don't... but it's not fair to him either.
> SARAH: If you go to any... we were never like... we still would never say, you know, our kid's so much better than your kid, you know.

Chad and Sarah ended their conversation with a reminder that they know not to state publicly that their White child is "better than" the children of Color who attended his magnet school. And yet, after losing their codes and making their views clear to a White interviewer, they did exactly that.

Chad and Sarah were not the only parents who neglected to keep their racism coded. The strongest examples of racism from a parent came from Kathleen, a married, middle-class, White mother of two children. Kathleen applied for her older child to attend her preferred magnet school several times, but when we met they had not yet won a spot. Kathleen lives in a gentrified downtown neighborhood, and was adamant that her child would not attend her neighborhood school. Their neighborhood school has a very low White enrollment and a very high economic need:

> KATHLEEN: But the whole, the whole motivation [to attend the magnet school] was that, um, we wanted him to have a decent spot for kindergarten because we didn't want to be in the exact position that we find ourself in now, which is our neighborhood school... I will not send him there.
> RYANE: Why is that?
> KATHLEEN: I had a nanny in my house that works after care there and said that he would get eaten alive.
> RYANE: Do you know what she meant by that?
> KATHLEEN: Yes. That there were many kids with lots of behavioral problems and although their student-teacher ratio is smaller than—it

is, because I investigated too. On paper it looks like, oh, they have the best student-teacher ratio in the district—[this] is because they have more problem children, more children with issues. And I mean, I don't have a perfect child. My kid is, I think, going to be a higher needs learner. Um, I want him to have more attention. Um, also there is a neighborhood Facebook group for downtown Albany parents. And something that really stuck with me is people always say, because I live right here in [this neighborhood], that you can't say you love the neighborhood if you don't love the neighborhood school. And I'm going to say something that's really not PC. [That is] not my neighborhood school. I did not choose to live in [a predominantly non-White, high-economic-need neighborhood]. I chose to live in [my gentrified neighborhood]. [My neighborhood] doesn't have a neighborhood school, it doesn't have preference in any of the sought-after magnet schools, and literally everyone who stays either does private school or magnet school. Someone posted in the downtown group who was in my position last year asking, Does anyone have any experience with either [nearby downtown school] because you know, we're looking for anyone with a positive experience and no one out of 350 people responded. The first people to say, "Oh, don't leave the city. Don't do the suburban White flight. . . ." The other thing with [that school] is I don't want my child to be one of three White kids in his class. Um, I, I want him to go to a diverse school. . . . I don't want to send him to a neighborhood school, because our neighborhood school . . . where he's not actually with peers. Um, or if there's going to be incidents of gang violence and other issues. . . . I don't consider many of those parents who send those, their children there to be my peers, you know, so I don't feel like there's much common ground where I can just go up to someone whose child goes to [that school] and say, "Hey, let's talk about your experience," because they have nothing in common with me.

This selection from Kathleen's interview shows a gradual change from coded language to the beginning of her losing that code. She begins with the same focus on behavioral problems that Chad and Sarah discussed at their magnet school. Kathleen, however, quickly moves to a combination of race and neoliberalism, when she explains that she did not "choose" to live in a neighborhood frequently referred to as the "ghetto." Her view, that her home in a gentrified neighborhood with housing prices well above the city's median is simply a matter of "choice," is a classic colorblind approach to the segregation that continues to infect many American cities.

Finally, Kathleen begins to lose her coding altogether when she indicates that the children who attend the school for which her neighborhood is zoned are not her son's peers, and those children's parents are not her peers. Kathleen assumes that she would have "nothing in common" with parents of children her own child's age, simply because they are from a different racial and economic background. This belief that people are inherently different from each other is the cornerstone of racism.

Kathleen continued to combine racism and neoliberalism as she weighed her options:

> I'm now trying to decide. Do I stay in the city or do we leave and go to the suburbs? Because I do not consider [my neighborhood school] a viable option for kindergarten. I will not send my child to the least privileged school in the city. You know . . . I don't live in the least privileged. . . . Not that I think that it should be this way, but like I live in a nice neighborhood. I would expect my neighborhood school to reflect that even if the neighborhood kids don't go there, like the city is collecting tax dollars from all of our houses. So why aren't they being distributed in a way where the schools appear more equal? Um, I, I don't know. And for me, like we're kind of . . . the places we're looking to move or weighing, you know, then the cuteness of our neighborhood that like I love the, I love the way there's community in my neighborhood, you know, different people of different ages and not so many different races truthfully, but like different ages, different socioeconomic backgrounds, different life experiences all come together and it really is kind of like Sesame Street, and I love that about my neighborhood. But I wish that there was a neighborhood school option that was just the default that felt like that to send my son to. And I don't know what the answer is because all of the kids from my neighborhood that stay go to [a magnet school], or like two families send them to [a different magnet school].

By now, Kathleen has largely given up the social norm of coding her racism. Rather than coding her language, she moves to another acceptable American structure—neoliberalism. She maintains that she has choice, and argues that her neighborhood is entitled to a better school because the homes there contribute significant amounts to the city tax rolls.

Kathleen's continued discussion suggests that Sarah was correct when she said that children learn attitudes from their parents. Aware of her own racism, she is concerned that her son would react negatively if placed in a school dominated by children of Color. She did not, however, have the same concern about a Black child surrounded by White children. Whiteness continues to maintain its hegemonic status as the unspoken norm against which "differences" are compared:[29]

> We looked at [a] charter school right here . . . because that was near . . . where my husband had worked and he didn't hear terrible things about it. And um, I knew that there was some racial diversity there. You know, the stereotype is that the charter schools are all little Black kids and I don't have a problem sending [my son] to a school that has a bunch of little Black kids, but just like, I'm sure that it's not a good experience to be the only one of your race in a school. I don't think that that's good, but specifically for [my son] because he's reactionary and he, you know, I worry about him.

Kathleen shows concern here that her own child might be "the only one of [his] race" if he was to attend a charter school, but did not suggest a similar concern for children of Color who may be enrolled in the predominantly White schools she was more interested in.

Like many parents, Kathleen had heard stories about Albany middle schools and the high school. Her framing, however, was stark: "I've heard fabulous things about Albany High School for gifted students who do AP and language . . . but I hear that the junior high years are a little bit like the jungle. I've heard from another [coworker] . . . that no learning happens at [a specific middle school]. Um, and then I've heard that it's not much better at [the other middle school]."

This comparison of a majority-minority middle school to a "jungle" is striking. A jungle is overrun with growth and wild animals. It is not neat, orderly, well-managed, or organized. The natural corollary to referring to a middle school as a "jungle" is to understand Kathleen's interpretation of the students there as uncontrollable wild animals. This connection between people of Color—particularly Black men—with animals is a traditional racist trope. Kathleen uses this language easily, baring her true views, because they are so internalized for her.

Kathleen comes back to her elementary school dilemma shortly thereafter. She continues to argue that her zoned neighborhood school is not acceptable to her, and compares its student population to those of other neighborhood schools that she would prefer:

> KATHLEEN: And [our zoned school is] a neighborhood school. Like I understand why [another elementary school] looks the way that [it] does because of the neighborhood that it's in. It's in a really nice privileged neighborhood. It's in a neighborhood I lived in. You don't see a lot of Black people, or people of Color. You also don't see a lot of Black people or people of Color in [my gentrified downtown neighborhood].
> RYANE: Right.
> KATHLEEN: So why? Why do my kids have to go, like, why are my kids the forced integration is how I feel and like why? Like the fact that everyone else seems to get their choice and I'm left with, I feel like no choice. It's really frustrating.

Kathleen continues to discuss schools from a position of White privilege, without ever acknowledging that she has that privilege. She also clearly indicates that a "nice privileged neighborhood" does not include Black or other people of Color. Barely hidden in this transcript is an argument that, because she lives in a "nice privileged neighborhood" without many people of Color, Kathleen should not have to send her children to a school that is majority Black. Her frustration is clear; other people in her "nice privileged neighborhood" are able to send their children to one of the city's magnet schools. Because her child did not get a spot in the lottery, she has "no choice."

"Choice," of course, is not always a part of public education. Kathleen's frustration would not be an issue had Albany not opened several magnet schools—available by choice—and had the city not seen a significant build-up of charter schools—also available by choice. Instead, the neoliberal dominance in public education has led parents like Kathleen to assume that they get to choose which public school their children will attend. And for Kathleen, a predominantly Black school is simply not her choice.

Kathleen applied for the same magnet school in the next year's lottery, and again did not receive a spot. She contacted me and requested a follow-up interview a year after our first one. Her views had not changed. After realizing that she would have to enroll her child in his zoned school or enroll him in private school (unless she opted to move out of Albany), she went to a community event at her zoned school. While she raved about the teacher's aide she spoke with, she did not feel any better about the school or the neighborhood in which it is located. Kathleen compared her wealthier neighborhood to the school's location, which she termed "ghetto": "I live in an established neighborhood with home values over three hundred thousand dollars, and I don't consider myself rich, but we're not in the ghetto, and that felt ghetto. My conversation with the teacher's aide, who was nice and delightful with my son, was stressing how inclusive they'd be for someone from our neighborhood, as if we were really different."

Kathleen continued to discuss her frustration with her school options. Her concerns included not only who her child would spend time with but also which parents would be her own potential friends. She was convinced that neither the students nor the parents at her zoned school would be accepting of her or her child, due to their racial background and higher economic status. And, although the Albany City School District offers significant choice—between magnet schools, neighborhood schools, open enrollment, and the nondistrict charter schools—not receiving a spot at her preferred magnet school made Kathleen feel as though she had no choice at all:

> It's work, because school is so much of what parents . . . It's gonna be a part of my social life too. I'm trying not to be so selfish about it, but where we choose to send [our child] to school, those are the moms I'm gonna meet. Those are gonna be my friends for the next eight years, that's it. So I feel like I do have to choose wisely too. I am not so idealistic to think that my son is going to be accepted at [our zoned school], that I'm going to be accepted at [that school], that I'm going to want to be accepted at [that

school], or that I'm going to want to be accepted at [our preferred magnet school]. It's kind of stratified.... You talk to anyone in the school district office and you have all of these choices. No, I don't ... What choice do I have? Beg for an opening at someone else's neighborhood school and try to use my influence? I know how to gain influence. I don't think that that has a place in education. That's where I draw my line.

The end of this statement is interesting. Kathleen has now spent multiple hours over two different interviews explaining how anxious she was to gain admission to her preferred magnet school. And yet, she completes her thoughts by stating that, even though she knows how to "gain influence," she did not think that would be appropriate in an educational setting. Kathleen's statements, until that point, had strongly implied that, had she had any method of giving her child an extra chance in the magnet lottery, she would have taken full advantage of that. Her concern does not seem to be with gaining or wielding influence, but rather that she does not wish to use any potential influence to gain acceptance for herself or her child at a predominantly Black school.

Stephanie, a neighbor of Kathleen's, had a child the same age as Kathleen's eldest. She heard about my project from Kathleen and reached out to me to volunteer for an interview. Although she was also interested in applying for the magnet lottery, Stephanie took a very different approach than Kathleen, and was not nearly as concerned about avoiding her zoned school. Her approach was that she would enroll her child in a magnet school if he got a spot, primarily because she knew he could always go back to his zoned school if they were not happy with the magnet. "Like nobody in our neighborhood Facebook group goes to [the neighborhood school]. And that's just depressing because, you know, if he goes there, I don't want him to be like isolated. I want there to be other neighborhood kids there. So it makes me think, and they all say, 'Oh yeah, [the school's] great, but we just wanted something else,' and like you almost sort of read behind those comments. Like, 'we wanted something better,' you know, and it makes me sort of defensive in advance."

While Stephanie had similar concerns as Kathleen about her child feeling isolated due to his race, she was also much more adept at understanding why students in her neighborhood did not attend their zoned school. She recognized that the middle- and upper-middle-class White families "wanted something better" than a predominantly Black, high-economic-need elementary school. Whereas Kathleen did not hide her contempt for the population she presumed to be at that school, Stephanie was much more critical of her neighbors who would not give the school a try. (Although Stephanie indicated a willingness to try the neighborhood school, her child won a lottery spot at a magnet school and she enrolled him there.)

Conclusion: Colorblindness, Coded Language, and Racism

The stories shared in this chapter show the progression of racism embedded within otherwise non-racially identifiable language. Language that once identified a speaker with racial justice and equality during the civil rights movement in the struggle for racial equality has been rearticulated to support racial hierarchy. It should be noted that none of the respondents I spoke with claimed to be racist, and only a few indicated that they saw themselves as somehow "better" than other members of the community. This is in keeping with the hegemonic colorblind ideology that has blanketed the United States for decades.

However, a careful examination of this language shows that colorblind language is hiding more traditional racist attitudes. Although it took respondents some time to get comfortable sharing their thoughts with me, the rapport we built up during the interview allowed several people the opportunity to drop their colorblind camouflage. The progression of language, both from and across individual respondents, makes it clear that colorblindness is simply modern-day racism.

Conclusion

Although recent scholarship bemoans the end of American democracy at the hands of race and capitalism,[1] something cannot end before it even begins. The United States was framed not as a great democratic experiment but as a slavocracy that allowed only a small handful of its residents to participate.[2] While policy changes temporarily included almost all adults as members of the voting public, the completed shift to neoliberalism shortly after those gains ensured that a full democracy would never develop. Where we once kept multiple populations from voting, running for office, or engaging in other public institutions, we now simply allow them to exit the polity altogether. A democracy includes everyone. It does not push out those who challenge it.

Democracy requires community. It might not always be pretty, but in a democratic society there must be enough trust between different groups that they can share power and plan for a common future. The genetic code of the United States, however, makes community difficult because of the divisions it maintains along multiple dimensions. I have argued throughout this book that race and class, so fundamental to the American founding (and even prefounding), continue to delineate policy options in all fields. This includes public education.

The double helix of race and neoliberalism that structures American foundations forms the very core of controversies that surround public schooling today. Like the genetic DNA that inspires its name, this double helix is invisible to the naked eye. Its very nature as a building block makes it hegemonic, and its hegemonic nature makes it difficult to see when this double helix shapes our politics. Public schools are political institutions that both (1) shape future citizens and workers; and (2) serve as sites for democratic (or nondemocratic) politics and permutations of power. Therefore, public schools can, and must, be studied politically.[3]

A political analysis of public schools requires that public schools be evaluated not only for their capacity to train or indoctrinate future citizens and workers but also as current sites of political decision making. In other words, we need to consider not just *civic education*, the commonly used moniker for understanding how schools train future citizens, but also *civic practice*, or the way in which schools facilitate or block democratic politics as institutions. This book relies on a deep case study of the charter school movement to understand how civic practice builds or limits democracy in the public institution that affects Americans so directly—their public schools.

The public narrative surrounding school choice, and market choices more generally, is that choice is equivalent to democracy. However, choice in a market is an economic decision, not a political one. While some claim that parents use school choice as an element of political agency,[4] making an economic decision in a market is different from making a political decision in a democracy. Parents who feel pushed out of their public schools and forced into a market decision instead provide evidence of the decline of democracy, not its improvement.

The irony of school choice, especially regarding the charter schools in Albany, is that it is an antidemocratic move that is overwhelmingly supported by people of Color. This creates a fundamental problem—while it might initially seem best to remove charter schools altogether, doing so would violate the preferences of a core population. Complete rejection of charter schools, now that they are so established in our communities of Color, would justifiably be interpreted as yet another attack on a population that has already been targeted by racism for centuries.

Rather than ending charter schools, therefore, I suggest that we find ways to further democratize what is currently a very neoliberal policy. Below, I provide four broad categories of changes that would begin this move.

Policy Suggestions

Because every state regulates charter schools differently, it is difficult to make policy suggestions that will work in every location. In New York, however, there are clear changes that will make charter school legislation more democratic. States whose charter school policies are similar to New York's should also take these ideas into consideration. None of these policy changes, it should be noted, will change the American DNA. These are ways to continue to make adjustments within a field limited by racial capitalism and colorblind individualism, not fundamental changes to our very structure.

1. PROVIDE A COMMUNITY VOICE. In New York, the local community does not have a vote on whether or not a new charter school opens. This is a fatal flaw. This policy means that outsiders can (and do) build new schools in areas that they know will attract people who feel underserved by public schools. The very predictable political result is that charter-school and traditional public-school communities do not interact with each other, and each accuses the other of taking or hoarding scant resources. Given the segregation in the Albany example, this pits Black against White, downtown against uptown, working class against middle class. None of this is conducive to democratic politics.

Providing a voice for the whole community will help to assuage this problem. New York State should require that those applying to open a new charter school hold multiple public hearings, held at different times to accommodate multiple work schedules. Providing childcare for these meetings will make it easier for more people to attend and participate. But this must be a real opportunity for community members—both those who support and those who oppose charter schools—to voice their concerns to the charter school developers and state institutions that have the ultimate decision-making power. If the charter school developers and charter-granting institutions listen to community members and make changes that the community supports, this will provide a feeling of inclusion and efficacy that is currently lacking.

2. ENSURE RELATIONSHIPS BETWEEN DISTRICT AND CHARTER SCHOOLS. Part of the logic behind schools of choice is that they will challenge traditional public schools to improve so they keep more of their students. This assumption is based on the ideology that a market leads to an equilibrium that naturally levels out supply and demand. However, even market ideology does not predict a positive relationship between charter and traditional schools, and this study certainly did not find a strong, working relationship between them. Both charter school leaders and school board members and employees made it clear that each had nothing to do with the other, and that neither institution sent representatives to learn from the other.

If a community is going to have two separate school systems, they might as well work together to build the best possible educational environment. If charter schools are doing something that "works" well, the whole community would benefit if the traditional schools studied that project. Similarly, if the charter schools are struggling with a particular issue, they should be able to rely on the expertise within the traditional school structure. Adjusting state policy to require a specific number of joint meetings, professional development sessions, or days that leaders from each type of school tour and visit with the other would help.

3. LISTEN TO PARENTS. While this recommendation is much broader than the first two, it is crucial that public institutions—here, public schools specifically—listen to their constituents. This is the crux of any democratic system. Although this should be the case for every aspect of public education and all other policies, in this case we should especially note the evidence of racism provided by many parents who chose to exit the public system. If the schools had listened to them when they brought up their concerns—if, for example, Billie had been treated with respect and dignity when she sat in the school office—there might be less of a drive to avoid public institutions. We should also remain cognizant that, when one person recognizes racism in action, the impact is not limited to that individual. Parents create their own communities and share knowledge, so that one racist act is magnified as its story is told.

More practically, parents in this study have made it clear that they need schools to remain open for longer days and longer years. This can be accomplished by providing free before- and after-school childcare, and using public school buildings for free day camps during the summer. Parents are also clearly interested in uniforms; even an optional uniform policy in public schools should be considered. Finally, parents do not feel part of the broader school community, they are not comfortable interacting with school personnel, and they do not think school leaders listen to their concerns. All of these problems must be addressed.

4. TRUST TEACHERS. Like the suggestion above, this one is also quite broad and not limited to charter school policy. However, it is imperative that New York, and the United States as a whole, treat teachers as the professionals that they are. Teachers' own professional knowledge is blocked at every turn, most clearly with the movement to standardized tests that has been part of federal education policies since No Child Left

Behind (2001). This trend is even stronger in New York, where students take not only the federally mandated exams but also Regents exams that are required for high school graduation.

Requiring these exams is not a way to promote greater rigor in education, as some political leaders claim, but a way to get around teachers' assessments of their own students. If a teacher believes a student has mastered the material in question, we should trust them to make that decision rather than subjecting children to an additional test (or group of tests). Avoiding standardized tests would also save money that can be reinvested directly into classrooms, potentially providing a way to respond to parents' concerns (as discussed in point number 3).

Context, Language, and Democracy

My own views on charter schools have changed dramatically in the ten years I have spent on this project. Admittedly, I was initially very critical of Albany charter schools because of the racial segregation they perpetuate. As a scholar of school desegregation policy, I viewed charter schools as moving us backward rather than forward. This research has reminded me of a mantra I often repeated to my undergraduate students: *context matters*. A segregated charter school that is composed of students whose parents deliberately chose that institution is fundamentally different from the typical pre-*Brown* segregated, Jim Crow school. While the student bodies might look similar, these schools are not analogous.

These institutions are different not only because parents choose them (and I remain convinced that this is an antidemocratic effect of racial capitalism) but because they celebrate people of Color rather than demean them. These are schools that are built around showing respect for African traditions and languages in a deliberate attempt to build community. The development of this community reflects the fact that so many students and their families did not feel that they were part of a community in their traditional public schools.

Racial capitalism and colorblind individualism divide community rather than build it. There was ample evidence of this division in Albany. It was incumbent on the school board, on the city, on the state, and even on the federal government to ensure that all students had access to the education they needed and desired. That none of these entities did so—and that they permit families to leave instead—should be read as evidence that the polity does not wish to include all community members within itself. Rather than working with multiple populations, these different levels of political structure have provided families with an exit option instead. And it is not difficult to understand why so many families take advantage of that option.

If Americans truly desire democratic governance, they must change how they approach public education and other policies. At this point, shutting down all charter schools would be read as punitive to those families who chose them, and that is hardly the goal. But all levels of political entities must fully invest in public education. This does not mean simply throwing more money at schools, though that is one part of the process. It also means trusting teachers as professionals instead of demanding constant standardized exams to prove that they are actually doing their jobs. It means providing full before- and after-school childcare so that children have a safe environment while their parents are working to support their families. It means providing children with healthy, delicious meals instead of prepackaged processed foods that lead students to crash before lunchtime. It means making schools an integral part of the community, not a place for students to "do their time" before they graduate and move on.

Although these moves would be important, they do not confront the double helix of race and class. The second thing Americans must do if they value democracy is to seriously challenge the nation's current distribution of resources. The slavocracy that developed into the contemporary United States privileges capital over labor, the wealthy over the economically struggling. This pattern did not change with the end of the Civil War or the civil rights movement, and is a remnant of our slave-owning past. A redistribution of resources would redirect our priorities.

The United States needs yet another Reconstruction. There are multiple political and economic avenues through which we can pursue this, but maintaining the status quo is not an option. Without redistributing political and economic resources, we will continue our progression of racial capitalism and colorblind individualism. These forces privilege the market over the community, promote segregation, and prevent democracy.

There is some early evidence that community-based challenges may be under development. We see this with the beginning of a shift in language. Trump notwithstanding, the American lexicon has broadly moved away from clearly racist speech. Instead, racist ideas are now hidden and coded by colorblind language. This remains the overall trend, and is now fully enshrined in American law with the Supreme Court's 2023 decisions that ended affirmative action. Nationally, race continues to divide us.

However, at the same time, we are beginning to see small challenges to colorblindness. Both Whites and people of Color occasionally use positive, race-conscious language that builds community rather than tearing it down. Although it can be misused like anything else, we may be at the beginning of a shift away from colorblindness and toward race consciousness. Because we must fully recognize race and racist language in order to fight racism, this is a positive move. If Albany proves to be a microcosm of the American city, perhaps a kernel of hope lies in the shifts documented in this book.

ACKNOWLEDGMENTS

No author writes a book solely on their own. Over the decade that I worked on various parts of this project, I learned from and relied on countless others. These individuals form my intellectual and personal communities, and I am grateful to all of you.

At the most intimate level of community, my family has been fully supportive as I struggled with developing the ideas I present here, especially as my own views changed throughout the writing process. My husband, Eric, who has been with me since my first year of college, provides a sounding board for every new thought I have. Thank you for insisting that I take breaks so we could walk our dog or eat one of your fabulous home-cooked meals. My children, Damian and Lucy, put up with my books, notes, and other items constantly strewn across the dining room table, and patiently moved them so we could all have dinner together. You are the core of my being. My own parents provided constant support, never doubting for a second that I would complete what frequently seemed like a mammoth, impossible undertaking. Thank you, Mom and Dad, for always believing in me.

My colleagues at the College of Saint Rose were phenomenal, and absolutely pushed me to expand my original thoughts about local charter schools. Our Friday morning women's writing group (with cheese and/or baked goods!) was truly my church. At various times, this interdisciplinary group of scholars included Susan Cumings (technically not from Saint Rose, but we adopted her), Eurie Dahn, Lisa Kannenberg, Angela Ledford, Silvia Mejia, and Bridgett Williams-Searle. Thank you for reading my early drafts and for providing challenging but supportive feedback.

More broadly, my colleagues at Saint Rose provided an intellectual foundation that helped me build my understanding of political, social, and historical processes. Thank you especially to Risa Faussette, Keith Haynes, Maureen Rotondi, and Carl Swidorski for challenging me and supporting me. I am also grateful to the Center for Citizenship, Race, and Ethnicity Studies and its leader, John Williams-Searle, for supporting the early part of this project.

Thank you, too, to the students I had over the years. Not only did you encourage me to push my own boundaries, but many of you came with a true open mind and thirst for your own intellectual development. My Racial and Ethnic Politics and Public Policy students served as my first audiences as I worked through interpretations of and arguments built on the interview data I shared in this book. Many provided probing questions and new ideas during class discussions. Several students in my Theories and Methods of Political Inquiry course contributed by transcribing full or partial interviews; thank you to Aileen Burke (one of my many former students who became a dear friend), Tyler Bushey, Reed Chronis, and Amnah Dhailia. I appreciate your work, and I hope you learned about the difficulties of qualitative research in the process!

Thank you to Sonia Tsuruoka, my editor at NYU Press, for believing in this project from the beginning. Without your original request to meet with me and your frequent assurances that, yes, this is going as expected, I would have given up long ago. Similar thanks go to the anonymous reviewers who read my original proposal and the full manuscript. This is a better book because of your insights, and I am grateful.

In addition to time and respondents, I needed a space to work. Although they went through many iterations in the process, several local Albany coffee shops provided me with a comfortable, friendly place to work on the manuscript and to conduct interviews. These included the Hudson River Coffee House, Ground Up, Muddy Cup, Uncommon Grounds, Bard and Baker, and others. Thank you for giving me a welcoming spot and for knowing what I would order before I even got to the counter. I conducted most parent interviews at several branches of the Albany Public Library; thank you, libraries, for being such amazing community spaces, and thank you, librarians, for keeping these spaces open to all.

Interview-based research requires dedicated time not only from the scholar leading the project but also from those she interviews. Sincere thanks to the elected officials, journalists, activists, and other policy leaders who comprised the first part of my sample. I deeply appreciate the time you provided me as you explained your understanding of how and why charter schools developed in Albany.

My deepest gratitude, however, goes to the parents who met with me. I am indebted to all of you who took time out of your busy work and family schedules to explain to me—a stranger—why and how you chose a school for your child(ren). That so many of you willingly shared your time to help me understand my own questions remains mind-boggling to me. This is true for all of you, but especially for those who chose charter schools. I realize that I had zero social capital in the charter school community before beginning this project, and I am grateful for and humbled by your trust in me.

APPENDIX A

Methods and the Case Study

You know why they're not replying, right? It's because you're an outsider.
—Interview, Albany, 2018

This book is about three large fields in the social sciences. The first two, race and class, create the space and form the boundaries for the third, public policy. In this study, I analyze how parents use school-choice policy to make intimate family decisions in a community structured by powerful forces that created, and continue to maintain, our current political and social world. This means that the national movement toward school choice, New York's charter school law, and Albany's implementation of that law are the center of the study. In that sense, this study takes a "policy centered perspective."[1]

The centrality of policy in this case study affects how people understand local power relations, deeply personal choices about where and how to educate their children, and the racial and class divisions that structure this context. For this project, I literally lived in the "policy milieu."[2] The policy under study—the New York State law that permits charter schools—had a direct impact on my own children, their peers, and our community. Although the political furor over charter schools has declined as some have closed, the city remains divided over charter schools. And, to this day, in 2024, these divisions are highly correlated with race and class.

Studying a policy while living in it provides an understanding of nuance that would otherwise be difficult to achieve. It also means that some of our most traditional research methodologies were inadequate for the task. Of all the questions asked by modern political scientists, some of the most divisive are those related to methodology. These divisions are essentially existentialist, because what we choose to study, and how we approach our questions and potential answers, conditions what we "find." There are multiple methodological questions within the field; the common quantitative/qualitative divide is simply the most visible. Whether a scholar chooses to approach their research by applying sophisticated statistical analyses, traditional qualitative inquiry, or a combination of both, a scholar's methodological approach is often the first indication of how they view the world.[3]

Quantitative scholars are especially adept at establishing patterns, discovering relationships, and narrowing down potential causal variables for some of our most important questions in a "directly observable" way.[4] However, as important as this knowledge is, quantitative scholarship struggles to understand the conditions of power that frame the precise variables under evaluation. These scholars are able to establish that relationships exist, explain why they exist, and measure their impact on dependent variables. But they do not have the tools to challenge how the identities upon which statistical relationships are based develop, or why they matter beyond their contribution to an equation. For most of these scholars, the world they study is a given, not a construction.[5] Even studies that acknowledge the social construction of identity-related variables generally ignore that construction as they test the strength of causal variables and seek to establish a chain of events. In other words, positivist, frequently quantitative-oriented scholars acknowledge that their variable of interest (such as race, gender, or ideology) is constructed and then treat it as though it were essentialist.

Quantitative scholarship is active across the social sciences, including many scholars who study school choice. However, as even these scholars attest, establishing quantitative relationships is only the first part of a broader research agenda. This is where the either/or dichotomy limits our conversations and knowledge; instead, scholars should work to see methodological approaches as a "both/and." As Zhang and Yang argue in their study of why charter schools developed in some parts of Florida and not others, "The data cannot show *how* politics and institutions affect charter school decisions or *how* charter school ideas are constructed in a larger discourse."[6] Rather, they suggest, qualitative scholars should build from these quantitative studies to learn more about the nuances of processes and, importantly, the role of power. These nuances are frequently based on the analysis of "unobservable relationships [which] can only be established indirectly."[7] It is these unobservable relationships that require a different approach.

As encouraged by quantitative scholars of charter school policy, this project is partly a response to the questions that arose through the work of previous scholars. But, as a qualitative scholar who views the social world as constructed and deeply entrenched with meaning and power, I do not attempt to provide simple answers to important questions. Parents who select a new school for their children do not do so in a vacuum. Their decisions are structured by a broader context that includes constructed knowledge of academic options within a world that is limited by power, race, and class.

INTERVIEWS AS "DATA" AND PROCESS

In this book, I rely heavily on interview data because I view the social world as a constructed entity, without solid answers to our most important questions. As with historians who rely on diaries and letters, interviews allow the researcher to "learn what people perceived and how they interpreted their perceptions."[8] Interviews provide a window not only to decisions made and actions completed, but—more importantly for the qualitative scholar—to the very *meaning* behind those decisions and actions. While quantitative scholarship is adept at narrowing down the causal variables behind political behavior, it cannot speak to how individuals understand their own behavior, their own actions, and their own limitations. To build this knowledge, we must rely on qualitative and interpretive scholarship.

To learn from individuals themselves, I took guidance from interpretive scholars.[9] While interpretive scholars frequently rely on qualitative methodologies such as interviews and textual and discourse analysis, interpretivism differs from other qualitative scholarship in that it fully rejects positivism and the very existence of a social world before it has been filtered through human understanding. My goal was to understand "a broader web of narratives" and "explore how individual comments fit together as parts of a more meaningful whole."[10] This meant that my interviews were not akin to surveys. Rather than asking respondents to select between options that would make it easier to confirm predetermined hypotheses, interview questions were deliberately open-ended.

During our in-depth interviews, or "guided conversation[s]," I also probed respondents for further discussion throughout our meetings. I deliberately allowed "informants to elaborate on their values and attitudes and account for their actions."[11] The open-ended questions meant that respondents rarely replied with a simple one-word answer or even a brief phrase; most questions led to long discussions and tangents. This approach allowed me to gain insight into how different communities within Albany view charter schools, both in their current state and during their rapid development. By leaving the questions open-ended and allowing tangents and storytelling, this methodology led to arguments and conclusions that would not have been possible otherwise.

THE SAMPLE

There is some controversy within political science about how to select respondents. While the gold standard for much of the field remains the random sample, that process works best when scholars attempt to identify a "typical" case or event. Instead of the norm, however, my goal here was to understand a broad range of actions and how different community members understood those actions. Nonprobability sampling is ideal "when . . . generalizations are not an aim, and the goal is rather to obtain information about highly specific events and processes."[12] Rather than the typical case, my goal was to understand a wide variety of viewpoints, or range.[13] Therefore, it was more important to identify a diverse group of participants than to construct and rely on a random sample.

Of course, nonprobability sampling has its own problems. Even when the goal is not to generalize to a larger population, selecting respondents always includes the possibility of developing a biased sample. There is little doubt that, had I spoken to fifty-five different people than I did, my "evidence" would look different than what I share throughout the text. I would have different quotations to include in the discussion, different parental backgrounds that help explain choice, and different viewpoints on charter development. However, it is also extremely *likely* that the overall story would remain very similar. None of my arguments are based on the statement of a single individual. All viewpoints are compared with the entire sample, correlated with documents and public discussions, and compared to other pieces of "evidence." In other words, in order to mitigate as much as possible the possibility that respondent selection impacted my argument, I triangulated the respondents and the data they provided. For both groups, I also attempted to speak with as diverse a population as possible.

RESPONDENTS

In all, I interviewed fifty-five individuals to learn about charter schools in Albany. All interviews were semistructured; respondents within each group were asked the same questions, but were always welcome to provide additional stories, details, and other tangents. Because there is no expectation that all respondents would view Albany charter schools in a similar way, I relied on qualitative interviewing techniques to "[learn] about the experiences of others."[14] This focus on understanding how different individuals view the social world and the choices they make within it is also a key part of interpretive methodologies.[15]

The First Group: Elite Interviews

My first research question was relatively straightforward. Given that all cities in New York State operate under the same charter school policy, why are there so many more charter schools, per capita, in Albany than in other cities in the same state? My primary approach to answer this question was to speak with policy entrepreneurs, elected officials, and activists on both sides of the charter school debate to "reconstruct" what occurred.[16] Elite interviews, or interviews with individuals who have specific knowledge of an event or process, "can shed light on the hidden elements of political action that are not clear from an analysis of political outcomes or other primary sources" on their own.[17]

For the first group of respondents, those with knowledge about the rapid development of charter schools in Albany, I wanted to speak with people from as many different backgrounds and viewpoints as possible. This group of twenty-three respondents includes individuals either who had direct involvement in the development of Albany charter schools, such as serving in leadership capacities and policy development, or who saw that development occur from a professional or activist position. Arguments built from this group of respondents are always based on what multiple people, from different sectors, expressed in our interviews. Including individuals with different roles in the development of charter schools ensured that the knowledge I gained from them is not biased toward or against a select group of people. Instead, it builds on multiple perspectives.

For the first group of respondents, I relied on a snowball sample to develop a diverse group. A snowball sample (in which the researcher begins with a small list of potential respondents, and asks those individuals for the names of additional people to interview) is helpful when it is not clear who would have the most knowledge about a particular event, and is a common way to develop a qualitative sample.[18] I began by interviewing current and previous elected members of the Albany City School District Board of Education and individuals who were identified by the local newspaper as being leaders in Albany charter schools. From these different groups, I built a carefully constructed sample to ensure that I met with a variety of individuals who had different types of knowledge. Thus, I met with policy entrepreneurs, elected officials at multiple levels, journalists, and activists. When twenty-three people from different backgrounds told a similar story, I was confident that this process led to an accurate portrayal. A summary of participants from Group 1 is shown in table A.1.

Group 2: Parents

My goal, however, was to learn not only how Albany became the home to so many charter schools but also why so many parents choose them. As a corollary to understanding why so many parents *do* choose charter schools, I also wanted to understand why so many—in fact, significantly more—parents do *not* choose charter schools. This necessitated speaking with a large number of parents, including both those who did and those who did not elect to send their children to charter schools.

Range was even more important for this population than for the first group of respondents. I had a narrower goal for the first group; I wanted to focus on those individuals who saw charter schools develop, whether from an activist, elected, or otherwise-involved viewpoint. For this second group, however, I wanted to include a wide range of available schools. As of spring 2024, there are twenty-three traditional and charter schools available within the city of Albany; my sample has experience with twenty of these. In addition to the twenty traditional and charter schools, members of the sample also had experience with now-closed public schools (one), now-closed charter schools (one), private schools

TABLE A.1. Composition of Respondents (Elite Interviews)

Current/Former School Board Members	6
Community Activists	5
State-Level Elected Officials	2
Current/Former District Employees	3
Journalists	1
Policy Entrepreneurs	3
Charter School Board Members	2
Black	5
White	17
Pro-Charter	10 (5 Black; 5 White)
Anti-Charter	9 (All White)
Neutral	3 (All White)

Note: This table reflects twenty-two individuals rather than twenty-three because one interview included two people. The primary respondent in that interview was an elected official, and the additional person was there as a policy expert from the office. The secondary individual did not add anything beyond what the primary individual stated.

(three respondents covering four schools), and home school (two). This diversity was possible because I sampled for range rather than for the typical case.

There are three distinct populations within the second group of respondents. The first includes the primary group of interest: parents (or guardians) who chose charter schools for their children. My desire to learn why people chose these schools and what other options they considered, as well as their experiences in the schools, made this a necessary population for this study.

Unlike the first group of respondents, who could speak to the development of charter schools in Albany, it was much more difficult to identify a first round of respondents of those who chose charter schools. Because each charter school is independently authorized and chartered, there is no comprehensive list of charter school students in Albany.[19] Nor would individual schools provide me with student lists and contact information. This made it difficult to reach out to parents directly.

I next tried outreach to the charter schools themselves. I sent emails and made phone calls to principals and other charter school leaders to ask them if they could identify parents who might be willing to speak with me. However, likely due to the significant political tension surrounding charter schools in Albany and the lack of social capital I have in the charter school community, this proved unfruitful. As one respondent, a mother with two children in charter schools, told me, "You know why they're not replying, right? It's because you're an outsider."[20] While a handful of people replied to my messages, it is unclear how many actually sent flyers home with students, posted them in public areas, or spoke with individual parents. Most of my emails went unanswered, and school receptionists refused to connect me with school leaders.

I next attempted to reach charter school populations without going through the schools directly. I placed flyers with tear-off portions that held my name and contact information in every library branch in Albany. The Albany public library consists of seven branches located throughout the city, and about two thirds of Albany residents possess a library card. The library system offers significant children's programming, as well, making it a logical place to reach out to parents.[21] I also posted the flyers at the Albany Jewish Community Center, which houses a daycare center and gym and offers family programming, and attempted to post them at the YMCA.[22] I also sent the flyer to historically Black churches in Albany. These efforts produced a small handful of respondents.

I was thus left with a large number of research questions and very few respondents. This led me to challenge the traditional methodologies of political science a bit more. Knowing that many people rely on social media for multiple purposes, I took to social media to find respondents. While this is a newer development for those conducting research, others have identified social media as a powerful tool for reaching hard-to-find populations.[23]

I focused on Facebook, because 68 percent of American adults use this site (and 76 percent of them check Facebook at least once a day), and it is the most popular social media site. Not only that, but the population I was interested in meeting with are, statistically speaking, high users of Facebook. Women, who are more likely to care for a child if there is only one parent present, use Facebook at higher rates than men.

There is very little difference among income groups; 84 percent of the lowest income group (under thirty thousand dollars) uses Facebook, and 77 percent of the highest group (over seventy-five thousand dollars) uses it. Further, 81 percent of urban residents use Facebook.[24] Thus, while there is some selection bias in relying on Facebook to find respondents, the effect is minimal.

The false intimacy provided by social networking also helped to assuage my outsider status. Social media, which now "occupies much of people's free time," "reinforce[s] bonds" through the sharing of content and "fostering constant tetheredness."[25] Some researchers have argued that the anonymity of the Internet makes it likely "to produce greater intimacy and closeness."[26]

I posted information about my study on the Facebook page for every charter school in Albany. While there is likely some overlap, the total "followers" of these pages tops twenty-one hundred. I posted information on my own page, made it public, and asked my networks to share it. I posted it on organizational pages that were targeted toward Albany as a whole or were likely to serve charter school students. These organizations included groups for Albany downtown parents, Albany Promise, the Albany Community Action Partnership, the Albany Social Justice Center, and the Capital District YMCA. All together, these groups had about 350,000 followers (again, there is likely significant overlap in these numbers). These attempts led to a few more respondents.

Finally, I began to make very direct requests. When an individual "reacted" or left a note on a charter school Facebook page, I contacted that individual through Facebook Messenger, an email-type messaging system that allows private communication between individuals on an otherwise very public site. Facebook works by connecting individuals who agree to be "friends"; both individuals have to agree to this relationship in order to see their full profile, updates, and comments. Messages sent to non-"friends" go directly into an "other" folder, so it is difficult to know how many of the eighty-one messages I sent this way were actually viewed. But this proved to be the most fruitful way to find respondents. Although a couple of potential respondents either declined to meet or stopped returning messages when I offered dates and times, most of the individuals who replied to my private Facebook messages did meet with me.

As with the first group of respondents, this one was also triangulated. Facebook was not my only source of respondents; I also posted the flyers and reached out to all members of the Albany City School Board and Albany Common Council. With these messages, I asked these officials to connect me with ward members or other connections who chose charter schools. While this resulted in a lower number of respondents than I had hoped, it did produce some. Most importantly, there was no discernible difference between respondents based on how I reached them.

In order to understand the context in which individuals chose charter schools, it was also necessary to learn more about those who chose different options, including public magnet schools and traditional neighborhood schools. It was much easier to locate respondents who chose Albany magnet and neighborhood schools than to locate respondents who chose charter schools. When I posted my request for respondents on Facebook and asked people to share it broadly, magnet school parents volunteered to participate at very high rates. A smaller group of neighborhood parents did the same. Although this was a smaller group, they provide the context necessary for understanding why others choose to leave. Table A.2 shows the coverage included in my parent/guardian interviews.

THE INTERVIEWS

For all interviews, I worked to develop a positive relationship between myself and the respondent.[27] Developing this relationship in the relatively short time span of one interview meant that interviews ran a bit long; especially with parent respondents, I wanted to establish trust before asking more difficult questions about their views on racial diversity. The two types of respondents also required slightly different relationships.

Group 1: Elite Interviews

For the most part, individuals in my first group of respondents were professionals who led the policy through the state legislature, oversaw its development in Albany, or were elected officials at the state or local level. My goal with this population was to learn why the New York State charter school policy was so heavily implemented in Albany, rather than other cities in New York. I was learning from these individuals as professionals. Discussions with them, therefore, required that I also

TABLE A.2. Respondent Coverage of Schools

School Type (Number Included in Sample)	Respondents*
Public Elementary Neighborhood Schools (8)	17
Public Elementary Magnet Schools (4)	16
Public Middle Schools (3)	10
Public High/Vocational Schools (2)	7
Charter Elementary Schools (7)	15
Charter Middle Schools (2)	7
Charter High Schools (2)	2
Private Schools (5)**	7
Home School	2
Lottery Applicants***	3

*"Respondents" refers to the number of individual interviews I held with people who sent their child(ren) to a particular school, either currently or previously. Because most of my respondents had more than one child and many of them had attended more than one school, this number is much larger than the total number of parents I spoke with.
**Private schools are included only when the respondent also had (a) child(ren) in an Albany neighborhood, magnet, or charter school.
***Individuals who had applied for a magnet slot in the district's pre-K or kindergarten lottery. At the time of our meeting, they had not yet heard where their child would attend school.

provide a professional persona. I did not shy away from my identity as a college professor; I provided information when they requested it, asked questions where necessary, and mentioned examples when appropriate.

Interviews with the first group of respondents averaged about one hour. Most occurred in a local café, while the remainder were at the respondent's home or office. All interviews were recorded and transcribed with the respondents' permission. Although I had a list of questions, I also allowed respondents to tell their own story. Some interviews had longer tangents, but I encouraged respondents to share with me as much as they were able.

Group 2: Parent Interviews

As with the first group, I worked to develop a strong, trusting relationship with the second group of respondents. However, I approached this population a bit differently. While almost all of the respondents worked,[28] my goal was not to learn from their professional experiences as I did with the first group. This time, I wanted to know much more personal information about how they felt they could best provide for their children, how much racial integration their children experienced, whether or not they found that important, what their neighborhood was like, and similar issues.

I worked to develop strong, trusting relationships by engaging in the "chat" that Rubin and Rubin suggest can lead to fuller, more truthful responses.[29] In these very personal conversations, I found it necessary to provide limited personal information, as well. While respondents shared stories about their children with me, I occasionally added to the conversation with similar stories about my own family and children, and my children's schools. My willingness to be open about myself, when I was asking the same of respondents, allowed them to open up and provide honest responses to very personal questions to a stranger.

The thirty-one interviews I conducted with thirty-two parents and guardians of children in Albany schools, including traditional neighborhood schools, charter schools, and magnet schools, averaged an hour each. The vast majority of these interviews took place in small, private study rooms at one of the seven branches of the Albany Public Library. A few others occurred at local coffee shops, at the respondent's request, usually to accommodate the respondent's work schedule.

* * *

All of the names in this book have been changed. Although some of the people with whom I spoke have been very public about their statements, I guaranteed anonymity to everyone. With permission from all respondents, I recorded our conversations and had them transcribed. I then reviewed each conversation carefully, looking for common themes and language to build a broader understanding of the development, impact, and usage of charter schools in Albany. I read this information against a broader context of published scholarship, journalism, web pages, census data, and other secondary information.

APPENDIX B

Charter School Enrollment in Capital Cities: An Extended View

TABLE A.3. Capital Cities with at Least 10 Percent Charter School Enrollment, 2006–2021.

	2006	2007	2008	2009	2010	2011	2012	2013	2014	2015	2016	2017	2020	2021
Albany, NY	15	17	18	24	23	26	27	26	26	16	24	24	26	27
Atlanta, GA						10	10	13	16	16	17	19	22	23
Austin, TX									11	12	16	17	19	19
Boise, ID													11	11
Boston, MA						10	13	15	17	19	20	21	24	24
Columbus, OH	13	15	17	18	20	21	23	25	25	22	26	27	30	31
Denver, CO				10	11	12	14	16	17	18	20	21	24	24
Indianapolis, IN		12	18	19	22	25	28	30	31	31	33	36	47	48
Lansing, MI				11	12	13	14	15	17	18	19	13	10	12
Little Rock, AR					12	13	12	12	13	13	16	18	22	23
Oklahoma City, OK		11	11	12	11	11	11	12	13	14	15	15	22	59
Phoenix, AZ, High Schools						22	24	21	21	21	26	27	24	25
Providence, RI							11	11			14	15	15	19
Sacramento, CA						11	12	16	12	14	12	13	13	
Salt Lake City, UT			15			11	14	10		13	13	18	14	
Santa Fe, NM							12	16	12	13	13	13	16	16
St. Paul, MI	13	14	16	17	18	19	20	22	23	25	26	28	32	33
Trenton, NJ		12	15	17	19		12	16	18	19	21	15	15	

The table shows the percent of students enrolled in charter schools in capital city school districts that have at least ten thousand students enrolled in both traditional public and charter schools, and at least 10 percent of their students in charter schools. Data from annual market share reports produced by the National Alliance for Public Charter Schools.
Note: Years indicate the start of an academic year. Data for academic years beginning 2018 and 2019 were not available. Data for the 2021–2022 academic year were the most recent available at the time of this writing.

NOTES

INTRODUCTION
1 Tushnet, 1996.
2 Frankenberg, 2024; Frankenberg et al., 2019; Orfield and Jarvie, 2020; Owens, 2020.
3 Fahle et al., 2020.
4 Mijs and Roe, 2021.
5 Guzman, 2020.
6 Neilsberg Research, 2024. Although of course there are middle-class Blacks and working-class Whites in Albany (and some of each are featured in this book), these examples break the larger patterns. When I speak of trends and aggregates, I frequently use shortcuts like "middle-class Whites" and "working-class Blacks" or, when speaking more broadly, "working-class people of Color."
7 Fessler, 2019.
8 New York State Education Department, n.d.
9 Official data uses the term "Hispanic" to refer to those of Spanish-language heritage, rather than the more contemporary term "Latinx."
10 City School District of Albany, n.d.
11 While the language is dated, it is not incorrect to refer to Albany as a "majority-minority" school district.
12 For the sake of transparency, when we bought our second home to keep our child in his elementary school, it was 52 percent White, 22 percent Black, 11 percent Latinx, and 8 percent Asian. New York State Education Department, 2015.
13 Bonilla-Silva, 2010; Omi and Winant, 2015.
14 Trump, quoted in Ye Hee Lee, 2015.
15 Peller, 1995.
16 Bonilla-Silva, 2010.
17 This means that my analysis of this phenomenon cannot be fully value free, though I am not convinced that any research is ever fully value free. Aware of my own bias in favor of public, integrated schools, I allow my respondents to speak for themselves as much as possible.

CHAPTER 1. REFRAMING SCHOOL CHOICE
1 A. Hacker, 2003.
2 I place "democratic" in quotation marks because I am not convinced that the United States is a democratic nation, nor do our policies frequently reflect

majority will. However, we frame the United States as a democracy and—at least publicly—claim to seek the common good.

3 Nikole Hannah-Jones also uses the term "DNA" to refer to the paradox of slavery and freedom in the United States, and David Brion claims that "racial exploitation and racial conflict have been part of the DNA of American culture" (Brion, 2006; Hannah-Jones, 2021, xxiii, 29). To my knowledge, no one else has used the double helix composition of DNA as an analogy for American structures of race and class.
4 Hannah-Jones, 2021.
5 C. I. Harris, 1995, 277.
6 Roediger, 2007, 11, emphasis added.
7 Crenshaw, 1995.
8 Roediger, 2007, 7, discussing Fields.
9 Kendi, 2016; Omi and Winant, 2015; Roediger, 2007.
10 Heng, 2018, 131.
11 Omi and Winant, 2015, 112–15.
12 Wilkerson, 2020.
13 Jacobson, 1999.
14 Jacobson, 1999; Wilkerson, 2020.
15 C. I. Harris, 1995, 285.
16 C. I. Harris, 1995; Lipsitz, 1998.
17 Du Bois, 2007 [1935].
18 Roediger, 2007.
19 C. I. Harris, 1995, 284.
20 Katznelson, 1981.
21 Massey and Denton, 1993; Rothstein, 2017.
22 Hartz, 1991.
23 Gramsci, 1973; Kendi, 2016; Omi and Winant, 2015.
24 Wilkerson, 2020, 18.
25 Omi and Winant, 2015.
26 Bonilla-Silva, 2010; Lawrence, 1995.
27 Durkheim, 1982; Lentin, 2020; Lipsitz, 1998; Omi and Winant, 2015.
28 Omi and Winant, 2015, 106; emphasis original.
29 Omi and Winant, 2015. Roediger, 2007.
30 Easton, 1965. A. L. Schneider and Ingram, 1997.
31 A. L. Schneider and Ingram, 1997.
32 Dye, 1972; Theodoulou, 1995, 2.
33 Dryzek, 2004; Edelman, 1985; Fischer, 2003.
34 Easton, 1965.
35 D. Stone, 2012.
36 Gamson, 1992, 3.
37 Fischer, 2003, viii.
38 Gamson, 1992; R. M. Straus, 2011.

39 E. Frankenberg et al., 2019; Monarrez, 2023; Orfield and Eaton, 1997; Orfield and Jarvie, 2020; Orfield and Yun, 1999; Owens, 2020; R. Straus and Lemieux, 2016.
40 Bertrand and Marsh, 2015; Stein, 2001.
41 Hyman, 2017; Jackson et al., 2016.
42 Tushnet, 1996.
43 Siegel-Hawley and Frankenberg, 2011.
44 E. Frankenberg et al., 2010; E. Frankenberg and Lee, 2003; Garcia, 2008b, 2008a; Monarrez et al., 2022; Whitehurst et al., 2016.
45 Hirschman, 1972.
46 D. Stone, 2012.
47 Scott, 2013, 6.
48 Ravitch, 2013.
49 Marsh and Furlong, 2002.
50 Two of these interviews included both parents. One of them was a repeat respondent, a parent who did not get her school choice for two years in a row and requested to meet with me again. In total, there are thirty families represented in this sample.
51 Private schools are included only if a parent had also chosen one of the three types of public schools.
52 Byrne, 2011, 213.
53 One of my respondents lives in Schenectady, about twenty-five minutes away. All others lived within the city of Albany.
54 For those who are interested in a deeper discussion of research methodology, I expand on this process in the appendix.

CHAPTER 2. NOT QUITE COLORBLIND

1 Stannard, 1992.
2 Hannah-Jones, 2021. Brockell, 2019; Guasco, 2017; Ponti, 2019.
3 Hannah-Jones, 2021.
4 Omi and Winant, 2015, 113. Though see Heng, *The Invention of Race in the European Middle Ages*, for an argument that the concept developed earlier.
5 Omi and Winant, 2015, 113.
6 Omi and Winant, 2015, 113, discussing Jordan 2012 [1968].
7 Du Bois, 2007 [1935], 5.
8 Kendi, 2016, 51.
9 Kendi, 2016, 32.
10 Du Bois, 2007 [1935], 5.
11 Sullivan and Rozsa, 2023.
12 Collier, 2015.
13 Lopez, 2022.
14 Romero, 2021.
15 Baptist, 2014; Beckert, 2015; Beckert and Rockman, 2016; Du Bois, 2007 [1935]; Schermerhorn, 2015.
16 J. Hacker and Pierson, 2020, 10.

17 Roediger, 2007, 11; emphasis added.
18 Bouie, 2022; Feagin, 2001; Madden, 2021; Suk, 2020.
19 Bhattacharyya, 2018; Mercado, 2022.
20 R. Straus and Lemieux, 2016.
21 Harvey, 2015.
22 Issar, 2021, 51.
23 Omi and Winant, 2015, 15.
24 Bachrach and Baratz, 1963; Dye, 1972; A. L. Schneider and Ingram, 1997; D. Stone, 2012; Theodoulou, 1995.
25 As Hudson (2018) points out, the first known use of the term "racial capitalism" actually came in 1979 in the journal *Ikwezi: A Black Liberation Journal of South African and Southern African Political Analysis*. Its usage in *Ikwezi*, however, was very different than Robinson's use. In *Ikwezi*, "racial capitalism" "is not to be celebrated and embraced as a critical counterweight to European Marxism. Instead it is a product of European Marxists' attempts to co-opt and condition black liberation struggles in southern Africa" (Hudson, 2018, 59). Nonetheless, the term "racial capitalism," particularly in its usage as a critique of capitalism as a race-based hermeneutic, is largely associated with Robinson.
26 C. Robinson, 2000, 2.
27 Hudson, 2018, 62.
28 Kelley, 2017, 7 (discussing Robinson).
29 Kelley, 2017, 7 (discussing Robinson).
30 C. Robinson, 2000, xxix; see also Omi and Winant, 2015.
31 See Beckert, 2015.
32 See especially Ralph and Singhal, 2019.
33 Fraser, 2023, 30.
34 Baptist, 2014; Beckert, 2015; Burden-Stelly, 2020; Du Bois, 2007 [1935]; Eschmann, 2023; Feagin, 2001; Marable, 1983. Melamed, 2015, 77.
35 Lipman, 2017, 4–5.
36 C. Robinson, 2000, 19, quoting Wallerstein, 1974; see also Feagin 2001.
37 Omi and Winant, 2015, 139.
38 Bowles and Gintis, 2011; Crenin, 1977, 28–29; Kaestle, 1983, 4; Zinn, 2005, 111.
39 Bowles and Gintis, 2011, 157–58.
40 Bowles and Gintis, 2011.
41 Pertusati, 1988.
42 Irons, 2002, ix.
43 Ficker, 1999, 303.
44 Kuo, 1998.
45 Du Bois, 2007 [1935].
46 Du Bois, 2007 [1935].
47 Katz, 1975.
48 Katz, 1975, 106; also quoted in Bowles and Gintis, 2011, 153.
49 Bowles and Gintis, 2011; Rooks, 2017.

50 Irons, 2002.
51 Bowles and Gintis, 2011, 181.
52 Bowles and Gintis, 2011, 186.
53 Bowles and Gintis, 2011; Oakes, 1986.
54 *Mendez v. Westminster*, 1947.
55 Omi and Winant, 1994, 82.
56 Feagin, 2001.
57 Bonilla-Silva, 2010; Omi and Winant, 2015.
58 Bonilla-Silva, 2010, 2.
59 This colorblindness was strengthened, especially in the field of education, with the Supreme Court's 2023 decisions in *Students for Fair Admissions, Inc. v. President and Fellows of Harvard College* and *Students for Fair Admissions, Inc. v. University of North Carolina*.
60 Bonilla-Silva, 2010.
61 Hagerman, 2018.
62 Eschmann, 2023, 81.
63 Eschmann, 2023, 35.
64 Bonilla-Silva, 2010; Eschmann, 2023; Myers, 2005.
65 Bonilla-Silva, 2010; Hagerman, 2018; Myers, 2005.
66 Hagerman, 2018; Myers, 2005.
67 Bonilla-Silva, 2010, 4.
68 Smith, 2014, 2930.
69 Ackerman, 2018. Smith, 2014.
70 *Parents Involved in Community Schools v. Seattle School District No. 1*, 2007, 748.
71 *Students for Fair Admissions, Inc. v. President and Fellows of Harvard College*, 2023; *Students for Fair Admissions, Inc. v. University of North Carolina*, 2023.
72 Omi and Winant, 2015, 110.
73 Omi and Winant, 2015, 110.
74 Bonilla-Silva, 2010.
75 *Students for Fair Admissions, Inc. v. University of North Carolina*, 2023.
76 Bonilla-Silva, 2010; Omi and Winant, 2015, 132.
77 Bonilla-Silva, 2010, 2.
78 Omi and Winant, 2015, 22.
79 Omi and Winant, 2015, 22.
80 Obama, 2008.
81 Alexander, 2010.
82 Examples of racist epithets for all groups abound. Many of these terms are among the most offensive words available in the English language.
83 Lipman, 2011, 34.
84 Lipman, 2011, 34.
85 In Lin-Manual Miranda's *Hamilton*, the character of Thomas Jefferson arrives at the beginning of the second act to ask, "What'd I Miss?"
86 Finkelman, 2015, x.

87 Hackworth, 2007, 3–4.
88 Melamed, 2015, 82, quoting Marx, "On the Jewish Question."
89 Renshaw, 1999.
90 Campbell, 2005; Renshaw, 1999.
91 Campbell, 2005, 195.
92 Campbell, 2005; Lipman, 2011.
93 See Hill, 1996.
94 Lipman, 2011.
95 Campbell, 2005. Lipman, 2011, 7.
96 Renshaw, 1999.
97 Hackworth, 2007, 9.
98 Omi and Winant, 2015, 211.
99 Harvey, 2007, 2.
100 Campbell, 2005, 188.
101 No matter the date of neoliberalism's takeover, Campbell (2005) notes that it took years of massaging the system to create the legal changes it required.
102 Hartnell, 2017, 2.
103 J. Hacker and Pierson, 2016.
104 Hartnell, 2017.
105 Hackworth, 2007, 9.
106 Campbell, 2005, 193.
107 Harvey, 2007; Spence, 2015.
108 Hackworth, 2007, 10.
109 Reagan, 1981.
110 Harvey, 2007.
111 J. Hacker and Pierson, 2016.
112 Harvey, 2007, 65.
113 Spence, 2015, 74.
114 Buras, 2015; N. Klein, 2007; Lubienski and Weitzel, 2010; Ravitch, 2013; Stahl, 2017.
115 Lubienski and Weitzel, 2010, 1.
116 Lipman, 2011, 10, discussing Harvey, 2005; see also Cohen, 2003.
117 Stone, 2012.
118 Lipman, 2011, 14.
119 Hirschman, 1972.
120 Hirschman, 1972, discussing Friedman 1962.
121 J. Hacker and Pierson, 2020, 1.
122 Fording and Schram, 2020; J. Hacker and Pierson, 2020.
123 E. Klein, 2020.
124 E. Klein, 2020; Levitsky and Ziblatt, 2018.
125 Levitsky and Ziblatt, 2018.
126 Levitsky and Ziblatt, 2018.
127 J. Hacker and Pierson, 2020.
128 Wilson, 2021.

129 D. Harris, 2020.
130 Lipman, 2011, 73.
131 Friedman, 1962.
132 Buras, 2015, 3.
133 Rooks, 2017.
134 Harvey, 2006, 2007.
135 Buras, 2015, 15.
136 Buras, 2015; Scott, 2013.

CHAPTER 3. SEGREGATION LIVES ON

1 White parents have a long history of deliberately choosing White schools. The US racial hierarchy makes this a different, not analogous, display and maintenance of power.
2 Baumgartner and Jones, 1993.
3 Given the construction of the Supreme Court in 2024, groups are now advocating legislative change rather than court challenges.
4 D. Stone, 2012.
5 Lasswell, 1936. Easton, 1965.
6 A. L. Schneider and Ingram, 1997.
7 A. L. Schneider and Ingram, 1997.
8 Peller, 1995.
9 Conneely, 2008; Siegel-Hawley and Frankenberg, 2011.
10 Civil Rights Project/Proyecto Derechos Civiles, n.d.
11 Hannah-Jones, 2021.
12 Hannah-Jones, 2016.
13 Serial Productions, 2020.
14 R. Straus and Lemieux, 2016.
15 J. Hacker and Pierson, 2014.
16 Schattschneider, 1975, 34.
17 J. Hacker and Pierson, 2014; Lowi, 1972.
18 Hannah-Jones, 2021.
19 For any who continue to doubt the veracity of this claim, the recent decision in *Dobbs v. Jackson Women's Health Organization* (2022) overturning *Roe v. Wade* (1973) should make it clear.
20 D. Stone, 2012.
21 J. Hacker et al., 2007.
22 A. L. Schneider and Ingram, 1997, 2.
23 Easton, 1965; Lasswell, 1936.
24 A. L. Schneider and Ingram, 1997.
25 A. L. Schneider and Ingram, 1997, 2.
26 Stone, 2012.
27 *Brown v. Board of Education*, 1954, 492–93.
28 *Brown*, 1954, 489.

29 *Brown*, 1954, 493.
30 *Brown*, 1954, 495.
31 Conneely, 2008; Library of Congress, n.d.
32 *Green v. New Kent County*, 1968, para 4.
33 *Green*, 1968, para. 14.
34 R. Straus and Lemieux, 2016.
35 Wolters, 2004, 321.
36 *Green*, 1968, para. 6.
37 *Green*, 1968, para. 6.
38 *Green*, 1968, para 6.
39 *Swann v. Charlotte-Mecklenburg Board of Education*, 1971, paras. 2, 30, 31.
40 Both quotations in *Swann*, 1971, para. 74.
41 *Swann*, 1971, para. 75.
42 Monarrez, 2023; Owens, 2020. K. Taylor and Frankenberg, 2021.
43 Massey and Denton, 1993; Rothstein, 2017; K.-Y. Taylor, 2019; Trochmann, 2021.
44 *San Antonio Independent School District v. Rodriguez*, 1973, syllabus part 1b.
45 History Channel, n.d.
46 R. Straus, 2005.
47 Blume, 2019.
48 Lindblom, 1959.
49 The Affordable Care Act (ACA), or Obamacare, is a classic example of incremental policy. The ACA works within the existing structure of private insurance companies and a patchwork of public options (primarily Medicare and Medicaid) to encourage more people to obtain health insurance. A sweeping change would have replaced the patchwork quilt with a public system; even a less incremental approach would have kept the public option that Obama originally wanted.
50 Orfield and Eaton, 1997, xxiii.
51 Tushnet, 1996.
52 See Orfield and Eaton, 1997, for a review
53 It is worth reading this statement twice. The Court said that the school district could not use race to promote racial integration. How else, one might legitimately wonder, might integration be promoted?
54 Orfield and Eaton, 1997.
55 *Parents Involved in Community Schools v. Seattle School District No. 1*, 2007, Syllabus.
56 *Swann v. Charlotte-Mecklenburg Board of Education*, 1971.
57 Richard Nixon Presidential Library and Museum, 2021.

CHAPTER 4. AN UNEQUAL CITY
1 Grondahl, 2021.
2 Pipkin, 2008, 331.
3 Manning, 1983.
4 Edelman, 1985; D. Stone, 2012.
5 A. L. Schneider and Ingram, 1993, 1997.

6 Lowi, 1972.
7 A. L. Schneider and Ingram, 1993, 1997.
8 Schneider and Ingram, 1997.
9 Albany Institute of History and Art, n.d.; Kennedy, 1983, 6.
10 Albany Institute of History and Art, n.d.
11 Kennedy, 1983, 14.
12 Albany Institute of History and Art, n.d.; Kennedy, 1983; Pipkin, 2008; Rabrenovic, 1996.
13 Albany Institute of History and Art, n.d.; Kennedy, 1983, 253; Underground Railroad Education Center, n.d.
14 Kennedy, 1983; Rabrenovic, 1996.
15 Kennedy, 1983, 65.
16 Rabrenovic, 1996.
17 Kennedy, 1983, 243.
18 Kennedy, 1983, 243; Rabrenovic, 1996, 41.
19 Kennedy, 1983, 47.
20 Keough, 2012, 40; Rabrenovic, 1996, 41.
21 New York State Board of Elections, n.d.
22 Grondahl, 2021.
23 Lynn, 1973.
24 Kennedy, 1983; Wilkinson, 1982.
25 Kennedy, 1983, 43–44.
26 Lynn, 1973.
27 Wilkinson, 1982.
28 Erie, 1990, 15.
29 Erie, 1990, 8.
30 Erie, 1990, 84.
31 Erie, 1990, 84–85.
32 Wilkinson, 1982.
33 Albany, New York, n.d.
34 Kennedy, 1983, 47.
35 Kennedy, 1983, 47.
36 Kennedy, 1983, 97.
37 Kennedy, 1983, 104.
38 Kennedy, 1983, 104.
39 Kennedy, 1983, 97.
40 Buras, 2015; Lipman, 2011.
41 Keough, 2012, 42.
42 Keough, 2012, 43.
43 Erie, 1990.
44 Erie, 1990, 119.
45 Erie, 1990.
46 Erie, 1990, 122.

47 Erie, 1990, 124.
48 Erie, 1990, 124.
49 Erie, 1990, 84.
50 Erie, 1990, 124.
51 In 2015, my family and I moved about a mile within city limits. Our new home was assessed at about 30 percent higher than what we paid for it. My realtor assured me that I could go to City Hall, meet with the assessor, and have the assessment lowered. He was correct; I walked into City Hall and spoke with one gentleman who filled out the form on my behalf, except for the requested assessed value—I had to do that part myself. The assessor recommended that I request a value lower than market value; the assessment board, he told me, prefers not to assess property as low as people request. Based on that advice, I requested an assessment for the value of our mortgage, which was about 20 percent below our contract price. Lo and behold, within weeks our home had been reassessed to the low value I requested. (It was changed to the purchase price a year later.) Although this one example cannot prove the existence of a remaining machine, I walked out of City Hall happy that I was a registered Democrat.
52 Erie, 1990, 169.
53 Keough, 2012, 42.
54 Mikati and Medina, 2021.
55 Erie, 1990, 169.
56 Erie, 1990, 169; Kennedy, 1983, 277–78; 342; Keough, 2012.
57 Williamson, 2009, 929.
58 Cazenave, 2007; Keough, 2012, 49.
59 Cazenave, 2007, 151.
60 Erie, 1990, 169; Kennedy, 1983, 342; Keough, 2012, 38.
61 Keough, 2012, 38.
62 Keough, 2012, 39.
63 Keough, 2012, 40.
64 Keough, 2012, 50.
65 Keough, 2012. Although my primary focus here is on the city of Albany, Albany mayors also essentially controlled the county during the machine's heyday (Kennedy, 1983, 337).
66 Keough, 2012.
67 Keough, 2012.
68 Keough, 2012, 53.
69 F. R. Robinson, 1977.
70 Kennedy, 1983, 341; Keough, 2012, 54.
71 Keough, 2012.
72 Keough, 2012, 58.
73 Kennedy, 1983, 261; Keough, 2012, 58.
74 Erie, 1990, 157.
75 Erie, 1990, 157,

76 Erie, 1990, 164.
77 Erie, 1990, 164.
78 Erie, 1990, 157–58.
79 Recall that Albany was settled by the Dutch and maintains a strong Dutch identity, at least symbolically. The Dutch queen was therefore seen as someone the city, and the state, wished to impress. Erie, 1990, 158; Grondahl, 2015; Keough, 2012, 45.
80 Erie, 1990, 157–60.
81 Erie, 1990, 159.
82 Erie, 1990, 159.
83 Erie, 1990, 159.
84 Erie, 1990, 160.
85 Grondahl, 2015.
86 Erie, 1990, 159.
87 Grondahl, 2015.
88 Mikati and Medina, 2021.
89 Mikati and Medina, 2021.
90 Erie, 1990, 159; Mikati and Medina, 2021.
91 Mikati and Medina, 2021.
92 Mikati and Medina, 2021.
93 Mikati and Medina, 2021.
94 Mikati and Medina, 2021.
95 Mikati and Medina, 2021.
96 Mikati and Medina, 2021.

CHAPTER 5. CITY POLITICS, POLICY, AND POWER

1 Lee and Foster, 1997, 146.
2 Omi and Winant, 2015.
3 National Alliance for Public Charter Schools, 2024.
4 N. Klein, 2007, 6.
5 N. Klein, 2007, discussing Milton Friedman.
6 Buras, 2015; N. Klein, 2007.
7 Buras, 2015, 2.
8 Buras, 2015.
9 Shibata, 2013.
10 Shibata, 2013.
11 Lipman, 2011; Shibata, 2013.
12 Melton and Sanchez, 1990.
13 Seth-Smith, 2013.
14 Seelye, 2011; Turbeville, 2013. United States Census Bureau, 2022.
15 Seelye, 2011.
16 Turbeville, 2013.
17 Nichols, 2014.
18 Hamlin, 2017.

19 Henig et al., 1999.
20 C. Stone, 1989.
21 Mossberger and Stoker, 2001; C. Stone, 1989, 1998.
22 C. Stone, 1989, 6.
23 Mossberger and Stoker, 2001.
24 Henig et al., 1999, 9.
25 Henig et al., 1999, 9.
26 Henig et al., 1999; C. Stone, 1998.
27 National Alliance for Public Charter Schools, 2024.
28 Butler et al., 2017; Clark, 1985; Jensen, 2003; Karch et al., 2016; Shipan and Volden, 2008; Walker, 1969.
29 SUNY Charter Schools Institute, n.d.
30 New York requires teachers to hold a bachelor's degree and a master's degree in order to obtain full certification.
31 Renzulli (2005) measures applications for new charter schools rather than their actual existence.
32 Glomm et al., 2005; Renzulli, 2005; Stoddard and Corcoran, 2007; Zhang and Yang, 2008.
33 Stoddard and Corcoran, 2007.
34 Glomm et al., 2005; Renzulli, 2005; Stoddard and Corcoran, 2007, 47; Zhang and Yang, 2008.
35 Stoddard and Corcoran, 2007.
36 Glomm et al., 2005.
37 Stoddard and Corcoran, 2007.
38 Stoddard and Corcoran, 2007.
39 Stoddard and Corcoran, 2007.
40 Zhang and Yang, 2008.
41 Zhang and Yang, 2008.
42 Zhang and Yang, 2008, 587.
43 Kingdon, 2003.
44 Mintrom, 2000.
45 Beland and Howlett, 2016; Cairney and Jones, 2016; Chow, 2014; Gearin et al., 2020; Mosier, 2013; Ridde, 2009; Stanifer and Hahn, 2020; Young et al., 2010.
46 See Jones et al., 2016, for a comprehensive review.
47 Kingdon, 1984, 92.
48 Kingdon, 1984, 129.
49 Mintrom, 2000, 114.
50 Lindblom, 1959.
51 Mintrom, 2000, 123.
52 Cobb and Elder, 1983; Edelman, 1985.
53 Mintrom, 2000, 130.
54 Goffman, 1974, 10.
55 Mintrom, 2000, 132.

56 Bachrach and Baratz, 1962; Cobb and Elder, 1983.
57 March and Olsen, 1989, 38.
58 March and Olsen, 1984, 738.
59 Lowi, 1972.
60 Edelman, 1985; March and Olsen, 1989, 1984.
61 March and Olsen, 1984, 739.
62 Erie, 1990, 2.
63 Erie, 1990, 142.
64 Bolton, 2004. In spite of local journalistic claims that the machine died with the election of David Soares, Albany residents, particularly those who identify as left of the Democratic Party, continue to make references to the Democratic machine.
65 Mayor Jennings is one of the very few people who refused an interview with me. His refusal of a research interview, even after his retirement, speaks to the continued political divisiveness of charter schools in the city of Albany.
66 Erie, 1990, 15.
67 Erie, 1990, 15
68 Erie, 1990, 157.
69 Erie, 1990, 157.
70 Erie, 1990, 157.
71 Erie, 1990, 160; Kennedy, 1983, 316.
72 Erie, 1990, 164; F. R. Robinson, 1977.
73 Charters in New York State are granted by either the Board of Regents or the SUNY (State University of New York) Charter School Institute.
74 Erie, 1990, 164; F. R. Robinson, 1977, 179.
75 New York Times, n.d.
76 Lackman, 2012; Waldman, 2012.
77 Lackman, 2012.
78 New York City, Buffalo, Rochester, Syracuse, and Yonkers.

CHAPTER 6. WHY PARENTS CHOOSE

1 Simon, 2005.
2 Schneider and Ingram, 1997.
3 Ellison and Aloe, 2019.
4 Ellison and Aloe, 2019.
5 Ellison and Aloe, 2019, 1147.
6 Ellison and Aloe, 2019, 1148.
7 Martinez and Thomas, 1994.
8 Carnegie Foundation for the Advancement of Teaching, 1992.
9 Altenhoften et al., 2016; Hausman and Goldring, 2000.
10 Hausman and Goldring, 2000.
11 M. Schneider et al., 2000.
12 Ellison and Aloe, 2019, 1149.
13 Ellison and Aloe, 2019, 1164; see also D. Stone, 2012.

14 Altenhoften et al., 2016; Carnegie Foundation for the Advancement of Teaching, 1992; Hastings et al., 2005; Lenhoff et al., 2020; M. Schneider et al., 2000; Smrekar and Goldring, 1999.
15 M. Schneider et al., 2000, 107.
16 Goldring and Hausman, 1999.
17 Ellison and Aloe, 2019.
18 Gallup, n.d.
19 See Pierce and Claybourn, 2023, for a discussion.
20 Bowles and Gintis, 2011, 10.
21 When I met with Janie, there were no single-sex charter middle schools available in Albany. The boys' and girls' charter middle schools closed in 2015.
22 The largest Catholic high schools in Albany and the surrounding region are single-sex.
23 Goyette, 2014; M. Schneider, 2001; Small, 2009.
24 Hamlin, 2020, 394.
25 Private schools are included only when a child also attended an Albany charter, magnet, or neighborhood school.

CHAPTER 7. DIVIDED BY CHOICE

1 Albany County Data, 2022.
2 Haney López, 2014, xii, referencing Bell, 1992.
3 Omi and Winant, 2015.
4 Bonilla-Silva, 2010.
5 Haney López, 2014.
6 Omi and Winant, 2015, 192.
7 Omi and Winant, 2015, 165.
8 Omi and Winant, 2015, 169.
9 King, 1963.
10 Roberts qtd. in Totenberg, 2023.
11 It is worth noting that the Court exempted the military academies from its ending of affirmative action. In a footnote, the Chief Justice notes that the federal government "contends that race-based admissions programs further compelling interests at our Nation's military academies." He does not explain why those "compelling interests" are not also important in all other American institutions (*Students for Fair Admissions, Inc. v. President and Fellows of Harvard College*, 2023, 22).
12 On the rare occasion when such claims are made, the pushback is vociferous. Witness the reaction to the publication of *The Bell Curve* in 1994, for example.
13 Haney López, 2014, 9.
14 Haney López, 2014, 10.
15 Haney López, 2014, 10.
16 Haney López, 2014, 4.
17 Haney López, 2014, 113.

18 See Lentin, 2020.
19 Bonilla-Silva, 2010.
20 Bonilla-Silva, 2010.
21 This interview was conducted in Spanish with the translation services of a native speaker.
22 Haney López, 2014.
23 For the 2020–2021 academic year, Albany High School was 21.67 percent White. Advanced placement courses were 41.45 percent White, while the International Baccalaureate courses were a staggering 53.68 percent White. Data are from New York State Education Department, n.d., "Albany High School at a Glance," for the school as a whole and New York State Education Department, n.d., "Albany High School 2020–21 AP/IB Report" for enrollment in AP and IB courses.
24 Gloria is referring to a McDonald's restaurant about a mile from the high school. High school students frequently stop there after school, although I am not aware of it ever shutting down because of them.
25 Chad and Sarah's interview was very unique. While every other parent I spoke with (including when both parents were present) waited to hear my prepared interview questions and seemed anxious to respond to them as fully as they could, Chad and Sarah barely allowed me to speak at all. Their conversation was also more jumbled than most, frequently moving between different topics. While they were not the only ones who repeatedly came back to specific themes—whether it was violence, segregation, academic preparation, or other—Chad and Sarah's interview transcript was difficult to read because they both continuously attempted to provide me with as many details as they could without any particular order. Their interview was more a collection of their frustrations with Albany schools than a clear response to an empirical research study.
26 It is worth noting that Sarah's understanding of the racial composition of her child's school was accurate; it was 11 percent White when her child attended.
27 This is the same "time out" room that angered Billie. Note that Sarah's and Billie's different experiences with the school district led them to understand this room in divergent ways.
28 As a frequent book fair volunteer, Sarah is likely aware that the point of these events is to place books in children's homes. That goal was reached in this situation.
29 R. Frankenberg, 1993.

CONCLUSION

1 Fording and Schram, 2020; J. Hacker and Pierson, 2020; Levitsky and Ziblatt, 2018; Wilson, 2021.
2 Hannah-Jones, 2021.
3 Anyon, 1997; Katznelson and Weir, 1988; Lipman, 2011; McDonnell, 2000; Morel, 2018; Tyack, 1974.
4 Ellison and Aloe, 2019.

APPENDIX A

1. Hacker et al., 2007.
2. Mintrom, 2000.
3. Marsh and Furlong, 2002; Yanow, 2006.
4. Marsh and Furlong, 2002.
5. There is a vast and varied literature on social construction, focusing on issues such as race, gender, and policy. For the fundamental text on social construction, see Berger and Luckmann, *The Social Construction of Reality*, 1966.
6. Zhang and Yang, 2008, 587; emphases mine.
7. Marsh and Furlong, 2002, 21–22.
8. Weiss, 1994, 1; see also Devine, 2002.
9. See especially Yanow and Schwartz-Shea, 2006.
10. Soss, 2006, 128–29.
11. Devine, 2002, 198.
12. Tansey, 2007, 768.
13. Weiss, 1994, 22–23.
14. Weiss, 1994, 3, ix.
15. Yanow and Schwartz-Shea, 2006.
16. Tansey, 2007, 766.
17. Tansey, 2007, 767.
18. Devine, 2002.
19. Interview, October 11, 2017.
20. Interview, January 22, 2018.
21. Albany Public Library, 2017.
22. My request at the YMCA was denied because, at the time, the organization shared a building with the Albany City School District. As the manager there told me (October 2017), he was concerned that placing a flyer advertising anything related to charter schools would produce a negative reaction from people who worked in the adjacent school district offices.
23. Baltar and Brunet, 2012.
24. Pew Research Center, 2016.
25. Schroder, 2018, 82.
26. McKenna et al., 2002, 9.
27. Devine, 2002; Rubin and Rubin, 2012; Weiss, 1994.
28. A handful of respondents focused on parenting and volunteer work, without outside paid employment. However, they had previous work experience or training in professional fields.
29. Rubin and Rubin, 2012.

REFERENCES

Ackerman, B. 2018. *We the People*. Volume 3, *The Civil Rights Revolution*. Belknap Press: An Imprint of Harvard University Press.
Albany County Data. 2022. *New York State Education Department*. https://data.nysed.gov.
Albany County Data. 2023. *New York State Education Department*. https://data.nysed.gov.
Albany Institute of History and Art. N.d. *Albany: One of America's First Cities*. Retrieved June 22, 2021, from www.albanyinstitute.org.
Albany, New York. N.d. *Albany Neighborhoods*. www.albanyny.gov, accessed August 30, 2024.
Albany Public Library. 2017, March. *Albany Public Library Fact Sheet*. www.albanypubliclibrary.org.
Alexander, M. 2010. *The New Jim Crow: Mass Incarceration in the Age of Colorblindness*. New Press.
Altenhoften, S., Berends, M., and White, T. G. 2016. School Choice Decision Making among Suburban, High-Income Parents. *AERA Open*, 2(1).
Anyon, J. 1997. *Ghetto Schooling: A Political Economy of Urban Educational Reform*. Teacher's College Press.
Bachrach, P., and Baratz, M. S. 1962. Two Faces of Power. *American Political Science Review*, 56(4), 947–52.
Bachrach, P., and Baratz, M. S. 1963. Decisions and Nondecisions: An Analytical Framework. *American Political Science Review*, 57(3), 632–42.
Baltar, F., and Brunet, I. 2012. Social Research 2.0: Virtual Snowball Sampling Method Using Facebook. *Internet Research*, 22(1), 57–74.
Baptist, E. E. 2014. *The Half Has Never Been Told: Slavery and the Making of American Capitalism*. Basic Books.
Baumgartner, F. R., and Jones, B. D. 1993. *Agendas and Instability in American Politics*. University of Chicago Press.
Beckert, S. 2015. *Empire of Cotton: A Global History*. Vintage Books.
Beckert, S., and Rockman, S., eds. 2016. *Slavery's Capitalism: A New History of American Economic Development*. University of Pennsylvania Press.
Beland, D., and Howlett, M. 2016. The Role and Impact of the Multiple-Streams Approach in Comparative Policy Analysis. *Journal of Comparative Policy Analysis: Research and Practice*, 18(3), 221–27.
Bell, D. 1992. *Faces at the Bottom of the Well: The Permanence of Racism*. Basic Books.

Berger, P. L., and Luckmann, T. 1966. *The Social Construction of Reality: A Treatise in the Sociology of Knowledge.* Penguin.

Bertrand, M., and Marsh, J. A. 2015. Teachers' Sensemaking of Data and Implications for Equity. *American Educational Research Journal,* 52(5), 861–93.

Bhattacharyya, G. 2018. *Rethinking Racial Capitalism: Questions of Reproduction and Survival.* Rowman and Littlefield International.

Blume, H. 2019, June 28. School Busing and Race Tore L.A. Apart in the 1970s. Now, Kamala Harris Is Reviving the Debate. *Los Angeles Times.* www.latimes.com.

Bolton, M. M. 2004, September 16. Soares Won in Altered County. *Albany Times-Union,* A1.

Bonilla-Silva, E. 2010. *Racism without Racists: Color-blind Racism and the Persistence of Racial Inequality in the United States.* Rowman and Littlefield.

Bouie, J. 2022, October 7. We Had to Force the Constitution to Accommodate Democracy, and It Shows. *New York Times.* www.nytimes.com.

Bowles, S., and Gintis, H. 2011. *Schooling in Capitalist America: Educational Reform and the Contradictions of Economic Life* (2nd ed.). Haymarket Books.

Brion, D. 2006. *Inhuman Bondage: The Rise and Fall of Slavery in the New World.* Oxford University Press.

Brockell, G. 2019, September 7. Before 1619, There Was 1526: The Mystery of the First Enslaved Africans in What Became the United States. *Washington Post.* www.washingtonpost.com.

Brown v. Board of Education, 347 U.S. 483 (United States Supreme Court 1954).

Buras, K. L. 2015. *Charter Schools, Race, and Urban Space: Where the Market Meets Grassroots Resistance.* Routledge.

Burden-Stelly, C. 2020. Modern U.S. Racial Capitalism. *Monthly Review,* 72(3). https://d1wqtxts1xzle7.cloudfront.net.

Butler, D. M., Volden, C., Dynes, A. M., and Shor, B. 2017. Ideology, Learning, and Policy Diffusion: Experimental Evidence. *American Journal of Political Science,* 61(1), 37–49.

Byrne, B. 2011. Qualitative Interviewing. In *Researching Society and Culture,* ed. C. Seale (206–26). Sage Publications.

Cairney, P., and Jones, M. D. 2016. Kingdon's Multiple Streams Approach: What Is the Empirical Impact of This Universal Theory? *Policy Studies Journal,* 44(1), 37–58.

Campbell, A. 2005. The Birth of Neoliberalism in the United States: A Reorganisation of Capitalism. In *Neoliberalism: A Critical Reader,* ed. A. Saad-Filho and D. Johnston (187–98). Pluto.

Carnegie Foundation for the Advancement of Teaching. 1992. *School Choice: A Special Report.* Carnegie Foundation for the Advancement of Teaching.

Cazenave, N. A. 2007. *Impossible Democracy: The Unlikely Success of the War on Poverty Community Action Programs.* State University of New York Press.

Chow, A. 2014. Understanding Policy Change: Multiple Streams and National Education Curriculum Policy in Hong Kong. *Journal of Public Administration and Governance,* 4(2), 46–64. https://doi.org/10.5296/jpag.v4i2.5184.

City School District of Albany. N.d. *Our Demographics*. Retrieved January 17, 2024, from www.albanyschools.org.

Civil Rights Project/Proyecto Derechos Civiles. N.d. www.civilrightsproject.ucla.edu, accessed August 27, 2024.

Clark, J. 1985. Policy Diffusion and Program Scope: Research Directions. *Publius*, 15(4), 61–70.

Cobb, R. W., and Elder, C. D. 1983. *Participation in American Politics: The Dynamics of Agenda-Building*. Johns Hopkins University Press.

Cohen, L. 2003. *A Consumers' Republic: The Politics of Mass Consumption in Postwar America*. Vintage Books.

Collier, K. 2015, October 5. Texas' Controversial Social Studies Textbooks under Fire Again. *Texas Tribune*. www.texastribune.org.

Conneely, N. 2008. After PICS: Making the Case for Socioeconomic Integration. *Texas Journal on Civil Liberties and Civil Rights*, 14(1).

Crenin, L. A. 1977. *Traditions of American Education*. Basic Books.

Crenshaw, K. W. 1995. Mapping the Margins: Intersectionality, Identity Politics, and Violence against Women of Color. In *Critical Race Theory: The Key Writings That Formed the Movement*, ed. K. Crenshaw, N. Gotanda, G. Peller, and K. Thomas (357–83). New Press.

Dahl, R. A. 1961. *Who Governs? Democracy and Power in an American City*. Yale University Press.

Devine, F. 2002. Qualitative Methods. In *Theory and Methods in Political Science* (2nd ed.). Palgrave Macmillan.

Dryzek, J. 2004. Review of *Reframing Public Policy: Discursive Politics and Deliberative Practices*. *Policy Sciences*, 37(1), 89–93.

Du Bois, W. E. B. 2007 [1935]. *Black Reconstruction in America: An Essay toward a History of the Part Which Black Folk Played in the Attempt to Reconstruct Democracy in America, 1860–1880*. Oxford University Press.

Durkheim, E. 1982. *The Rules of Sociological Method*. Free Press.

Dye, T. 1972. *Understanding Public Policy*. Prentice Hall.

Easton, D. 1965. *A Systems Analysis of Political Life*. John Wiley and Sons.

Edelman, M. 1985. *The Symbolic Uses of Politics*. University of Illinois Press.

Ellison, S., and Aloe, A. M. 2019. Strategic Thinking and Positioned Choices: Parental Decision Making in Urban School Choice. *Educational Policy*, 33(7), 1135–70. https://doi.org/10.1177/0895904818755470.

Erie, S. 1990. *Rainbow's End: Irish-Americans and the Dilemmas of Urban Machine Politics, 1840–1985*. University of California Press.

Eschmann, R. 2023. *When the Hood Comes Off: Racism and Resistance in the Digital Age*. University of California Press.

Fahle, E., Reardon, S. F., Kalogrides, D., Weathers, E. S., and Jang, H. 2020. Racial Segregation and School Poverty in the United States, 1999–2016. *Race and Social Problems*, 12, 42–56.

Feagin, J. R. 2001. *Racist America: Roots, Current Realities, and Future Reparations*. Taylor & Francis.

Fessler, P. 2019, December 28. In Nearly Every U.S. Metro Area, New Data Show Opportunity Lags for Kids of Color. *National Public Radio*. www.npr.org.

Ficker, D. 1999. From *Roberts* to *Plessy*: Educational Segregation and the "Separate but Equal" Doctrine. *Journal of Negro History*, 84(4), 301–14.

Finkelman, P. 2015. *Slavery and the Founders: Race and Liberty in the Age of Jefferson* (3rd ed.). Routledge.

Fischer, F. 2003. *Reframing Public Policy: Discursive Politics and Deliberative Practices*. Oxford University Press.

Fording, R. C., and Schram, S. F. 2020. *Hard White: The Mainstreaming of Racism in American Politics*. Oxford University Press.

Frankenberg, E. 2024, January 5. 70 Years after *Brown vs. Board of Education*, Public Schools Still Deeply Segregated. *The Conversation*. https://theconversation.com.

Frankenberg, E., Ee, J., Ayscue, J. B., and Orfield, G. 2019. *Harming Our Common Future: America's Segregated Schools 65 Years after* Brown. Civil Rights Project/Proyecto Derechos Civiles, UCLA. https://civilrightsproject.ucla.edu.

Frankenberg, E., and Lee, C. 2003. Charter Schools and Race: A Lost Opportunity for Integrated Education. *Education Policy Analysis Archives*, 11(32).

Frankenberg, E., Siegel-Hawley, G., and Wang, J. 2010. *Choice without Equity: Charter School Segregation and the Need for Civil Rights Standards*. Civil Rights Project/Proyecto Derechos Civiles, UCLA. https://civilrightsproject.ucla.edu.

Frankenberg, R. 1993. *White Women, Race Matters: The Social Construction of Whiteness*. University of Minnesota Press.

Fraser, N. 2023. *Cannibal Capitalism: How Our System Is Devouring Democracy, Care, and the Planet and What We Can Do about It*. Verso.

Friedman, M. 1962. *Capitalism and Freedom*. University of Chicago Press.

Gallup. N.d. *In Depth: Topics A to Z; Education*. Retrieved April 3, 2024, from https://news.gallup.com.

Gamson, W. A. 1992. *Talking Politics*. Cambridge University Press.

Garcia, D. 2008a. Academic and Racial Segregation in Charter Schools: Do Parents Sort Students into Specialized Charter Schools? *Education and Urban Society*, 40(5), 590–612.

Garcia, D. 2008b. The Impact of School Choice on Racial Segregation in Charter Schools. *Educational Policy*, 22(6), 805–29.

Gearin, B., Turtura, J., Kame'enui, E. J., Nelson, N. J., and Fien, H. 2020. A Multiple Streams Analysis of Recent Changes to State-Level Dyslexia Education Law. *Educational Policy*, 34(7), 1036–68. https://doi.org/10.1177/0895904818807328.

Glomm, G., Harris, D., and Lo, T.-F. 2005. Charter School Location. *Economics of Education Review*, 24(4), 451–57.

Goffman, E. 1974. *Frame Analysis: An Essay on the Organization of Experience*. Harvard University Press.

Goldring, E., and Hausman, C. 1999. Reasons for Parental Choice of Urban Schools. *Journal of Education Policy*, 14(5), 469–90.

Goyette, K. 2014. Setting the Context. In *Choosing Homes, Choosing Schools*, ed. A. Lareau and K. Goyette (1–24). Russell Sage Foundation.

Gramsci, A. 1973. *Selections from the Prison Notebooks*. International Publishers.

Green v. New Kent County, 391 U.S. 430 (United States Supreme Court 1968).

Grondahl, P. 2015, May 26. Reassessing the Legacy of the Empire State Plaza. *Albany Times Union*. www.timesunion.com.

Grondahl, P. 2021, February 3. How 100 Years of the Democratic Rule Has Shaped the City of Albany. *Albany Times Union*. www.timesunion.com.

Guasco, M. 2017, September 3. The Misguided Focus on 1619 as the Beginning of Slavery in the U.S. Damages Our Understanding of American History. *Smithsonian Magazine*. www.smithsonianmag.com.

Guzman, G. 2020. *Household Income by Race and Hispanic Origin: 2005–2009 and 2015–2019* (acsbr19–07). United States Census Bureau. www.census.gov.

Hacker, A. 2003. *Two Nations: Black and White, Separate, Hostile, Unequal*. Scribner.

Hacker, J., Mettler, S., and Soss, J. 2007. The New Politics of Inequality: A Policy-Centered Perspective. In *Remaking America: Democracy and Public Policy in an Age of Inequality*, ed. J. Hacker, S. Mettler, and J. Soss (3–23). Russell Sage Foundation.

Hacker, J., and Pierson, P. 2014. After the "Master Theory": Downs, Schattschneider, and the Rebirth of Policy-Focused Analysis. *Perspectives on Politics*, 12(3), 643–62.

Hacker, J., and Pierson, P. 2016. *American Amnesia: How the War on Government Led Us to Forget What Made America Prosper*. Simon and Schuster.

Hacker, J., and Pierson, P. 2020. *Let Them Eat Tweets: How the Right Rules in an Age of Extreme Inequality*. Liveright.

Hackworth, J. 2007. *The Neoliberal City: Governance, Ideology, and Development in American Urbanism*. Cornell University Press.

Hagerman, M. A. 2018. *White Kids: Growing Up with Privilege in a Racially Divided America*. New York University Press.

Hamlin, D. 2017. Are Charter Schools Safer in Deindustrialized Cities with High Rates of Crime? Testing Hypotheses in Detroit. *American Educational Research Journal*, 54(4), 725–56.

Hamlin, D. 2020. Flight to Safety in Deindustrialized Cities: Perceptions of School Safety in Charter and Public Schools in Detroit, Michigan. *Education and Urban Society*, 52(3), 394–414.

Haney López, I. 2014. *Dog Whistle Politics: How Coded Racial Appeals Have Reinvented Racism and Wrecked the Middle Class*. Oxford.

Hannah-Jones, N. 2016, June 9. Choosing a School for My Daughter in a Segregated City: How One School Became a Battleground over Which Children Benefit from a Separate and Unequal System. *New York Times Magazine*. www.nytimes.com.

Hannah-Jones, N., ed. 2021. *The 1619 Project: A New Origin Story*. One World.

Harris, C. I. 1995. Whiteness as Property. In *Critical Race Theory: The Key Writings That Formed the Movement*, ed. K. Crenshaw, N. Gotanda, G. Peller, and K. Thomas (276–91). New Press.

Harris, D. 2020. *Charter School City: What the End of Traditional Public Schools in New Orleans Means for American Education*. University of Chicago Press.

Hartnell, A. 2017. *After Katrina: Race, Neoliberalism, and the End of the American Century*. State University of New York Press.

Hartz, L. 1991. *The Liberal Tradition in America* (2nd ed.). Mariner Books.

Harvey, D. 2005. *A Brief History of Neoliberalism*. Oxford University Press.

Harvey, D. 2006. *Spaces of Global Capitalism: Towards a Theory of Uneven Geographical Development*. Verso.

Harvey, D. 2015. *Seventeen Contradictions and the End of Capitalism*. Oxford University Press.

Hastings, J. S., Kane, T. J., and Staiger, D. O. 2005. *Parental Preferences and School Competition: Evidence from a Public School Choice Program* (Working Paper 11805). National Bureau of Economic Research.

Hausman, C., and Goldring, E. 2000. Parent Involvement, Influence, and Satisfaction in Magnet Schools: Do Reasons for Choice Matter? *Urban Review*, 32(2), 105–21.

Heng, G. 2018. *The Invention of Race in the European Middle Ages*. Cambridge University Press.

Henig, J. R., Hula, R. C., Orr, M., and Pedescleaux, D. S. 1999. *The Color of School Reform: Race, Politics, and the Challenge of Urban Education*. Princeton University Press.

Hill, H. 1996. The Problem of Race in American Labor History. *Reviews in American History*, 24(2), 189–208.

Hirschman, A. O. 1972. *Exit, Voice, and Loyalty: Responses to Decline in Firms, Organizations, and States*. Harvard University Press.

History Channel. N.d. Violence Erupts in Boston over Desegregation Busing. *This Day in History*. Retrieved April 4, 2023, from www.history.com.

Hudson, P. J. 2018, February 20. Racial Capitalism and the Dark Proletariat. *Boston Review*, 59–65.

Hyman, J. 2017. Does Money Matter in the Long Run? Effects of School Spending on Educational Attainment. *American Economic Journal: Economic Policy*, 9(4), 256–80.

Irons, P. 2002. *Jim Crow's Children: The Broken Promise of the Brown Decision*. Penguin.

Issar, S. 2021. Listening to Black Lives Matter: Racial Capitalism and the Critique of Neoliberalism. *Contemporary Political Theory*, 20, 48–71. https://doi.org/10.1057/s41296-020-00399-0.

Jackson, C. K., Johnson, R. C., and Persico, C. 2016. The Effects of School Spending on Educational and Economic Outcomes: Evidence from School Finance Reforms. *Quarterly Journal of Economics*, 131(1), 157–218.

Jacobson, M. F. 1999. *Whiteness of a Different Color: European Immigrants and the Alchemy of Race*. Harvard University Press.

Jensen, J. L. 2003. Policy Diffusion through Institutional Legitimation: State Lotteries. *Journal of Public Administration Research and Theory: J-PART*, 13(4), 521–41.
Jones, M. D., Peterson, H. L., Pierce, J. J., Herweg, N., Bernal, A., Raney, H. L., and Zahariadis, N. 2016. A River Runs through It: A Multiple Streams Meta-Review. *Policy Studies Journal*, 44(1), 13–36. https://doi.org/10.1111/psj.12115.
Jordan, Winthrop D. 2012 [1968]. *White over Black: American Attitudes toward the Negro, 1150-1812* (2nd ed.). University of North Carolina Press.
Kaestle, C. F. 1983. *Pillars of the Republic: Common Schools and American Society, 1780–1860.* Hill and Wang.
Karch, A., Nicholson-Crotty, S. C., Woods, N. D., and O'M. Bowman, A. 2016. Policy Diffusion and the Pro-Innovation Bias. *Political Research Quarterly*, 69(1), 83–95.
Katz, M. B. 1975. *Class, Bureaucracy, and Schools: The Illusion of Educational Change in America.* Praeger Publishers.
Katznelson, I. 1981. *City Trenches: Urban Politics and the Patterning of Class in the United States.* University of Chicago Press.
Katznelson, I., and M. Weir. 1988. *Schooling for All: Race, Class, and the Decline of the Democratic Ideal.* University of California Press.
Kelley, R. D. G. 2017, January 12. What Did Cedric Robinson Mean by Racial Capitalism? *Boston Review* (5–8).
Kendi, I. X. 2016. *Stamped from the Beginning: The Definitive History of Racist Ideas in America.* Bold Type Books.
Kennedy, W. 1983. *O Albany! Improbable City of Political Wizards, Fearless Ethnics, Spectacular Aristocrats, Splendid Nobodies, and Underrated Scoundrels.* Penguin.
Keough, B. 2012. Politics as Usual or Political Change: The War on Poverty's Community Action Program in Albany, N.Y., 1959–1967. *University Libraries Faculty Scholarship*, 31.
King, M. L., Jr. 1963. *I Have a Dream*. National Archives. www.archives.gov.
Kingdon, J. 1984. *Agendas, Alternatives, and Public Policies* (1st ed.). Little, Brown.
Kingdon, J. 2003. *Agendas, Alternatives, and Public Policies* (2nd ed.). Longman.
Klein, E. 2020. *Why We're Polarized.* Avid Reader Press.
Klein, N. 2007. *The Shock Doctrine: The Rise of Disaster Capitalism.* Picador.
Kozol, J. 1991. *Savage Inequalities: Children in America's Schools.* Crown Publishers.
Kuo, J. 1998. Excluded, Segregated, and Forgotten: A Historical View of the Discrimination of Chinese Americans in Public Schools. *Asian Law Journal*, 5, 181–212.
Lackman, A. H. 2012. The Collapse of Catholic School Enrollment: The Unintended Consequences of the Charter School Movement. *Albany Government Law Review*, 6(1), 1–20.
Lasswell, H. D. 1936. *Politics: Who Gets What, When, How.* Whittlesey House.
Lawrence, C. I. R. 1995. The Id, the Ego, and Equal Protection: Reckoning with Unconscious Racism. In *Critical Race Theory: The Key Writings That Formed the Movement*, ed. K. Crenshaw, N. Gotanda, G. Peller, and K. Thomas (235–57). New Press.
Lee, S., and Foster, C. 1997. Trustbusters. *Forbes*, 159(11), 146–52.

Lenhoff, S. W., Singer, J., Pogodzinski, B., and Cook, W. 2020. Exiting Detroit for School: Inequitable Choice Sets and School Quality. *Journal of Education Policy*, 37(4), 590–612. https://doi.org/10.1080/02680939.2020.1856932.
Lentin, A. 2020. *Why Race Still Matters*. Polity Press.
Levitsky, S., and Ziblatt, D. 2018. *How Democracies Die*. Broadway Books.
Library of Congress. N.d. *The Civil Rights Act: A Long Struggle for Freedom*. Retrieved April 4, 2023, from www.loc.gov.
Lindblom, C. 1959. The Science of "Muddling Through." *Public Administration Review*, 19(2), 79–88.
Lipman, P. 2011. *The New Political Economy of Urban Education: Neoliberalism, Race, and the Right to the City*. Routledge.
Lipman, P. 2017. The Landscape of Education "Reform" in Chicago: Neoliberalism Meets a Grassroots Movement. *Education Policy Analysis Archives*, 25(54). https://files.eric.ed.gov.
Lipsitz, G. 1998. *The Possessive Investment in Whiteness: How White People Profit from Identity Politics*. Temple University Press.
Lopez, B. 2022, June 30. State Education Board Members Push Back on Proposal to Use "Involuntary Relocation" to Describe Slavery. *Texas Tribune*. www.texastribune.org.
Lowi, T. J. 1972. Four Systems of Policy, Politics, and Choice. *Public Administration Review*, 32(4), 298–310.
Lubienski, C., and Weitzel, P. C. 2010. Two Decades of Charter Schools: Shifting Expectations, Partners, and Policies. In *The Charter School Experiment: Expectations, Evidence, and Implications*, ed. C. Lubienski and P. C. Weitzel (1–14). Harvard Education Press.
Lynn, F. 1973, February 10. Political Machine Grinds On in Albany City Hall. *New York Times*.
Madden, D. P. 2021. *The Constitution and American Racism: Setting a Course for Lasting Injustice*. McFarland.
Manning, R. H. 1983. "Herald of the Albany Regency: Edwin Crosswell and the 'Albany Argus,' 1823–1854." Ph.D. dissertation, Miami University.
Marable, M. 1983. *How Capitalism Underdeveloped Black America*. South End Press.
March, J. G., and Olsen, J. P. 1984. The New Institutionalism: Organizational Factors in Political Life. *American Political Science Review*, 78(3), 734–49.
March, J. G., and Olsen, J. P. 1989. *Rediscovering Institutions: The Organizational Basis of Politics*. Free Press.
Marsh, D., and Furlong, P. 2002. A Skin, Not a Sweater: Ontology and Epistemology in Political Science. In *Theory and Methods in Political Science*, ed. D. Marsh and G. Stoker (2nd ed., 17–41). Palgrave Macmillan.
Martinez, V., and Thomas, K. 1994. Who Chooses and Why: A Look at Five School Choice Plans. *Phi Delta Kappan*, 75(9), 678.
Massey, D. S., and Denton, N. A. 1993. *American Apartheid: Segregation and the Making of the Underclass*. Harvard University Press.

McDonnell, L. 2000. Defining Democratic Purposes. In *Rediscovering the Democratic Purposes of Education*, ed. L. McDonnell, P. M. Timpane, and R. Benjamin (1-18). University Press of Kansas.
McKenna, K. Y. A., Green, A. S., and Gleason, M. E. J. 2002. Relationship Formation on the Internet: What's the Big Attraction? *Journal of Social Issues*, 58(1), 9-31.
Melamed, J. 2015. Racial Capitalism. *Critical Ethnic Studies*, 1(1), 76-85.
Melton, R. H., and C. Sanchez. 1990, January 18. D.C.'s War on Violence Succeeding, Barry Says. *Washington Post*.
Mendez v. Westminster, 161 F.2d 774 (United States Court of Appeals 1947).
Mercado, B. 2022. Review of *Rethinking Racial Capitalism: Questions of Reproduction and Survival*. *Sociology of Race and Ethnicity*, 8(4), 557-58. https://doi.org/10.1177/2332649220904061.
Mijs, J. J. B., and Roe, E. L. 2021. Is America Coming Apart? Socioeconomic Segregation in Neighborhoods, Schools, Workplaces, and Social Networks, 1970-2020. *Sociology Compass*, 15(6). https://doi.org/10.1111/soc4.12884.
Mikati, M., and Medina, E. 2021, June 6. A City Divided: How New York's Capital City Was Splintered along Racial Lines. *Albany Times Union*. www.timesunion.com.
Mintrom, M. 2000. *Policy Entrepreneurs and School Choice*. Georgetown University Press.
Monarrez, T. E. 2023. School Attendance Boundaries and the Segregation of Public Schools in the United States. *American Economic Journal: Applied Economics*, 15(3), 210-37.
Monarrez, T. E., Kisida, B., and Chingos, M. 2022. The Effect of Charter Schools on School Segregation. *American Economic Journal: Economic Policy*, 14(1), 301-40.
Morel, D. 2018. *Takeover: Race, Education, and American Democracy*. Oxford University Press.
Mosier, S. L. 2013. Cookies, Candy, and Coke: Examining State Sugar-Sweetened-Beverage Tax Policy from a Multiple Streams Approach. *International Review of Public Administration*, 18(1), 93-120.
Mossberger, K., and Stoker, G. 2001. The Evolution of Urban Regime Theory: The Challenge of Conceptualization. *Urban Affairs Review*, 36(6), 810-35.
Moynihan, D. P. 1969. *Maximum Feasible Misunderstanding: Community Action in the War on Poverty*. Free Press.
Murray, C. A. 1984. *Losing Ground: American Social Policy, 1950-1980*. Basic Books.
Myers, K. 2005. *Racetalk: Racism Hiding in Plain Sight*. Rowman and Littlefield.
National Alliance for Public Charter Schools. 2005-2024. *Charter School Data Dashboard*, http://data.publiccharters.org, accessed August 30, 2024.
Neilsberg Research. 2024, January 4. *Albany, NY Median Household Income by Race*. Neilsberg. www.neilsberg.com.
New York State Board of Elections. N.d. *Enrollment by County*. www.elections.ny.gov, accessed August 29, 2024.
New York State Education Department. 2015. *New Scotland Elementary School Enrollment (2014-2015)*. http://data.nysed.gov, accessed August 29, 2024.

New York State Education Department. N.d. *Albany High School at a Glance, 2022-23.* https://data.nysed.gov, accessed August 31, 2024.

New York State Education Department. N.d. *Albany High School 2020-21 AP/IB Report.* https://data.nysed.gov, accessed August 31, 2024.

New York State Education Department. N.d. *NY State Data.* Retrieved January 17, 2024, from https://data.nysed.gov.

New York Times. N.d. *Mapping the 2010 U.S. Census.* Retrieved October 31, 2014, from http://projects.nytimes.com.

Nichols, J. 2014, July 17. Standing Up to Disaster Capitalism in Detroit. *The Nation.* www.thenation.com.

Oakes, J. 1986. *Keeping Track: How Schools Structure Inequality.* Yale University Press.

Obama, B. 2008, June 15. Fatherhood Speech (transcript), *Politico,* www.politico.com.

Omi, M., and Winant, H. 1994. *Racial Formation in the United States: From the 1960s to the 1990s* (2nd ed.). Routledge.

Omi, M., and Winant, H. 2015. *Racial Formation in the United States* (3rd ed.). Routledge.

Orfield, G., and Eaton, S. 1997. *Dismantling Desegregation: The Quiet Reversal of Brown v. Board of Education.* New Press.

Orfield, G., and Jarvie, D. 2020. *Black Segregation Matters: School Resegregation and Black Educational Opportunity.* Civil Rights Project/Proyecto Derechos Civiles, UCLA. www.civilrightsproject.ucla.edu.

Orfield, G., and Yun, J. T. 1999. *Resegregation in American Schools.* Civil Rights Project, Harvard University. www.civilrightsproject.ucla.edu.

Owens, A. 2020. Unequal Opportunity: School and Neighborhood Segregation in the USA. *Race and Social Problems, 12,* 29–41. https://doi.org/10.1007/s12552-019-09274-z.

Parents Involved in Community Schools v. Seattle School District No. 1, 551 U.S. 701 (United States Supreme Court 2007).

Peller, G. 1995. Race-Consciousness. In *Critical Race Theory: The Key Writings That Formed the Movement,* ed. K. Crenshaw, N. Gotanda, G. Peller, and K. Thomas (127–58). New Press.

Pertusati, L. 1988. Beyond Segregation or Integration: A Case Study from Effective Native American Education. *Journal of American Indian Education, 27*(2), 10–20.

Pew Research Center. 2016, November 11. Social Media Update. *Internet & Technology.* www.pewinternet.org.

Pierce, E., and Claybourn, C. 2023, August 29. Private School vs. Public School. *US News and World Report.* www.usnews.com.

Pipkin, J. S. 2008. "Chasing Rainbows" in Albany: City Beautiful, City Practical, 1900–1925. *Journal of Planning History, 7*(4), 327–53.

Ponti, C. 2019, August 14. America's History of Slavery Began Long before Jamestown. *History.com.* www.history.com.

Rabrenovic, G. 1996. *Community Builders: A Tale of Neighborhood Mobilization in Two Cities*. Temple University Press.

Ralph, M., and Singhal, M. 2019. Racial Capitalism. *Theory and Society*, 48(6), 851–81.

Ravitch, D. 2013. *Reign of Error: The Hoax of the Privatization Movement and the Danger to America's Public Schools*. Vintage Books.

Reagan, R. 1981. Inaugural Address. Ronald Reagan Presidential Foundation & Institute. www.reaganfoundation.org.

Renshaw, P. 1999. Was There a Keynesian Economy in the USA between 1933 and 1945? *Journal of Contemporary History*, 34(3), 337–64.

Renzulli, L. A. 2005. Organizational Environments and the Emergence of Charter Schools in the United States. *Sociology of Education*, 78(1), 1–26.

Richard Nixon Presidential Library and Museum. 2021. *Nixon and the Supreme Court*. www.nixonlibrary.gov.

Ridde, V. 2009. Policy Implementation in an African State: An Extension of Kingdon's Multiple-Streams Approach. *Public Administration*, 87(4), 938–54.

Robinson, C. 2000. *Black Marxism: The Making of the Black Radical Tradition* (2nd ed.). University of North Carolina Press.

Robinson, F. R. 1977. *Machine Politics: A Study of Albany's O'Connells*. Transaction Books.

Roediger, D. R. 2007. *The Wages of Whiteness: Race and the Making of the American Working Class*. Verso.

Romero, S. 2021, May 20. Texas Pushes to Obscure the State's History of Slavery and Racism. *New York Times*. www.nytimes.com.

Rooks, N. 2017. *Cutting School: Privatization, Segregation, and the End of Public Education*. New Press.

Rothstein, R. 2017. *The Color of Law: A Forgotten History of How Our Government Segregated America* (1st ed.). Liveright.

Rubin, H. J., and Rubin, I. S. 2012. *Qualitative Interviewing: The Art of Hearing Data* (3rd ed.). Sage.

San Antonio Independent School District v. Rodriguez, 411 U.S. 1 (United States Supreme Court 1973).

Schattschneider, E. E. 1975. *The Semi-Sovereign People: A Realist's View of Democracy in America*. Cengage Learning.

Schermerhorn, J. L. 2015. *The Business of Slavery and the Rise of American Capitalism, 1815–1860*. Yale University Press.

Schneider, A. L., and Ingram, H. 1993. Social Construction of Target Populations: Implications for Politics and Policy. *American Political Science Review*, 87(2), 334–47.

Schneider, A. L., and Ingram, H. 1997. *Policy Design for Democracy*. University Press of Kansas.

Schneider, M. 2001. Information and Choice in Education Privatizations. In *Privatizing Education: Can the Marketplace Deliver Choice, Efficiency, Equity, and Social Cohesion?*, ed. H. Levin. Westview.

Schneider, M., Teske, P., and Marschall, M. 2000. *Choosing Schools: Consumer Choice and the Quality of American Schools*. Princeton University Press.

Schroder, R. 2018. *Social Theory after the Internet: Media, Technology, and Globalization*. UCL Press.

Scott, J. 2013. A Rosa Parks Moment? School Choice and the Marketization of Civil Rights. *Critical Studies in Education*, 54(1), 5–18.

Seelye, K. Q. 2011, March 22. Detroit Census Confirms a Desertion like No Other. *New York Times*. www.nytimes.com.

Serial Productions. 2020. *Nice White Parents*. Podcast.

Seth-Smith, N. 2013, December 17. Detroit: From Disaster to Salvation? *Open Democracy*. www.opendemocracy.net.

Shibata, K. 2013, February 24. Charter Schools and Disaster Capitalism. *Salon*. www.salon.com.

Shipan, C. R., and Volden, C. 2008. The Mechanisms of Policy Diffusion. *American Journal of Political Science*, 52(4), 840–57.

Siegel-Hawley, G., and Frankenberg, E. 2011. Redefining Diversity: Political Responses to the Post-PICS Environment. *Peabody Journal of Education*, 86(5), 529–52.

Simon, D. 2005. *"The Target" Commentary Track* [DVD]. HBO.

Small, M. L. 2009. *Unanticipated Gains: Origins of Network Inequality in Everyday Life*. Oxford University Press.

Smith, R. M. 2014. Ackerman's Civil Rights Revolution and Modern American Racial Politics. *Yale Law Journal*, 123(8), 2906–40.

Smrekar, C., and Goldring, E. 1999. *School Choice in Urban America: Magnet Schools and the Pursuit of Equity*. Teachers College Press.

Soss, J. 2006. Talking Our Way to Meaningful Explanations: A Practice-Centered View of Interviewing for Interpretive Research. In *Interpretation and Method: Empirical Research Methods and the Interpretive Turn*, ed. D. Yanow and P. Schwartz-Shea (127–49). M.E. Sharpe.

Spence, L. K. 2015. *Knocking the Hustle: Against the Neoliberal Turn in Black Politics*. Punctum Books.

Stahl, G. 2017. *Ethnography of a Neoliberal School: Building Cultures of Success*. Routledge.

Stanifer, S. R., and Hahn, E. J. 2020. Analysis of Radon Awareness and Disclosure Policy in Kentucky: Applying Kingdon's Multiple Streams Framework. *Policy, Politics, & Nursing Practice*, 21(3), 132–39. https://doi.org/10.1177/1527154420923728.

Stannard, D. E. 1992. *American Holocaust: The Conquest of the New World*. Oxford University Press.

Stein, S. J. 2001. "These Are Your Title I Students": Policy Language in Educational Practice. *Policy Sciences*, 34(2), 135–56.

Stoddard, C., and Corcoran, S. P. 2007. The Political Economy of School Choice: Support for Charter Schools across States and Districts. *Journal of Urban Economics*, 62, 27–54.

Stone, C. 1989. *Regime Politics: Governing Atlanta, 1946–1988*. University Press of Kansas.
Stone, C. 1998. Introduction: Urban Education in Political Context. In *Changing Urban Education*, ed. C. Stone (1–20). University Press of Kansas.
Stone, D. 2012. *Policy Paradox: The Art of Political Decisionmaking* (3rd ed.). Norton.
Straus, R. 2005. "Reconstructing Magnet Schools: Social Construction and the Demise of Desegregation." Ph.D. dissertation, University of California–Irvine.
Straus, R., and Lemieux, S. 2016. The Two *Browns*: Policy Implementation and the Retrenchment of *Brown v. Board of Education*. *New Political Science*, 38(1), 44–60.
Straus, R. 2011. Citizens' Use of Policy Symbols and Frames. *Policy Sciences*, 44(1), 13–34.
Students for Fair Admissions, Inc. v. President and Fellows of Harvard College, 600 U.S. 181 (United States Supreme Court 2023).
Students for Fair Admissions, Inc. v. University of North Carolina, 601 U.S. 181 (United States Supreme Court 2023).
Suk, J. C. 2020, October 26. Our Undemocratic Constitution. *Boston Review*. www.bostonreview.net.
Sullivan, K., and Rozsa, L. 2023, July 22. DeSantis Doubles Down on Claim That Some Blacks Benefited from Slavery. *Washington Post*. www.washingtonpost.com.
SUNY Charter Schools Institute. N.d. *Frequently Asked Questions*. Retrieved April 4, 2023, from www.newyorkcharters.org.
Swann v. Charlotte-Mecklenburg Board of Education, 402 U.S. 1 (United States Supreme Court 1971).
Tansey, O. 2007. Process Tracing and Elite Interviewing: A Case for Non-probability Sampling. *PS: Political Science and Politics*, 40(4), 765–72.
Taylor, K., and Frankenberg, E. 2021. Student Assignment Policies and Racial and Income Segregation of Schools, School Attendance Zones, and Neighborhoods. *Educational Administration Quarterly*, 57(5), 747–75.
Taylor, K.-Y. 2019. *Race for Profit: How Banks and the Real Estate Industry Undermined Black Homeownership*. University of North Carolina Press.
Theodoulou, S. Z. 1995. The Contemporary Language of Public Policy: A Starting Point. In *Public Policy: The Essential Readings*, ed. S. Z. Theodoulou and M. A. Cahn (1–9). Prentice Hall.
Totenberg, N. 2023, June 29. Supreme Court Guts Affirmative Action, Effectively Ending Race-Conscious Admissions. *National Public Radio*. www.npr.org.
Trochmann, M. 2021. Identities, Intersectionality, and Otherness: The Social Constructions of Deservedness in American Housing Policy. *Administrative Theory & Praxis*, 43(1), 97–116.
Turbeville, W. 2013. *The Detroit Bankruptcy*. Demos.
Tushnet, M. V. 1996. The "We've Done Enough" Theory of School Desegregation. *Howard Law Journal*, 39(3), 767–79.
Tyack, D. 1974. *The One Best System: A History of American Urban Education*. Harvard University Press.

Underground Railroad Education Center. N.d. *Stephen and Harriet Myers Residence*. Retrieved March 19, 2024, from https://undergroundrailroadhistory.org.
United States Census Bureau. 2022. *Quick Facts*. www.census.gov.
Waldman, S. 2012, September 24. Parochial Schools Feel Pinch. *Times Union*. www.timesunion.com.
Walker, J. 1969. The Diffusion of Innovations among the American States. *American Political Science Review*, 63(3), 880–99.
Wallerstein, I. 1974. *The Modern World System*. Academic Press.
Weiss, R. S. 1994. *Learning from Strangers: The Art and Method of Qualitative Interview Studies*. Free Press.
Whitehurst, G. J. "Russ," Reeves, R. V., and Rodrigue, E. 2016. *Segregation, Race, and Charter Schools: What Do We Know?* Center on Children and Families at Brookings. www.brookings.edu.
Wilkerson, I. 2020. *Caste: The Origins of Our Discontents*. Random House.
Wilkinson, T. 1982, December 26. Yes, Virginia, There Is One Old-Time Political Machine. *Washington Post*.
Williamson, T. 2009. Review: *Impossible Democracy: The Unlikely Success of the War on Poverty Community Action Programs*. *American Journal of Sociology*, 115(3), 928–31.
Wilson, C. A. 2021. *Trumpism: Race, Class, Populism, and Public Policy*. Lexington Books.
Wolters, R. 2004. From *Brown* to *Green* and Back: The Changing Meaning of Desegregation. *Journal of Southern History*, 70(2), 317–26.
Yanow, D. 1996. *How Does a Policy Mean? Interpreting Policy and Organizational Actions*. Georgetown University Press.
Yanow, D. 2006. Thinking Interpretively: Philosophical Presuppositions and the Human Sciences. In *Interpretation and Method: Empirical Research Methods and the Interpretive Turn*, ed. D. Yanow and P. Schwartz-Shea. M.E. Sharpe.
Yanow, D., and Schwartz-Shea, P., eds. 2006. *Interpretation and Method: Empirical Research Methods and the Interpretive Turn*. M.E. Sharpe.
Ye Hee Lee, M. 2015, July 8. Donald Trump's False Comments Connecting Mexican Immigrants and Crime. *Washington Post*. www.washingtonpost.com.
Young, T. V., Shepley, T. V., and Song, M. 2010. Understanding Agenda Setting in State Educational Policy: An Application of Kingdon's Multiple Streams Model to the Formation of State Reading Policy. *Education Policy Analysis Archives*, 18, 15. https://doi.org/10.14507/epaa.v18n15.2010.
Zhang, Y., and Yang, K. 2008. What Drives Charter School Diffusion at the Local Level: Educational Needs or Political and Institutional Forces? *Policy Studies Journal*, 36(4), 571–91.
Zinn, H. 2005. *A People's History of the United States*. Harper Perennial Modern Classics.

INDEX

Page numbers in italics indicate Figures and Tables

AAVE. *See* African American Vernacular English
ACA. *See* Affordable Care Act
academic programs: charter school choice influenced by, 146–53; magnet school choice influenced by, 146; school choice influenced by, 121, 124, 154, 155
academic support: charter school choice influenced by, 151; of public school, 149–50
ACAP. *See* Albany Citizens Against Poverty
affirmative action programs, US Supreme Court ending, 33, 34, 158, 201, 234n11
Affordable Care Act (ACA), 228n49
African American Vernacular English (AAVE), 176
Afrocentric charter schools, 4–5, 37, 52, 53, 56
after-school programs: charter school choice influenced by, 122; school choice influenced by, 122, 123, 125, 126
Agendas, Alternatives, and Public Policies (Kingdon), 102
Albany, New York. *See specific topics*
Albany Citizens Against Poverty (ACAP), 86–87
Albany Economic Opportunity Commission (EOC), 86
Albany Times-Union, 74
Aloe, A. M., 120–22
American polity, racial capitalism structuring, 26–27, 29–31, 51

Apostolic Church of God (Chicago, Illinois), 35
Asian persons, racism against, 4
assimilationism, 158, 159
authoritarianism, of Trump, 47

Baltimore (Maryland), 118
behavioral problems, 186–87
The Bell Curve (Herrnstein and Murray) (1994), 234n12
biracial identity, 165, 169
Black community: Obama blaming, 35; policy design undervaluing, 77–78
Black Is Beautiful, 37, 54, 55
Black Lives Matter, 37, 54
Black Marxism (Robinson), 28
Black men, Obama blaming, 35
Blackness, 12
Black persons, White persons achievement differences from, 159
Black population, 79–80; in Albany neighborhoods, 83, 88–89; O'Connell Democratic machine war with, 84–88
Black Power, 37, 158, 159
Black Reconstruction (Du Bois), 30
Black voters, O'Connell Democratic machine ignoring, 85
Board of Education of Oklahoma City Public Schools v. Dowell (1991), 69
Bonilla-Silva, E.: on colorblind racism, 33, 170; on hesitant language, 171
book fair, 183, 235n28

251

Brion, David, 222n3
the Brothers, 87, 89
Brown v. Board of Education (1954), 1, 43, 52; Afrocentric charter schools evolving from, 53; context surrounding, 59–60, 62; enforcement of, 63–64; Green v. New Kent County and Swann v. Charlotte-Mecklenberg Board of Education going beyond, 63–66, 66; legacy of, 71–72; rules of, 63; shortcomings of, 57–58, 60–61; trend away from, 68, 69–71; Warren on, 15, 56, 57. See also desegregation, school
building approval, Jennings' control of, 110
bullying: in public school, 108; uniforms avoiding, 133, 134
Bureau of Indian Education, federal, 29
bus, charter school choice influenced by, 126–27, 129, 146–47
busing: school desegregation, 67; school segregation, 63

CAA. See Community Action Agency
California, Proposition 13 in, 77
California's School Law (1860), 30
CAP. See Community Action Program
capital city status, charter school development influenced by, 114–16, 219
capitalism: individualism in, 27, 38–45; racism intertwined with, 13, 26; slavery encouraging, 28–29; slavocracy relationship with, 25–26. See also disaster capitalism; Keynesian economics; race and capitalism double helix; racial capitalism
Capitalism and Freedom (Friedman) (1962), 93
Catholic private schools, 108–9; charter school development influenced by, 111–14; closures of, 113, 119; racial composition of, 111–12; single-sex education, 234n22; voucher program for, 112, 113

Cazenave, N. A., 85
charter school choice, 18, 43–44, 48, 123, 212, 213; academic programs regarding, 146–53; after-school programs and, 122; discipline and structure influencing, 153–54; economic need regarding, 49; location influencing, 129–30; parent involvement relationship with, 137–41; private school attributes regarding, 130–32, 135–36; race consciousness of, 4–5; racial composition and, 156, 171, 189; safety informing, 141, 145; school bus relationship with, 126–27, 129, 146–47; school communication influencing, 140, 148; school days informing, 124–27, 147, 151–52; school year informing, 124–25, 127–29; single-sex education and, 134–36, 234n21; social network relationship with, 136–37; uniforms influencing, 132–34
charter schools, 2, 7, 22, 101, 138, 233n65; Afrocentric, 4–5, 37, 52, 53, 56; capital city status influencing, 114–16, 219; Catholic private schools influencing, 111–14; colorblind individualism promoting, 27; community language invoked by, 17–18; demographics associated with, 100–101; disaster capitalism leading to, 94–95, 95, 96; institutional structures leading to, 93, 105–16, 117; interview respondent inquiries to, 214; market influencing, 17–18, 45, 47; under neoliberalism, 43, 133–34; O'Connell Democratic machine influencing, 106–11; parents of Color choosing, 18, 48–49; paycheck rewards at, 44–45; policy entrepreneurs on, 102–6, 114–15, 116–17, 139; population size influencing, 115–16; public policy and, 16–18, 196–99, 207; public school competition with, 97–98, 149–51, 197–98; racial composition of, 3, 37–38, 128; racial hierarchies

personified by, 16, 18; racism against, 166; segregation of, 6, 18, 49–50, 197, 199; segrenomics of, 48; state legislative foundations of, 98–100; target groups of, 119–20; urban regime theory on, 96–98. *See also* school days, charter; school year, charter

Chicago (Illinois): Apostolic Church of God in, 35; disaster capitalism and charter school development in, 95

childcare, 124, 198, 200; school day and, 125–26, 128, 152, 153; school year and, 128

civic capacity, public-private coalitions building, 97

civic education, 196

civic practice, 196

Civil Rights Act (1964), 13, 15, 33, 63–64

civil rights movement, 157; backlash to, 13, 159; in politics, 13–14

Civil War, 29; Du Bois on, 30; public school after, 30–31

class hierarchies, 9, 16, 23

class size, charter school choice influenced by, 148

coded language: about special needs students, 181, 184; about theft, 183–84

coded racism, 158, 168; about African American Vernacular English, 176; about Albany neighborhoods, 175–76, 177–78, 187–88, 190; culture used in, 159–60, 172; in interviews, 20–21; about magnet school, 180–86, 192; neoliberalism invoked in, 188–89; about parents of Color, 179–80, 184–85; about public school, 170–71, 173–76, 177, 186–87; racism hidden by, 180–93; about safety, 175, 176, 178–79, 235n24; on school segregation, 174; about students of Color, 182–83, 184, 185–86

College and Career prep class, in public school, 173–74

colorblind ideology, 158, 159

colorblind individualism, 21, 26, 31–32, 155; charter schools promoted by, 27; democracy relationship with, 45–50; *Green v. New Kent County* highlighting, 64; of *PICS*, 70–71; policy design motivated by, 75–76, 76, 77–79; school choice constrained by, 22; school segregation condoned by, 56. *See also* racial capitalism

colorblind language, 157, 158, 159–61, 201; of charter schools, 37; racial discourse using, 33–34, 36, 37; White parents using, 36

colorblind market, 48

colorblindness, 4, 5, 13, 27; individualized racism of, 167–70, 193; nonracist, 169; race consciousness compared to, 37–38, 168, 201; of schools, 54–55; US Supreme Court rulings strengthening, 225n59

colorblind racism, 22, 169; Bonilla-Silva on, 33, 170; racial hierarchy maintained by, 32; of White persons, 4, 33

Columbus, Christopher, 24–25

communication, school: charter school choice influenced by, 140, 148; magnet school choice influenced by, 141

community: charter school language invoking, 17–18; voice, 197. *See also* Black community

Community Action Agency (CAA), 86, 87

Community Action Program (CAP), 85; ACAP application for, 87; O'Connell Democratic machine applications for, 86

Constitution, US, 39

Corning, Erastus, II, 74–75, 77; O'Connell's relationship with, 80, 81; property taxes increased by, 87; term of, 106

culture: coded racism using, 159–60, 172; race compared to, 34

Cutting School (Rooks), 24

Dahl, Robert, 58
decision-making: political and economic, 10; in public policy, 14, 15, 17
deficit, national, 41–42
democracy, 195, 199–201, 221n2; colorblind individualism relationship with, 45–50; neoliberalism redefining, 46; school choice relationship with, 196
Democracy in America (de Tocqueville), 39
Democratic party, 74, 99. *See also* O'Connell Democratic machine
demographics, 79, 90, *90*, 100–101
deregulation, charter school development from, 43
DeSantis, Ron, 25
desegregation, school, 16; busing, 67; Civil Rights Act on, 63–64; public policy, 52, 54; *San Antonio v. Rodriguez* impacting, 66–67; shortcomings on, 57–58, 60–61; US Supreme Court stance on, 33 34, 56, *66*, 72–73; White parents against, 57. *See also Brown v. Board of Education*; integration, school; segregation, school
Detroit (Michigan): disaster capitalism and charter school development in, 96; school segregation in, 68
Detroit Water and Sewage Department, 96
disaster capitalism: charter school development from, 94–95, *95*, 96; in Detroit, 96; in New Orleans, 94–95
discipline: charter school choice influenced by, 153–54; coded racism about, 182, 183; parent involvement in, 139
displacement, by South Mall government plaza, 89
dispossession, accumulation by, 48
diversity, Albany, 79
Dobbs v. Jackson Women's Health Organization (2022), 227n19

dog whistles, 158; Haney Lopez on, 160–61, 172, 173; in politics, 160
Du Bois, W. E. B., 21, 30
Dutch immigrants, 79, 231n79

economic disparity, in Albany neighborhoods, 90–91
economic need, charter school choice influenced by, 49
economics: decision-making in, 10; Keynesian, 39–40, 41, 43; politics double helix with, 10–11, 13–14; school choice influenced by, 122
elite interviews, 211–12, *213*, 216–17
Ellison, S., 120–22
Empire State Plaza, 88, 89
Engels, Friedrich, 28
English as a New Language (English with New Learners) (ENL), 181–82
English immigrants, 79
EOC. *See* Albany Economic Opportunity Commission
Equal Protection Clause, of Fourteenth Amendment, 1, 15
Erie, Steven, 106
ethnic residential patterns, 82–83
European immigrants, 79

Facebook, interview respondent outreach on, 214–16
Fair Housing Act (1968), 33
Father's Day speech, by Obama, 35
fight, public school, 141, 143–44, 177
Forbes, on Giffen Memorial Elementary School, 92–93
Fourteenth Amendment, 1, 15, 33, 62, 71
Frame Analysis (Goffman), 104
Fraser, Nancy, 28
freedom schools, racial identification in, 54, 55–56
Freeman v. Pitts (1992), 69
Friedman, Milton, 48, 93
funding, school, 66–67, 68, 72

German immigrants, 79
ghetto, 36, 37, 171; charter schools perceived as, 166; public school described as, 191
Giffen Memorial Elementary School, Forbes on, 92–93
Goffman, Erving, 104
government, Reagan's distrust of, 41–42, 130, 131
Green v. New Kent County (1968): colorblind individualism highlighted by, 64; school integration through, 57, 63–66, 66, 68, 69, 72

Hamilton, 24, 74, 225n85
Hamilton, Alexander, 24, 74
Haney Lopez, Ian, 160–61, 172, 173
Hannah-Jones, Nikole, 11, 57, 222n3
Harvey, David, 40
Herrnstein, Richard J., 234n12
homeowners, White middle-class, 75, 76–77, 78–79, 84–85
Home Owners' Loan Corporation, redlining by, 89
Hudson, P. J., 224n25
human rights abuse, in Detroit, 96
hunger, 91
Hurricane Katrina, 94–95

identity, biracial, 165, 169
Ikwezi (1979), 224n25
incrementalism, of public policy, 69
Indigenous peoples, 79; public school for, 29; racial othering of, 24–25
individualism: in capitalism and neoliberalism, 27, 38–45; Marx critiquing, 39
institutions: charter school development influenced by, 93, 105–16, 117; racial capitalism basis of, 29; venue shopping for, 52–53. *See also* political institutions
integration, school: through *Green v. New Kent County* and *Swann v. Charlotte-Mecklenburg Board of Education*, 57, 63–66, 66, 68, 69, 72; Hannah-Jones on, 57; *PICS* inhibiting, 70, 228n53. *See also* desegregation, school
interpretivism, 19, 142, 165, 209
intersectionality, 11
interviews, 207, 223n50, 223n53, 235n21, 235n25; coded racism in, 20–21; as data, 209–10; elite, 211–12, 213, 216–17; Facebook outreach for, 214–16; identity relationship with, 19–21, 221n17; interpretivist approach to, 142; Jennings refusal of, 233n65; with parents, 212–16, 217, 217, 218, 236n22, 236n28; with parents of Color, 20, 21; relationship building for, 216–18; respondents for, 211–13, 213, 214–16; sample for, 210–11, 212
Irish immigrants, 79, 80

Jackson, Ketanji Brown, 34
Jefferson, Thomas, 24, 39, 225n85
Jennings, Gerald: building approval under, 110; charter school development under, 106, 109–10; interview refused by, 233n65
Jim Crow schools, 54, 54; charter schools compared to, 199; *PICS* ruling on, 71; racial identification in, 55; Warren on, 15, 56
judicial branch, 61–63. *See also* Supreme Court, US

Kennedy, William: *O Albany!* by, 82; on O'Connell Democratic machine, 80–81
Kerner Commission, 9
Keyes v. School District No. 1 (1973), 65–66
Keynesian economics, 39–40, 41, 43
kindergarten, charter, 151
King, Martin Luther, Jr., 158–59
Kingdon, J.: *Agendas, Alternatives, and Public Policies* by, 102; multiple streams framework of, 102–3; on policy entrepreneur, 105

Klein, Naomi, 94
Kozol, Jonathan, 16

Latinx, 221n9
laundry operation, policy entrepreneur running, 118, 119
legislative foundations, state, 98–100
liberalism, classical, 39
library system, interview respondent outreach in, 214
location: charter school choice influenced by, 129–30; polling, 144

magnet school choice, 130; academic programs informing, 146; parent involvement relationship with, 139–40, 141; school communication influencing, 141; social networks and, 136–37
magnet schools, 5, 216; coded racism about, 180–86, 192; racial composition of, 180–81, 192, 235n26
market: charter schools influenced by, 17–18, 45, 47; colorblind, 48; democracy in, 46; neoliberalism's stance on, 41; school choice influenced by, 47, 93, 120, 124, 196
Marx, Karl: individualism critiqued by, 39; Robinson critiquing, 28
Marxism, European, 224n25
Massachusetts Supreme Judicial Court, school segregation ruling of, 29–30
meaning, 102, 116–17
Medicaid, 228n49
Medicare, 228n49
Mendez v. Westminster (1947), 31
methodology, divisions about, 207–8
middle class, 91; White homeowners, 75, 76–77, 78–79, 84–85; White parents, 2, 221n6
Milliken v. Bradley (1974), 68, 69, 70
Mintrom, M., 103–5
Miranda, Lin-Manual, 24, 74

Missouri v. Jenkins (1995), 69–70
multiple streams framework, 102–3
Murray, Charles, 234n12

The National Association for the Advancement of Colored People (NAACP), 53
National Public Radio (NPR), 1–2, 57
A Nation at Risk (1983), 42–43
neighborhoods, Albany, 82; Black population in, 83, 88–89; coded racism about, 175–76, 177–78, 187–88, 190; economic disparity in, 90–91. See also South End
neoliberalism, 26, 226n101; charter schools under, 43, 133–34; coded racism invoking, 188–89; democracy redefined by, 46; government viewed through, 41–42; Harvey on, 40; individualism in, 27, 38–45; market stance of, 41; plutocracy supported by, 47; public policy under, 47–48; public school under, 42–43; taxpayer perspective of, 162
new institutionalism, 105
New Kent County school desegregation (Virginia), 63–64. See also *Green v. New Kent County*
New Orleans (Louisiana): charter schools in, 115; disaster capitalism in, 94–95
New World: colonization of, 11–12; racial othering in, 24–25
New York State: charter schools in, 98–100, *101*, 196; Office of Economic Opportunity, 86, 87
Nixon, Richard, 72
nonprobability sampling, 210
NPR. See National Public Radio

O Albany! (Kennedy), 82
Obama, Barack, 35, 157
Obamacare, 228n49

O'Connell, Dan, 74, 80, 81
O'Connell Democratic machine, 91, 230n51; Black population's war with, 84–88; Black voters ignored by, 85; CAP applications by, 86–87; charter school development influenced by, 106–11; Kennedy on, 80–81; property taxes kept low by, 75, 76, 77, 82, 107; public school patronage mill of, 107–8, 109, 111; Soares' election ending, 106, 233n64; White middle-class homeowners privileged by, 75, 76–77, 78–79, 84–85; working-class benefits shift of, 81
Office of Economic Opportunity (OEO), 86, 87
Omi, M.: on culture and race, 34; on rearticulation, 158
online racism, 32
open-ended questions, for interviews, 210
opioid epidemic, school safety relationship with, 145–46
organized interests, public policy influenced by, 58–59
othering, 24–25, 172

parent involvement: charter school choice influenced by, 137–41; in disciplinary issues, 139; magnet school choice influenced by, 139–40, 141; in public schools, 198
parents: interviews with, 212–16, 217, 217, 218, 236n22, 236n28; public school dissatisfaction of, 110; social network of, 191; workshops for, 137–38. *See also* charter school choice; magnet school choice; school choice; White parents
Parents Involved in Community Schools v. Seattle School District No. 1 (2007) (PICS), 72; colorblind individualism of, 70–71; school integration inhibited by, 70, 228n53; on Seattle, 16, 33, 56, 70–71

parents of Color: charter schools chosen by, 18, 48–49; coded racism about, 179–80, 184–85; interviews with, 20, 21; racism against, 166–67, 198; working class, 2, 221n6
Pataki, George E., 49, 50, 99
paycheck rewards, at charter schools, 44–45
PICS. See *Parents Involved in Community Schools v. Seattle School District No. 1*
Plessy v. Ferguson, 62
pluralism, 58–59
plutocracy, 47
police, White parents calling, 184–85
policy: milieu, 102, 104, 207; problems, 104; suggestions, 196–99; window, 103
policy design: Black community undervalued by, 77–78; colorblind individualism motivating, 75–76, 76, 77–79; context of, 61; on judicial branch, 61–63; politics relationship with, 76; on property taxes, 75, 76, 77; target groups in, 119; taxpayers privileged by, 76–78
policy entrepreneurs: on charter schools, 102–6, 114–15, 116–17, 139; laundry operation run by, 118, 119; Mintrom on, 103–5; on school segregation, 156
Policy Entrepreneurs and School Choice (Mintrom) (2000), 103
Polish immigrants, 83
political institutions: public school as, 195–96; US Supreme Court as, 60–61
politics: civil rights movement in, 13–14; decision-making in, 10; discourse-oriented approaches to, 14; dog whistles in, 160; economics double helix with, 10–11, 13–14; elite interviews illuminating, 211; institutions influencing, 105; public policy relationship with, 53, 75–76, 76; value allocation in, 53
polling locations, schools serving as, 144
polygenesis theory, 25

population size, charter school development influenced by, 115–16
poverty, 84–88, 89, 90–91
power: Black Power, 37, 158, 159; the state maintaining, 59; White parents' school choice maintaining, 227n1
primary election, school polling locations for, 144
prison, school symbolism invoking, 162, 167, 179, 180
private schools, 223n51, 234n25; charter school choice influenced by, 130–32, 135–36; public opinion on, 130–32; safety of, 142–43; school choice for, 137. *See also* Catholic private schools
property rights, 58
property taxes: Corning increasing, 87; O'Connell Democratic machine keeping low, 75, 76, 77, 82, 107; public school relationship with, 107, 108; school funding through, 66–67, 68, 72; tax exemptions for, 82
Proposition 13 (California), 77
public policy: charter schools and, 16–18, 196–99, 207; colorblind individualism framing, 27; decision-making in, 14, 15, 17; incrementalism of, 69; multiple streams framework for, 102–3; neoliberal, 47–48; organized interests influencing, 58–59; politics relationship with, 53, 75–76, 76; race and capitalism double helix framing, 54, 54; in race and class double helix, 14–15, 18–19; racial capitalism maintained through, 27, 31; racially neutral, 65; school desegregation, 52, 54
public-private coalitions, civic capacity built by, 97
public schools: academic support of, 149–50; alternative choices to, 112, 113–14, 190–91; bullying in, 108; charter school competition with, 97–98, 149–51, 197–98; after Civil War, 30–31; coded racism about, 170–71, 173–76, 177, 186–87; College and Career prep class in, 173–74; fight in, 141, 143–44, 177; for Indigenous peoples, 29; investing in, 200; under neoliberalism, 42–43; O'Connell Democratic machine patronage mill of, 107–8, 109, 111; parent involvement in, 198; parents dissatisfied with, 110; as political institutions, 195–96; property tax relationship with, 107, 108; public opinion on, 130–32; race and class double helix shaping, 195; racial composition of, 111, 174, 190, 235n23; racism, 161–67, 189–90; safety of, 143–45, 175, 176; school choice away from, 121, 141, 147–49, 150–51, 161–62, 192–93; segregation of, 120, 174, 197; single-sex education in, 135; tenure system of, 44

qualitative scholars, 208–9
quantitative scholars, 208–9

race, 35–37; culture compared to, 34; interviews influenced by, 20–21; social construct of, 32–33, 34
race and capitalism double helix, 56–57, 157; *Brown v. Board of Education* context of, 60; in policy design, 76; public policy change framed by, 54, 54
race and class double helix, 1, 11–13, 119, 207, 222n3; public policy in, 14–15, 18–19; public school shaped by, 195; safety fears involving, 142; school choice influenced by, 122; slavocracy and capitalism influencing, 25–26
race consciousness, 22–23; of Black Is Beautiful, 37, 54, 55; of Black Lives Matter, 37, 54; of charter school choice, 4–5; colorblindness compared to, 37–38, 168, 201

racial capitalism, 6, 23, 26, 32, 199; American polity structured by, 51; Du Bois on, 30; in *Ikwezi*, 224n25; institutions based on, 29; public policy maintaining, 27, 31; Robinson on, 28, 224n25; school choice constrained by, 22; US Supreme Court entrenched in, 21–22. *See also* colorblind individualism

racial composition, 221n12; of Catholic private schools, 111–12; charter school choice influenced by, 156, 171, 189; of charter schools, 3, 37–38, 128; of magnet schools, 180–81, 192, 235n26; *PICS* stance on, 70–71; of public schools, 111, 174, 190, 235n23

racial discourse: colorblind language used for, 33–34, 36, 37; White persons avoiding, 32, 33

racial divisions, 81

racial hierarchies, 9, 23, 157–58; charter schools personifying, 16, 18; colorblind language maintaining, 37; colorblind racism maintaining, 32; New World colonization leading to, 11–12

racial identification: in freedom schools, 54, 55–56; in Jim Crow schools, 55; of school segregation, 54

racial inequality theories, slavery justified by, 25

racialism, 26

racial othering, in New World, 24–25

racism, 26–27, 31, 225n82; against Asian persons, 4; capitalism intertwined with, 13, 26; against charter schools, 166; coded racism hiding, 180–93; market relationship with, 48; online, 32; against parents of Color, 166–67, 198; about peers, 188; public school, 161–67, 189–90; slavocracy justified with, 24–25; structural, 157; of teachers, 163, 164, 165. *See also* coded racism; colorblind racism; dog whistles

racism, individualized, 160; colorblindness, 167–70, 193; racist language of, 168, 193, 201; of Trump, 157. *See also* coded racism

racist language, 168, 193, 201

Rainbow's End (Erie) (1990), 106

raises, legislator, 99

Reagan, Ronald, 41–42, 130, 131

rearticulation: of King, 158–59; Omi and Winant on, 158

Reconstruction, 13, 71, 200

redlining, by Home Owners' Loan Corporation, 89

renters, O'Connell Democratic machine deprioritizing, 75

Republican party, 74, 80, 99

residential segregation, 82–83, 88–90, 91

Roberts, John: on *PICS* ruling, 33, 56, 71; on *Students for Fair Admissions* decision, 158, 234n11

Roberts, Sarah, 29–30

Robinson, Cedric, 21; *Black Marxism* by, 28; on racial capitalism, 28, 224n25

Rockefeller, Nelson, 88

Roe v. Wade (1973), 227n19

Rooks, Noliwe, 24

Rubin, H. J., 218

Rubin, I. S., 218

safety: charter school choice informed by, 141, 145; coded racism about, 175, 176, 178–79, 235n24; opioid epidemic relationship with, 145–46; of private schools, 142–43; of public school, 143–45, 175, 176; school choice informed by, 141–46

San Antonio v. Rodriguez (1973): on property taxes, 66–67, 68, 72; school desegregation impacted by, 66–67

Sandy Hook Elementary School (Newtown, Connecticut), 141, 144

Savage Inequalities (Kozol) (1991), 16

Schenectady (New York): neighborhood in, 177; public schools in, 150–51; safety in, 145–46
school choice, 2, 207; academic programs influencing, 121, 124, 154, 155; after-school programs influencing, 122, 123, 125, 126; democracy relationship with, 196; Ellison and Aloe on, 120–22; Friedman on, 93; location influencing, 130; market influencing, 47, 93, 120, 124, 196; for private schools, 137; against public school, 121, 141, 147–49, 150–51, 161–62, 192–93; push and pull factors in, 120–22, 123–24; racial capitalism and colorblind individualism constraining, 22; safety informing, 141–46; social networks influencing, 136–37; of White parents, 227n1. *See also* charter school choice; magnet school choice
school days, charter: charter school choice influenced by, 124–27, 147, 151–52; childcare and, 125–26, 128, 152, 153
schools. *See specific topics*
school year, charter: charter school choice influenced by, 124–25, 127–29; childcare and, 128
Seattle (Washington), 16, 33, 56, 70–71
segregation: Kerner Commission on, 9; residential, 82–83, 88–90, 91; the state creating, 68
segregation, de jure school, 62, 70; *Board of Education of Oklahoma City Public Schools v. Dowell* on, 69; *Keyes v. School District No. 1* ruling of, 65–66
segregation, school, 1, 3, 31; busing, 63; California's School Law on, 30; of charter schools, 6, 18, 49–50, 197, 199; coded racism on, 174; colorblind individualism condoning, 56; de facto, 62, 64; Massachusetts Supreme Judicial Court ruling on, 29–30; *Milliken v. Bradley* on, 68; NPR on, 57; policy entrepreneur on, 156; of public school, 120, 174, 197; racial identification of, 54; *Savage Inequalities* on, 16. See also *Brown v. Board of Education*; desegregation, school
segrenomics, of charter schools, 48
SENCAP. *See* South End Neighborhood Community Action Project
shock doctrine, 94–95, 96
shooting, at Sandy Hook Elementary School, 141, 144
Simon, David, 118
single-sex education: Catholic private school, 234n22; charter school choice influenced by, 134–36, 234n21; in public schools, 135
1619 Project, 25
slaveholders' compact, US Constitution as, 39
slavery: capitalism's reliance on, 28–29; racial inequality theories justifying, 25; Robinson on, 28
slavocracy, 11, 51, 200; capitalism relationship with, 25–26; democracy compared to, 195; racial capitalism and colorblind individualism evolution from, 21; racism justifying, 24–25
snowball sample, 212
Soares, David, 106, 233n64
social construct, 32–33, 34, 236n5
socialist movement, 12
social media, 214–15
social movements, of 1960s and 1970s, 40
social networks: charter and magnet school choice influenced by, 136–37; of parents, 191
South End (Albany neighborhood), 82; Black population in, 83, 88–89; South Mall government plaza in, 88, 89
South End Neighborhood Community Action Project (SENCAP), 87

South Mall government plaza, in South End, 88, 89
special needs students, coded language about, 181, 184
standardized tests, 148–49, 198–99
the state, 66–67; organized interests influencing, 59; segregation created by, 68
Stone, Clarence, 97
Stone, Deborah, 46
structural racism, 157
structure, charter school choice influenced by, 153–54
Students for Fair Admissions, US Supreme Court decision, 158, 234n11
students of Color, 68; *Brown v. Board of Education* ruling for, 62, 63; coded racism about, 182–83, 184, 185–86
substitute teacher, 142
Supreme Court, US, 15–16; affirmative action programs ended by, 33, 34, 158, 201, 234n11; *Board of Education of Oklahoma City Public Schools v. Dowell* and *Freeman v. Pitts* ruling of, 69; colorblindness strengthened by, 225n59; *Dobbs v. Jackson Women's Health Organization* ruling of, 227n19; *Milliken v. Bradley* ruling of, 68, 69, 70; *Missouri v. Jenkins* ruling of, 69–70; Nixon's appointees to, 72; as political institution, 60–61; racial capitalism entrenched in, 21–22; *Roe v. Wade* overturned by, 227n19; school desegregation stance of, 33, 34, 56, 66, 72–73; *Students for Fair Admissions* decision by, 158, 234n11; in 2024, 227n3. See also *Brown v. Board of Education*; *Green v. New Kent County*; *Parents Involved in Community Schools v. Seattle School District No. 1*; *San Antonio v. Rodriguez*
suspensions, 163
Swann v. Charlotte-Mecklenburg Board of Education (1971), 57, 63–66, 66, 68, 69, 72

target groups, of charter schools, 119–20
taxpayers: neoliberal perspective of, 162; policy design privileging, 76–78
teachers: bathroom refusal of, 164; coded racism about, 182–83; racism of, 163, 164, 165; substitute, 142; trust in, 198–99, 200; unions, 125
tenure system, public school, 44
Texas, property tax school funding in, 66–67
theft, coded language about, 183–84
Thomas, Clarence, 158
time-out room, dark, 163, 235n27
de Tocqueville, Alexis, 39
Trinity Institution (Trinity Alliance), 86–87
Trump, Donald, 13, 131; authoritarianism of, 47; inauguration protests of, 45–46; individualized racism of, 157
Trump administration, 4, 5

uniforms, 198; bullying avoided with, 133, 134; charter school choice influenced by, 132–34
United States. *See specific topics*
urban regime theory, on charter school development, 96–98

Virginia, New Kent County in, 63–64
vote buying, 87
Voting Rights Act (1965), 13, 33
voucher programs, school, 92–93, 112, 113

War on Poverty, 84–88
Warren, Earl, 15, 56, 57
Washington, DC, 95–96
White children, 68
White flight, 89
White middle-class homeowners, 75, 76–77, 78–79, 84–85
Whiteness, 12

White parents, 68; colorblind language used by, 36; middle-class, 2, 221n6; police called by, 184–85; against school desegregation, 57; White schools chosen by, 227n1

White persons: Black persons achievement differences from, 159; colorblind racism of, 4, 33; interviews with, 20–21; racial discourse avoided by, 32, 33

White privilege, 190

White saviorism, 50

White schools, White parents choosing, 227n1

Who Governs? (Dahl) (1961), 58

Winant, H.: on culture and race, 34; on rearticulation, 158

The Wire, 118

workforce, uniform preparation for, 133–34

working class: O'Connell Democratic machine shifting away from, 81; parents of Color, 2, 221n6

workshops, for parents, 137–38

Yang, K., 208

Young Men's Christian Association (YMCA), 214, 215, 236n22

Zhang, Y., 208

ABOUT THE AUTHOR

RYANE MCAULIFFE STRAUS is an Empire State Fellow in Albany, New York. Previously, she was a Professor of Political Science at the College of Saint Rose, which closed in 2024.